DAILY LIFE IN

THE EARLY AMERICAN REPUBLIC, 1790–1820

DAILY LIFE IN

THE EARLY AMERICAN REPUBLIC, 1790–1820

CREATING A NEW NATION

DAVID S. HEIDLER AND JEANNE T. HEIDLER

The Greenwood Press "Daily Life Through History" Series

GREENWOOD PRESS
Westport, Connecticut • London

Library of Congress Cataloging-in-Publication Data

Heidler, David Stephen, 1955–
  Daily life in the early American republic, 1790–1820 / David S. Heidler
and Jeanne T. Heidler.
    p. cm. — (The Greenwood Press "Daily life through history" series)
  Includes bibliographical references and index.
  ISBN 0–313–32391–7
  1. United States—Social life and customs—1783–1865. I. Heidler, Jeanne T. II.
Title. III. Series.
  E164.H44   2004
  973.4—dc22   2004011771

British Library Cataloguing in Publication Data is available.

Library of Congress Catalog Card Number: 2004011771
ISBN: 0–313–32391–7
ISSN: 1080–4749

First published in 2004

Greenwood Press, 88 Post Road West, Westport, CT 06881
An imprint of Greenwood Publishing Group, Inc.
www.greenwood.com

Printed in the United States of America

The paper used in this book complies with the
Permanent Paper Standard issued by the National
Information Standards Organization (Z39.48–1984).

10 9 8 7 6 5 4 3 2 1

To
Our students
A major part of our daily life for more than two decades

CONTENTS

A map and photo essay follows page 94.

INTRODUCTION

The years spanning 1790 to 1820 were both seminal and transitional for the United States. In the course of founding a new government and stabilizing a fragile economy, the country experienced both subtle shifts and profound changes. Although many Americans regarded their daily routines as a set of fixed practices that differed little from those of their colonial forebears, their lives were markedly different in the philosophies that guided them. They were also steadily changing from undeveloped and unrealized possibilities of the eighteenth century to the dynamic market economy of the 1800s. Some of these changes derived from the formation of a new government under the Constitution. Others resulted from shifting economic climates and transformed modes of production and consumption. Abundant land and natural resources afforded new economic opportunities and spurred national expansion. All had the effect of impinging on and modifying the daily habits of citizens. By the end of the period, many Americans were not just poised to embark on a vast adventure; they sensed they had already begun it.

This book will look at various aspects of that transitional time and the way the various people called Americans lived in it. Chapter 1 presents an overview of the important historical events of the period to supply a basis for references that occur in subsequent chapters. Those chapters explore the range of rituals and routines that characterized the daily lives of most Americans. In chapter 2, we take a general look at how couples courted, married, and raised families, examining their houses as well as their health and hygiene, and finally concluding with ceremonies of death and mourning.

Most Americans lived on farms during these years, and chapter 3 describes agricultural life and the ways it varied regionally. Here the reader will see how American ingenuity achieved agricultural improvements that set the country on the road to modernity, paving the way for it to become the breadbasket of the world. Here also the reader will see how southern agriculture became tragically reliant on slave labor, the implications of which were as morally repugnant as they were politically disastrous.

Chapter 4 describes the old economy of artisanship that was slowly being transformed into the modern one of industrial capitalism, and chapter 5 looks at the leisure pursuits of all the classes. The early Republic was an age of sincere piety and fervent religious faith, from the quiet devotions of unique sects, such as the Quakers and Moravians and Mennonites, to the raucous revivalism of frontier evangelists. Chapter 6 describes the wide range of faith that existed in America and explores how religion provided moral instruction, gave comfort, exerted a civilizing influence, and formed the seedbed for the great reform movements of temperance and abolition.

Communities exclusive to the American culture existed both within and apart from American society during these years, sometimes by choice and occasionally by fiat. Chapter 7 describes those groups who lived beyond the mainstream of the American experience, including Indians, African American slaves, free blacks, pioneers, and immigrants. Chapter 8 examines life in the U.S. military at a time when Americans were at best ambivalent about, and frequently hostile to, the concept of a standing army and costly navy. An epilogue provides general conclusions about the period as a whole and especially about the momentous changes and understated shifts that marked the lives of those who lived through it. A bibliography serves as a guide for readers interested in specifically investigating particular topics.

As always, we are grateful to friends and colleagues who have encouraged us in this project as enthusiastically as they have in others. Several scholars have read the manuscript in whole or in part, and their suggestions have improved it. The editorial staff at Greenwood has been characteristically patient and supportive. We are indebted to Michael Hermann for his good cheer throughout and for the extra days at the end.

CHRONOLOGY

1789

General	Publications: William Hill Brown's *The Power of Sympathy* is the first American novel; *Gazette of the United States*
	Culture: The first association advocating temperance is organized in Litchfield County, Connecticut
January	Georgetown University, the first Catholic college in the United States, is founded
February	Electors cast ballots in the first presidential election
March	Pennsylvania lifts its ban on stage plays
April 30	George Washington inaugurated as the first president of the United States
May 7	U.S. Protestant Episcopal Church is established
May 12	Society of Saint Tammany founded in New York City
September 29	Congress establishes an army of 1,000 men
October	George Washington tours New England
November 26	The first national Thanksgiving Day

1790

General   First U.S. census tallies a population of 3,929,625

Culture: Prison reformers apply the idea of rehabilitation at Philadelphia's Walnut Street Prison; Duncan Phyfe begins making furniture in New York City; revivals that foreshadow the Second Great Awakening begin in New England

Publications: Mercy Otis Warren's *Poems, Dramatic and Miscellaneous*; the *Universal Asylum, and Columbian Magazine* begins publication in Philadelphia; and the *New-York Magazine; or, Literary Repository* first appears

Notable deaths: Benjamin Franklin (April 17) at age 84

February   Quakers petition Congress to abolish slavery

March   In Philadelphia, John Martin gives the first major stage performance by an actor born in America

May   Adherents of Universalist religious doctrines meet in Philadelphia; Washington signs into law the nation's first copyright statute; the *Philadelphia Spelling Book* is the first book to receive a copyright under the new law

August   The merchant vessel *Columbia* arrives in Boston after circumnavigating the globe; John Carroll becomes America's first Roman Catholic bishop

October 18   Gen. Josiah Harmar's expedition against northwestern Indians is defeated near Fort Wayne

December   Congress relocates the national capital from New York City to Philadelphia; in Pawtucket, Rhode Island, Samuel Slater opens America's first cotton mill, the start of U.S. industrialism

1791

General   Publications: John Adams's *Discourses of Davila*; William Bartram's *Travels*; Thomas Paine's *Rights of Man*; Benjamin Banneker begins publishing an almanac

Culture: Massachusetts Historical Society is founded

Inventions: John Fitch receives a patent for a steamboat

Notable Births: Peter Cooper (February 12); Francis Preston Blair (April 12); James Buchanan (April 23)

February   The Bank of the United States is chartered

April–June   Washington tours the South

November 4   Northwestern Indians defeat a U.S. force under General Arthur St. Clair

December   Virginia ratifies the Bill of Rights, providing the necessary approval by three-quarters of the states to make it part of the U.S. Constitution

1792

General   Publications: Thomas Paine's *Rights of Man*, part 2; Jedidiah Morse's *The American Geography, or, a View of the Present Situation of the United States of America*; Noah Webster's *An American Selection of Lessons in Reading and Speaking*; the *Lady's Magazine and Repository of Entertaining Knowledge* appears in Philadelphia; *Old Farmer's Almanac* appears for the first time

Commerce: The Boston Crown Glass Company begins producing window glass

Notable births: Thaddeus Stevens (April 4); Sarah Grimké (November 26)

Notable deaths: Naval hero John Paul Jones (July 18) at age 45

April   Kentucky rejects measures that would exclude slavery and enters the Union as the 15th state in June; the National Coinage Act establishes a mint at Philadelphia, a decimal system for coins, and a 15:1 ratio of silver to gold in the U.S. dollar

May   Robert Gray sails his ship *Columbia* into the mouth of the great watercourse he will dub the Columbia River; the New York Stock Exchange is established

August–   Opposition to the government's excise tax on whiskey
September   grows in Pennsylvania and certain parts of the South

November   The second presidential election takes place and when electoral votes are counted in December will return George Washington for a second term

1793

General   Publications: St. John de Crèvecoeur's *Letters from an American Farmer*; the periodical the *New Hampshire Magazine: Or, The Monthly Repository of Useful Information*; published quarterly in New York, the *Free Universal Magazine*

addresses religious topics; the first daily newspaper is Noah Webster's *American Minerva,* published in New York

Culture: Samuel Slater opens a Sunday school for children working in his Pawtucket factory to teach them basic educational skills

Inventions: Eli Whitney's cotton gin

Notable births: Lucretia Mott (January 3), Sam Houston (March 2), Stephen F. Austin (November 3)

Notable deaths: John Hancock (October 8) at age 56

January   First hot air balloon flight in the United States takes place in Philadelphia

February 1   France declares war on Great Britain, Spain, and the Netherlands

February 12   Congress passes Fugitive Slave Act

April 22   Washington declares American neutrality concerning the European war

July 31   Thomas Jefferson resigns as secretary of state, to become effective on December 31

September 18   Washington lays the cornerstone for the U.S. Capitol in the new federal capital

November   Slave riots break out in Albany, New York

1794

General   Publications: *The Monthly Miscellany, or Vermont Magazine* begins publication

Notable births: Matthew Perry (April 10), Edward Everett (April 11), Cornelius Vanderbilt (May 27), William Cullen Bryant (November 11)

Notable deaths: Richard Henry Lee (June 19) at age 62

March   U.S. Navy is established

April   Pennsylvania abolishes capital punishment except for murder

May   Philadelphia shoemakers organize the first trade union in the United States

July   Whiskey Rebellion breaks out in Pennsylvania; it is quickly suppressed

August 20	U.S. Army defeats northwestern Indians at the Battle of Fallen Timbers
November	Jay's Treaty with Great Britain is concluded

1795

General	Publications: several periodicals begin publication in Philadelphia, including the *American Monthly Review* and the *Philadelphia Minerva*
	Transportation: An inclined wooden railroad is built on Beacon Hill in Boston
	Notable births: James Knox Polk (November 2)
	Notable deaths: William Prescott, who commanded at Breed's Hill in 1775 (October 13) at age 69
January 31	Alexander Hamilton resigns as secretary of the treasury
June 24	Jay's Treaty is ratified despite its unpopularity
August	Treaty of Greenville signed with Ohio Indian tribes
October	Treaty of San Lorenzo (Pinckney's Treaty) is concluded with Spain

1796

General	Publications: Amelia Simmons's *American Cookery* is the first American cookbook
	Notable births: Horace Mann (May 4), Reverdy Johnson (May 21), George Catlin (July 26)
March	The U.S. Supreme Court rules on the constitutionality of a 1794 congressional statute, the first time that the Court renders such a decision; Pinckney's Treaty is ratified
May	Congress passes a land law to facilitate the sale of public lands in the Northwest Territory
June 1	Tennessee becomes a state
September 17	George Washington's Farewell Address appears in the Philadelphia *Daily American*
October	The *Otter* is the first American ship to explore the California coastline
November	France suspends diplomatic relations with the United States
December	John Adams is elected third president of the United States

1797

General	Publications: Jedidiah Morse's *The American Gazetteer*
	Notable births: Mary Lyon (February 28)
	Notable deaths: Oliver Wolcott (December 1) at age 71
January	New York moves its capital to Albany
March 4	John Adams becomes the second president
May	The frigate *United States,* the first vessel in the new U.S. Navy, is launched
June	Charles Newbold patents a cast-iron plow
September	The frigate *Constellation* is launched
October	The French rebuff an American peace commission unless it offers bribes, a continuing demand that will result in the XYZ Affair; the frigate *Constitution,* destined to become known as "Old Ironsides" during the War of 1812, is launched

1798

General	Notable births: Future wife of Millard Fillmore, Abigail Powers (March 13); naval commander Charles Wilkes (April 3)
January– March	Negotiations in Paris break down completely
April	President Adams reports on the XYZ Affair to Congress; the Mississippi Territory, which embraces the eventual states of Alabama and Mississippi, is created
June	Congress abolishes debtor prisons
June–July	Congress passes the Alien and Sedition Acts
July	As potential war looms with France, George Washington is appointed commander in chief of the U.S. Army; Congress creates the U.S. Marine Corps and establishes the forerunner of the U.S. Public Health Service
September	Benjamin Bache, Benjamin Franklin's grandson, is arrested under the Sedition Act for allegedly libeling President John Adams
November	The Kentucky Resolutions protesting the Alien and Sedition Acts are adopted by the Kentucky legislature

December   The Virginia Resolutions protesting the Alien and Sedition Acts are adopted by the Virginia legislature

1799

General   Culture: Deerfield Academy is founded in Massachusetts

Labor: The shoemakers' trade union in Philadelphia (officially the Federal Society of Cordwainers) stages the first successful strike in American history

Notable births: Mountain man Jedediah Smith (January 6); Amos Bronson Alcott (November 29)

Notable deaths: Patrick Henry (June 6) at age 63; George Washington (December 14) at age 67

January   Congress passes the Logan Act, making it unlawful for American citizens to engage in private diplomacy with foreign governments

February   Congress passes the first law authorizing federal help to cities implementing health quarantines; a taxpayer revolt led by Pennsylvanian John Fries collapses after his arrest

March   New York enacts measures to facilitate the gradual emancipation of slaves within its borders

May   After months of undeclared war on the high seas, France offers to open peace talks

1800

General   The second U.S. census counts about 5.3 million people, marking an increase of 35 percent in the population

Publications: The *Waverly Magazine* and the *Literary News, a Monthly Journal of Current Literature* begin publication

Agriculture: Pennsylvanian John Chapman begins his 50-year campaign to grow and tend apple trees in the Ohio River valley, a vocation that will earn him the nickname "Johnny Appleseed"

Inventions: Eli Whitney begins an attempt to make guns with interchangeable parts

Customs: George Washington's widow Martha is granted free mail service

Culture: Congress founds the Library of Congress

Notable births: Millard Fillmore (January 7); educator William McGuffey (September 23); historian George Bancroft (October 3); inventor Charles Goodyear (December 29); Nat Turner (either January 22 or October 2)

Notable deaths: Composer William Billings (September 29) at age 53

January   Philadelphia free blacks unsuccessfully petition Congress to end slavery and repeal all legislation supporting it

April   The first Federal Bankruptcy Act is enacted

May   The Land Act of 1800 revises policies for the sale of public lands

June   The federal government moves from Philadelphia to the new capital at Washington, D.C.

August   The Gabriel Prosser slave rebellion is prevented outside Richmond, Virginia, when it is prematurely discovered; Prosser hangs on October 7

September   France and the United States end their undeclared naval war with the Treaty of Mortefontaine to take effect on December 21

November   Congress meets for the first time in Washington, and John Adams moves into the unfinished Executive Mansion

December   The quadrennial presidential election is held, but electoral ballots are not counted until the following February

1801

General   Publications: *The American Ladies' Pocket-Book* appears, describing itself as "an useful register of business and amusement, and a complete repository of fashion, literature, the drama, painting, and music"

Culture: The New York Academy, a public art museum, is founded but will cease to exist in 1805

Notable births: Painter Thomas Cole (February 1); William H. Seward (May 16); Brigham Young (June 1); David Farragut (July 5)

Notable deaths: Benedict Arnold (June 14)

January   John Marshall appointed chief justice of U.S. Supreme Court

February 17   Thomas Jefferson becomes the third president-elect after a tie with Aaron Burr in the Electoral College throws the election into the House of Representatives

February   Judiciary Act revising the federal court system is passed

March 4   Jefferson is inaugurated as president

August   A massive camp meeting revival at Cane Ridge, Kentucky, gives momentum to the Second Great Awakening in the West

December 8   Jefferson establishes the custom of sending annual messages (the equivalent of the State of the Union message) to Congress rather than delivering them in a speech, a tradition that continues until Woodrow Wilson departs from it in 1913

1802

General   Publications: *Catalogue of the Books, Maps, and Charts, Belonging to the Library of the Two Houses of Congress: Apr, 1802*

Culture: John James Beckley becomes first Librarian of Congress

Inventions: James Stevens designs a screw propeller

Notable births: Educator Mark Hopkins (February 4); abolitionist Lydia Maria Child (February 11); Dorothea Dix (April 4); Gideon Welles (July 1); missionary Marcus Whitman (September 4); abolitionist Elijah Lovejoy (November 9)

March   Congress repeals the Judiciary Act of 1801; Congress authorizes the establishment of the United States Military Academy at West Point, New York; the Peace of Amiens temporarily ends the European war

April   Rumors circulate that Spain has ceded Louisiana to Napoleon's France

July 4   The United States Military Academy formally opens

October   Spain unexpectedly closes New Orleans to American commerce, a violation of Pinckney's Treaty

November   In preparation for statehood, Ohio holds a state constitutional convention

1803

General	Notable births: Albert Sidney Johnston (February 2); Ralph Waldo Emerson (May 25); inventor John Ericsson (July 31); future wife of James Polk, Sarah Childress (September 4)
	Notable deaths: Revolutionary leader Samuel Adams (October 2) at age 81
February	The Supreme Court ruling in *Marbury* v. *Madison* establishes the principle of judicial review
March 1	Ohio becomes the 17th state
April	Spain restores the right of deposit at New Orleans
May 2	The Louisiana Purchase Treaty is signed in Paris
August	The Corps of Discovery led by Meriwether Lewis and William Clark starts its westward journey beginning on the Ohio River
December 20	The United States takes possession of the Louisiana Territory

1804

General	Publications: The first part of John Marshall's five-volume biography of George Washington appears, to continue through 1807
	Culture: The New York Historical Society is established
	Notable births: John Deere (February 7); mountain man James (Jim) Bridger (March 17)
	Notable deaths: Caesar Rodney (February 2) at age 62
February	New Jersey institutes the gradual emancipation of its slaves
March	Congress revises land policy with the Land Act of 1804
May	The Lewis and Clark expedition embarks from St. Louis; Napoleon Bonaparte crowns himself emperor of France
July 11	Aaron Burr mortally wounds Alexander Hamilton in a duel at Weehawken, New Jersey
August 20	Charles Floyd succumbs to appendicitis, the only member of the Lewis and Clark expedition to die on the journey
December 5	Thomas Jefferson is reelected president

1805

General   Publications: Mercy Otis Warren's three-volume *The Rise, Progress, and Termination of the American Revolution*

Culture: Charles Wilson Peale founds the Pennsylvania Academy of Fine Art, a public art museum

Commerce: Ice is first exported from New England to the Caribbean

Notable births: Abolitionist Angelina Grimké (February 20); Alexis de Tocqueville (July 29); sculptor Horatio Greenough (September 6): archaeologist John Stephens (November 28); William Lloyd Garrison (December 10); Wells Fargo cofounder Henry Wells (December 12); Mormon Joseph Smith Jr. (December 23)

January   Part of the Indiana Territory is used to create the Michigan Territory

March 1   The Senate acquits impeached Supreme Court justice Samuel Chase

March 4   Jefferson is inaugurated for his second term as president

May   A strike for higher wages by the trade union of Philadelphia shoemakers fails when its leaders are arrested; the Lewis and Clark expedition sights the Rocky Mountains

July   Britain restricts U.S. trade with the French West Indies

August   Lt. Zebulon Pike leads an exploratory expedition into the Minnesota region

November   Lewis and Clark see the Pacific Ocean and establish a winter encampment at the mouth of the Columbia River

1806

General   Publications: Noah Webster's *Compendious Dictionary of the English Language*

Culture: Williams College students found the Brethren, the first American society to promote foreign missionary journeys

Notable births: Cherokee leader Stand Watie (December 1806)

Notable deaths: George Wythe (June 8) at age 79; Benjamin Banneker (October 9) at age 74

January 17	The first child born in the new Executive Mansion is Thomas Jefferson's grandson, James Madison Randolph
March	Congress authorizes the construction of the National Road from Cumberland, Maryland, to Wheeling, Virginia
April	Congress begins a long experiment using commercial restriction to persuade Britain and France to respect American commercial rights
May 30	Andrew Jackson kills Nashville attorney Charles Dickinson in a duel
July	Zebulon Pike leads another exploratory expedition, this time into the Southwest
September	The Lewis and Clark expedition arrives in St. Louis
November	Zebulon Pike's expedition sights the mountain that will later be named Pikes Peak; Napoleon issues the Berlin Decree
December	Jefferson requests that Congress prohibit slave importation as of January 1, 1808

1807

General	Publications: Essays by New Yorkers Washington Irving, William Irving, and James Kirk Paulding inaugurate a style that features American subjects and is gradually identified as the Knickerbocker school
	Inventions: Robert Fulton's *Clermont* is the first successful steamboat
	Notable births: Ezra Cornell (January 11); Robert E. Lee (January 19); Henry Wadsworth Longfellow (February 27); John Greenleaf Whittier (December 17)
January	Britain's Orders in Council restrict American shipping in response to Napoleon's Berlin Decree
February	Aaron Burr is arrested in the Mississippi Territory and will later be indicted for treason
March	Congress prohibits the foreign slave trade, to take effect on January 1, 1808
June	The British frigate *Leopard* fires on and boards the USS *Chesapeake* to remove alleged British deserters
September	Aaron Burr is acquitted of treason in Richmond, Virginia

December	Napoleon issues the Milan Decree, an additional insult to American neutrality; Congress enacts the Embargo Act, which bans all trade with foreign countries
1808	
General	Culture: The *Missouri Gazette* of St. Louis becomes the first newspaper west of the Mississippi; the public art museum is revived in New York with the establishment of the New York Academy of Fine Arts; the opulent opera house Theatre d'Orleans opens in New Orleans; a temperance society is formed in New York City
	Notable births: Salmon P. Chase (January 13); Jefferson Davis (June 3)
January 1	The foreign slave trade is abolished
July	William Clark and others establish the Missouri Fur Company in St. Louis
December	James Madison is elected fourth president of the United States
1809	
General	Publications: Washington Irving's *History of New York* is published under the pseudonym Diedrick Knickerbocker
	Transportation: James Stevens's steamboat cruises from Hoboken, New Jersey, to the Delaware River, the first ocean journey by a steamboat
	Notable births: Edgar Allan Poe (January 19); Abraham Lincoln (February 12); Oliver Wendell Holmes (August 29); Christopher (Kit) Carson (December 24)
	Notable deaths: Thomas Paine (June 8) at age 72; Meriwether Lewis (October 11), rumored a suicide at age 35
January	Congress enacts legislation to enforce the increasingly unpopular embargo
February	Anger about, and resistance to, the embargo increases, especially in New England
March	Jefferson signs legislation that repeals the embargo and replaces it with less severe restrictive measures; the Illinois Territory, embracing present-day Illinois, Wisconsin, and eastern Minnesota, is created
March 4	James Madison is inaugurated as president

July   The Shawnee Tecumseh begins laying plans for an Indian confederation to resist American expansion in the Northwest

1810

General   The third census shows a 36.4 percent increase in the U.S. population to 7,239,881

Culture: The Boston Philharmonic Society establishes America's first symphony orchestra

Commerce: One hundred cotton mills are operating in Rhode Island and Pennsylvania

Inventions: Hot air balloonists A. R. Hawley and Augustus Post travel more than one thousand miles from St. Louis to Canada

May   Congress passes Macon's Bill No. 2, yet another variation of its increasingly ineffective effort to coerce British and French respect for American neutral rights

Notable births: Phineas Taylor Barnum (July 5); clipper ship designer Donald McKay (September 4)

July   The New York trial of striking shoemakers in that city follows Philadelphia's 1806 lead in determining that such strikes are criminal conspiracies

September   Americans in the western part of West Florida rebel against Spanish authority and request annexation by the United States, a request to which the Madison administration consents in the following month

October   Country fairs have their origin in the Berkshire Cattle Show in Massachusetts

1811

General   Astoria, the first permanent American settlement in the Pacific Northwest, is established at the mouth of the Columbia River

Transportation: The steamboat *New Orleans* completes a four-month passage from Pittsburgh to New Orleans and commences riverboat service between New Orleans and Natchez

Notable births: Horace Greeley (February 3); AME bishop Daniel Payne (February 24); painter George Caleb Bingham (March 20); elevator inventor Elisha G. Otis (August

3); utopian John Humphrey Noyes (September 3); abolitionist Wendell Phillips (November 29)

Notable deaths: Supreme Court justice Samuel Chase (June 19) at age 70

January	Congress secretly authorizes the annexation of Spanish East Florida if residents agree or if another foreign power moves to occupy the province
March 4	The Bank of the United States closes because Congress has refused to renew its charter
November 7	William Henry Harrison's force fights the Battle of Tippecanoe and destroys the principal village of Tecumseh's confederation
November	Construction of the National (Cumberland) Road commences
December 16	Centered at New Madrid, Missouri, one of the strongest earthquakes to occur in North America rocks the Mississippi River valley

1812

General	Publications: David Rice's pamphlet *A Kentucky Protest against Slavery*
	Notable deaths: Lewis and Clark interpreter Sacagawea (December 20)
January 23	Another, stronger earthquake occurs at New Madrid, Missouri
February	Massachusetts governor Elbridge Gerry signs a bill that creates voting districts deliberately drawn for partisan advantage; their cartographic resemblance to a salamander gives rise to the term "gerrymander" to describe the practice of using redistricting to marginalize political opponents
February 7	Possibly the most powerful earthquake ever to occur in North America strikes New Madrid, Missouri, causing the Mississippi River to flow backward and resulting in thousands of aftershocks
April	As war looms with Britain, Congress enacts an embargo and authorizes President Madison to call up the militia
April 20	Vice President George Clinton's death leaves that office vacant for the remainder of Madison's first term; Elbridge

	Gerry will become vice president–elect in December upon Madison's reelection
April 30	Louisiana enters the Union with its capital of New Orleans the fifth largest city in the country
June 19	The United States declares war on Great Britain, thus beginning the War of 1812
July–August	Opposition in New England prompts Connecticut and Massachusetts to withhold their militias from the American war effort
August 16	Detroit is surrendered to British forces
August 19	USS *Constitution* defeats HMS *Guerrière* and is dubbed "Old Ironsides"
September	The Russian tsar offers to mediate the Anglo-American war
October 25	USS *United States* defeats HMS *Macedonian*
December	James Madison wins reelection to the presidency; the British Royal Navy blockades the mid-Atlantic coast
December 29	USS *Constitution* defeats HMS *Java*
1813	
General	Notable births: Henry Ward Beecher (June 24)
	Notable deaths: Benjamin Rush (April 19) at age 67; Zebulon Pike (April 27), in battle at age 34
January 22	Following an American defeat at Frenchtown just west of Lake Erie, Indians massacre American prisoners on the River Raisin
March 4	James Madison is inaugurated for a second term
March	The United States accepts the Russian mediation offer, but Britain rejects it
April	U.S. forces occupy Spanish Mobile
April 27	U.S. forces burn York (modern Toronto)
May	The British extend their blockade southward into the Gulf of Mexico
June 1	HMS *Shannon* defeats USS *Chesapeake*; American captain James Lawrence is fatally wounded but shouts, "Don't give up the ship!"

September 10	Capt. Oliver Hazard Perry's U.S. squadron defeats its British counterpart in the Battle of Lake Erie
October 5	William Henry Harrison defeats the British and their Indian allies at the Battle of Thames, where Tecumseh is reportedly killed
November	In the Creek War that overlaps the War of 1812, Tennessee militia forces under Andrew Jackson converge on the Creek Nation to fight a series of bloody but indecisive battles against nativist Indians there
December	The Niagara frontier becomes the scene of retaliatory violence by American and British forces

1814

General	Industry: At Waltham, Massachusetts, Francis Lowell opens the first factory that integrates powered textile machinery for spinning and weaving, the forerunner of his factory complex at Lowell, Massachusetts
	Notable births: sculptor Thomas Crawford (March 22)
	Notable deaths: Elbridge Gerry (November 23) at age 70
March 27	Andrew Jackson ends the Creek War by decisively defeating nativist Creeks at the Battle of Horseshoe Bend
April	Napoleon Bonaparte is defeated and removed from power, freeing British veterans for the American war; the Royal Navy extends its blockade to New England
July 25	A stalemate at Lundy's Lane near Niagara Falls is the bloodiest battle of the war
August 9	The Treaty of Fort Jackson cedes 23 million acres of Creek land to the United States
August 24–25	British forces occupy Washington, D.C., and burn its public buildings, including the Executive Mansion
September 11	A British invasion of New York is repulsed at Plattsburgh
September 12–14	The British effort to take Baltimore fails after an extended bombardment of Fort McHenry; Francis Scott Key writes "The Star-Spangled Banner" to commemorate the American victory
December	The British begin their campaign against New Orleans; New England Federalists convene at Hartford, Connecticut, to protest the war

| December 24 | Peace commissioners meeting at Ghent sign a treaty ending the War of 1812 |

1815

General	Publications: The *North American Review* is published in Boston; Jedidiah Morse's pamphlet *Review of American Unitarianism* traces the growing controversy caused by the doctrine
	Inventions: John Stevens receives the first charter in the United States to build a railroad, but the project will languish for more than a decade; Baltimore's streets are illuminated by gaslights as the city's Gas Light Company becomes the first firm of its kind
	Notable births: Anna Ella Carroll (August 29); surgeon Crawford Williamson Long (November 1); suffragist Elizabeth Cady Stanton (November 12)
	Notable deaths: Robert Fulton (February 24) at age 51
January	The Hartford Convention adjourns after adopting resolutions that oppose the war and seek to redress New England's waning political influence
January 8	Andrew Jackson defeats the British at the Battle of New Orleans and becomes a national hero
February 17	The War of 1812 officially ends with the exchange of ratifications of the Treaty of Ghent
February–March	Congress reduces the army and navy
July–August	The U.S. Navy forces the North African sponsor states of the Barbary pirates to sign treaties
December	Madison proposes a public works program and the establishment of another national bank

1816

General	Publications: John Pickering's *Vocabulary* catalogs indigenous American words and phrases
	Notable births: Henry David Thoreau (July 12)
March	Congress establishes the second Bank of the United States
April	The African Methodist Episcopal Church is established in Philadelphia

June–August	Volcanic eruptions in Indonesia alter the world's climate, depriving New England of a growing season as almost a foot of snow falls in June and hard frosts occur throughout July and August
December	James Monroe is elected president; the American Colonization Society is organized to colonize freed blacks in Africa; Indiana is admitted to the Union; Boston's Provident Institution is the first savings bank in the United States

1817

General	Publications: John Kenrick's *Horrors of Slavery*
	Transportation: Henry Shreve's steamboat *Washington* begins commercial service between Louisville, Kentucky, and New Orleans
January	The second Bank of the United States (known as the BUS) opens for business
March	Work begins on the Erie Canal to connect the Hudson River with Lake Erie, a project that will be completed in 1825; the Alabama Territory is created out of the eastern portion of the Mississippi Territory
March 4	James Monroe is inaugurated as president
December	Mississippi enters the Union

1818

General	Transportation: The steamboat *Walk-in-the-Water* begins carrying passengers on Lake Erie from Buffalo to Detroit
	Notable deaths: Abigail Adams (October 28), wife of John Adams, at age 73
March	Congress passes legislation granting lifetime pensions to all Revolutionary War veterans
March–May	Andrew Jackson leads an army into Spanish Florida to punish Seminole Indians, but in violation of his orders, he seizes Spanish forts and towns
June	Connecticut ends property ownership as a requirement for voting rights
December	Illinois enters the Union

1819

General	Commerce: A serious financial panic ushers in a wide-ranging depression that sets off many bank failures and foreclosures throughout the year
	Transportation: The *Savannah* steams part of the way and sails the rest from Savannah, Georgia, to Liverpool, England, completing the first transatlantic voyage of a steamship
	Culture: William Ellery Channing delivers a seminal sermon on Unitarianism
	Notable births: James Russell Lowell (February 22); Julia Ward Howe (May 27); Walt Whitman (May 31); Herman Melville (August 1); Allan Pinkerton (August 25)
	Notable deaths: Hero of the Battle of Lake Erie Oliver Hazard Perry (August 23) at age 34
January	Congress refuses to condemn Andrew Jackson's behavior during the Florida invasion
February	A crisis over slavery in the prospective state of Missouri develops; Spain formally agrees to cede Florida to the United States for $5 million
March	Congress enacts measures to stop slave smuggling
June	An expedition under Maj. Stephen H. Long departs from Pittsburgh to explore the region south of the Missouri River, the Great Plains, and part of the Rocky Mountains
December	Alabama enters the Union

1820

General	Notable births: William Tecumseh Sherman (February 8); Susan B. Anthony (February 15); John Bartlett, editor of *Bartlett's Quotations* (June 14)
	Notable deaths: Naval hero Stephen Decatur (March 22), killed in a duel at age 41; Daniel Boone (September 26) at age 85
January	Eighty-six free blacks embark from New York bound for the British colony of Sierra Leone
February– March	After a lengthy process of negotiation and adjustment, Congress enacts the Missouri Compromise, which temporarily quells arguments over the slavery question; the

agreement to admit Missouri to the Union as a slave state is balanced by the admission of Maine as a free state

March   New England missionaries arrive in Hawaii

April   Congress revises the policy and procedures for the sale of public lands with the Public Land Act

December   James Monroe is reelected president of the United States

PROLOGUE: THE TIME OF THEIR LIVES

Imagine a place where there was no "time" as we now know it. Such a place would be, even in our imaginations, so alien to our sense of routine, so exotic in comparison to the schedules of modern life, that it would be difficult to picture and even more difficult to understand. Yet such a place does not exist only in the realm of imagination. It is not a product of fiction or fantasy. It existed in the relatively near reach of our own history. The period covered by this book—the early Republic of the revolutionary generation's waning days and industrial capitalists' infant ones—was without time as we understand it.

Of course, the people of the early Republic had ways of measuring the passing of their lives and of gauging the march of the abstraction made tangible as time. For the most part they were a farming people and accordingly adjusted the considerable labor and little leisure that filled their lives to the seasons. For as long as anyone could remember, it had been thus. Seasonal events—spring planting, summer cultivation, fall harvest, winter chores—dictated people's lives as much as defined them. Within the larger seasons that ordered their years, the smaller units of time were gauged in accuracy inversely proportional to their size: the smaller the unit, the less certain its measure. In keeping with colonial New England's Puritan heritage, farmers in that part of the country did not celebrate holy days, not even Christmas, but they observed Sunday as a day of rest. The practice helped to order a week in which one day seemed much like another, except Sunday, which helped to sort the other days into their proper places. But in measuring hours, these Americans remained blithely imprecise. Watches were rare, expensive, and cumbersome. If they were not cumbersome, they were costly and fragile. Even people who did have watches owned imperfect mechanical novelties that kept time eccentrically. At the opening of the period, even the mantel clock was a luxury, although that would gradually change as men like Eli Terry of Connecticut anticipated mass production by using interchangeable parts, another development of these remarkable years. By the end of the period, Terry's "scroll and pillar" mantel clocks were becoming fixtures throughout the country. They seem cheap to modern pocketbooks—an average clock cost about $15—but in 1800 that was quite a sum of money, the equivalent of about $225 today. That households were willing to bear the burden of an expensive clock is a testament to time's growing importance in the scheme of things. Clocks would outnumber watches until the mid-nineteenth century as the principal mechanical means of telling time.

Before Terry's clock there was the sun. People set sundials according to almanacs, which in addition to the Holy Bible were the staple of every household. *The Farmer's Almanac* began publication in 1792 and eventually had so many imitators that it was forced to change its name to *The Old Farmer's Almanac* in 1832. Published annually, almanacs contained complicated tables almost indecipherable to modern eyes but indispensable to the people who used them to determine sunrises and sunsets, as well as the moon's cycle of waxing and waning. Along with horticultural lore, almanacs provided extended weather forecasts (for the entire year) that according to some were remarkably accurate. They also recommended the best herbs for remedying various illnesses and told the best time of the year to use them.

But it was mainly by making time measurable for farmers that the almanac proved essential. Almanac publisher Nathaniel Law boasted that "twenty gentlemen in company will hardly be able, by the help of their thirty-guinea watches, to guess within two hours of their true time of night...whilst the poor peasant, who never saw a watch, would tell you the time to a fraction by the rising and setting of the moon, which he learns from his almanack."[1]

For farming folk, the sun's appearance in the morning signaled the start of work. Its traverse of the sky directed work's course. Varying tasks from milking to collecting eggs to tilling to weeding and reaping all fell into allotted spans measured not by spring-driven cogged gears but by the chore itself and the shadows cast while completing it. The sun's disappearance closed the workday on the farm. Activities after dark were brief, and bedtimes early, for artificial light was expensive and could be dangerous.

In the towns and villages of the early Republic, the sun held sway as well, even when prosperous and growing communities installed clocks in courthouse towers. These clocks required frequent, sometimes daily, adjustments, not only because they gained or lost noticeable increments of time each week but also because they had to be brought into accordance with the master timekeeper, the sun. The synchronization of mechanical clocks was made more precise by the indispensable almanac. Accounting for seasonal changes, noon would have to fall in the middle of the day, as celestially determined. Noon by the clock was expected to match the sun's zenith in the sky, and thus apparent or natural time dictated the settings of clock time in every locality, making the measurement of time and its sense of passage a uniquely local affair. One village's noon was never the same as that of another.[2] The people living under such a varied system were neither physically discomfited nor confused by it. Clocks and watches were not mysteries. They were devices that provided ways of marking time, but they were not really time itself, any more than a portrait was the actual person being depicted. The concept of time was unique to each locale, whether it was a village or a homestead.

People who lived in towns were really only a few steps from a rural setting, but in terms of time, they lived differently from their farmer neighbors. City life simply posed different circumstances of interdependence because markets, courts, theaters, and businesses required people to match their activities more carefully. To gather at an appointed time, no matter how roughly figured it was, required a more exact sense of where the day was. Yet while some people might work beyond daylight in the city, and all were more aware of the time as indicated by clockworks and tolling chimes, they knew it was a marking of time unique to their locality, and they accommodated those from beyond their locality accordingly. Appointments were general in their circumstance, usually made for a day rather than an hour.

Not that it much mattered. Communication and travel were slow by any measure. Messages traveled by mail and moved only as fast as the conveyances that carried them. In 1776 news of the Declaration of Independence took almost a month to travel from Philadelphia to Charleston, South Carolina, a situation that was not much improved more than two decades later. Reports of George Washington's death took almost a week to travel from Mount Vernon to Philadelphia and almost a month to reach Lexington, Kentucky. Horses continued to plod over land, sailing vessels still rode swells at sea, and current-driven barges or keelboats drifted lazily on inland waters as they had during colonial times. In 1800 a mail coach in good working order could race along at the impressive speed of seven miles per hour, depending on the condition of the road, always a significant variable. Most roads, in fact, were little more than dirt paths. Any traffic on them raised billowing clouds of dust in dry weather, and rain turned them into muddy bogs. If falling trees did not block the way, or if bridges had not washed out, a traveler in a horse-drawn vehicle could cover about 25 miles in a long day. Short journeys for errands—the only reason most people left their homes at all—were made on foot. Poor folks thought nothing of walking five to six miles to attend church or go to school. The more affluent rode horses, but children almost always walked, regardless of their class. In New England, most farming families lived close enough to a town to visit it daily if necessary, but in the rural South, people might be far enough from a town to go an entire month before visiting it for a special market day.

In any case, distance was not measured in miles but gauged instead by the time it took to cover it. A destination was so many days' ride or walk from where one started. And there were many places so difficult to get to that they qualified for the fabled "you can't get there from here" designation. There was no direct road from Albany to Detroit during the whole of the period, for instance, and the mail between those points had to be hauled by horsemen plodding around Lake Erie and through the perilous Black Swamps of the Maumee River region. Before the advent of steam power, waterborne traffic depended on the vagaries of wind and weather or the tedious application of animals or manpower to get from one place to another. Schedules were at best vague promises that nobody considered very binding, and later when relatively dependable steamboats were introduced, the novelty of having something show up when it was supposed to led to their special description as "packets."

Geographical regions did more than physically separate Americans; they made them distinctive types that defied generalization, even within their regions. The New England Yankee, the mid-Atlantic farmer, the western pioneer, the poor white southerner, the urban professional, the elite planter—all could be different in the way they dressed, the way they spoke, and, in some cases, the way they thought. And there were not many of them. In 1790 about 4 million people lived in all 13 states of the American Republic, most of them on farms that were less than a week's journey from the Atlantic Ocean. There were few real cities—Philadelphia and New York had populations of 42,000 and 33,000 respectively—and well over 90 percent of the people lived in villages or towns of a couple thousand or less. Growth was limited by physical factors. The lack of any semblance of a national transportation network meant that village populations were constrained by the amount of food local farms could produce.

Distance and geographical diversity also meant differences in the basic stuff of life, such as language, or at least the way it was spoken. Pronunciations differed across the country, and speaking could instantly identify a person's region and sometimes his or her locality within that region. Rural New Englanders spoke through their noses to say "eend" instead of "end" or "Gawd" instead of "God" and inserted barely perceptible extra syllables in some words, so that cow became "keow." Southerners and westerners broadened their vowels to make "where" into "whar" or "there" into "thar." Americans were a rural people, and regardless of region, they unwittingly fashioned a dialect peculiar to their country, "delightsome" (delightful) to some, "curous" (curious) to others, revealing a woeful lack of "larnin" (learning) to foreigners. A careless person wading across a swift "crick" (creek) might get "drownded." A cook should mind her "kittle" lest it "bile" over. Creatures were "critters" that one either hunted or "cotch'd" (caught), a different animal altogether from a "varmint," the term for vermin. Daughters were "darters," who were taught to be "perlite" so they could attract suitable "bachelders" (bachelors). The New England farmer talked of the "ruff" (roof) over his head as his "hum" (home) and the "stuns" (stones) he had cleared from his rocky fields with "stiddy" (steady) labor. Fireplace smoke went up the "chimbly" whether in the South, North, or West—or, in a word, "everywheres." And if one were feeling ill, it might be a "tech" (touch) of "rheumatiz" (rheumatism). The common tongue, like a common sense of time, was equally intangible for these Americans.

Although their hours were not rapidly paced or measured by a universal standard, they were not empty. On the broad canvas of the national experience, great and profoundly important events moved with magisterial deliberateness. The Constitution ushered in a new government, the merchant class struggled to cope with the financial burdens of new nationhood, farmers watched the skies and tilled the ground, pioneers pulled up stakes and trudged toward the western wilderness. All of this passed minute to minute, hour to hour, in the long span of years beginning with George Washington's inauguration and proceeding through the uncertainties, fears, and hopes of the country's first three decades. The men and women living through these events did not see them as starkly marking the end of historically significant chapters or the start of important eras. They were merely part of the stuff of their lives, frequently pushed to the margins of more personal experiences, rarely occupying center stage for them as these events do in our historical memory. As the sun rose and set on their seasons of birth, youth, planting, reaping, enfeeblement, and death, the Americans of the early Republic cried over their sorrows, laughed over their joys, despaired over their failures, and took comfort in the affection of their families and the kindness of their friends. Later times would listen to the rhythmic tick of mechanical clocks, the precise click of quartz movements, or gaze upon shimmering, digitized numerals of increasingly sophisticated and accurate devices to mark the divisions of their days. Later times would have those mechanical or electronic tools to sustain the sensation that life is fleeting. For Americans in the early years of their country, there was something else. Their lives were not simpler because they were less ordered, sorted, and categorized. Their lives were differently arranged, not less varied, complex, or bewildering than our own. For those Americans, the inescapable verities were the same as they are today, reminding us that the human condition, both in earlier times and in ours, binds us all together. In a world without watches, the heart is a clock of sorts.

NOTES

1. Quoted in Michael O'Malley, *Keeping Watch: A History of American Time* (New York: Viking, 1990), 5.

2. Eli Terry patented an apparent clock in 1797—the second patent issued in the United States—that through clever gearing could tell two types of time at once. A minute hand indicated the clock, or mechanical, time while another showed the natural, or apparent, time according to the sun. Because of its complexity and consequent expense, the clock remained only a novelty.

1

HISTORICAL
NARRATIVE

The Americans of the early Republic lived through some of the most exciting and perilous years of the nation's history. Having successfully gained independence from Great Britain, a feat whose sheer audacity astonished the world, Americans suddenly found themselves facing an even sterner challenge. They would have to shape diverse elements, different religions, and enormous geographical spaces into a new nation that could remain politically free and become economically prosperous. The great figures and events that shaped their country's destiny moved on a larger stage while they, American individuals, went about their daily routines.

Many Americans understood the momentous questions of their time with great clarity. Arguably, they understood their time better than many modern Americans immersed in the Internet and round-the-clock cable news understand theirs. Many, for instance, entirely grasped the arguments that caused the American Revolution, especially because years of closely followed debate had broken those arguments down to their barest essentials. The quarrel between Great Britain and its North American colonies is popularly depicted as centering on taxes levied by London, but taxes were a symptom of a more basic argument. Many colonists were disturbed by what they perceived as the steady erosion of their political rights under policies designed by distant and faceless authorities. In the years before the American Revolution, a series of measures by the British king and Parliament sought to strengthen and organize the British Empire, but many Britons in North America were increasingly alienated by this policy. Finally, the belief that their liberty was being systematically weakened caused Americans to take up arms and then, after considerable debate, to declare their independence.

In its simplest terms, the American War of Independence was fought to secure the right to regulate one's own affairs. To understand this is the key to understanding the political events that unfolded during and after the Revolution. The colonies that had transformed themselves into states during the conflict were not willing to relinquish local control to another distant and faceless authority merely because it was based in Philadelphia or New York. Committed to protecting themselves from intrusive regulations imposed by any remote authority, the states agreed only to a central government so weak that it turned out to be ineffective. From 1781 to 1789, the United States government operated under a document called the Articles of Confederation, which denied the central government the power to tax, always the most irritating manifestation of regulation. Other attitudes etched by the revolutionary experience also appeared in the Articles. They did not create an executive (or president) because a president resembled a king. The government instead consisted of a unicameral legislature in which state delegations voted as blocs, each having one vote regardless of its size or population. Small states consequently felt protected from behemoths such as New York or Virginia or Pennsylvania.

This system satisfied people who worried over losing what they had fought for—the right to regulate their own localities as they saw fit—but the system's weakness gradually became so apparent that it compelled reevaluation. Most ominous was the financial emergency that engulfed the government and disrupted the economy. The United States carried a staggering debt from the Revolution, and without the power to levy taxes, the Confederation government had no way to fund that debt. The government's sinking credit created uneasiness in the states, whose own debts were frequently just as much a problem. Commerce was crippled, and some states contemplated erecting separate economic systems, a sure prelude to their breaking away from the United States to establish separate political systems. The experiment in liberty, won with great patriotic sacrifice, seemed fated to fail in its first decade. European monarchies, especially Britain, looked on with unconcealed pleasure.

Scholars continue to argue over how close to collapse the American government actually was during the Confederation period. Although some claim that the economic and governmental problems were not really that dire, a sense of growing alarm nevertheless prompted Americans to amend the Articles of Confederation. Ultimately, a major convention of virtually all the states (Rhode Island did not attend) elected to discard the Articles of Confederation and craft a new instrument of government. The result was the Constitution of the United States of America, drafted in 1787 and ratified by the states in the months that followed. Under the Constitution, three separate and distinct branches of the national government would each serve to regulate the behavior of the other two. The legislative branch, consisting of a bicameral congress, would make laws, regulate the currency, and levy taxes; the executive would administer and enforce domestic laws and, subject to the consent of Congress, direct foreign policy; and the judiciary would administer justice by hearing disputes arising from the law. Each branch would exercise vigilance to make sure that the Constitution, both in spirit and in letter, was protected from abridgment or change unless under clearly prescribed processes. The Constitution made the central government strong enough to fulfill its function, but its system of internal checks and balances prevented the government from becoming so powerful as to threaten the liberty of the people.

Of course, people went about the everyday business of expanding the new nation as the Constitution established this new government. In 1790 the first official census counted the American population at nearly 4 million people, a figure that doubled in the 30 years that followed. About nine-tenths of America remained rural, but cities like Philadelphia (42,000 people), New York (33,000), Boston (18,000), Charleston (16,000), and Baltimore (13,000) were ripening into a rough urbanity along the edge of the vast American frontier. In 1790 few Americans lived beyond the Appalachian Mountains—95 percent of the population resided east of that rolling range—and those who had moved west were mostly in Kentucky, Tennessee, and Ohio, but their growing numbers made it possible for those regions to become states in only a few years rather than many generations. Foreigners observing the rough-and-ready life of American city dwellers and their wilderness cousins were more frequently carping than complimentary. Yet they grudgingly admitted that the strange people in this exotic new land were an enterprising and assured lot, blessed with abundant resources and possessed of the will to make the most of them.

It is worth remembering that the business of establishing another new government did not always proceed smoothly. Despite the promising opportunities provided by the land's sheer size and the citizens' intention to use it, that sheer size also posed a problem. Americans' traditional distrust of central authority was especially pronounced in the West, where hardy and self-sufficient pioneers cleared forests, slept lightly, and nursed deep suspicions about losing their independence to distant influences. The Mississippi River, more accessible and useful than rough trails through dark forests and over rugged mountains, was their lifeline to the outside world, including the eastern United States, but the Mississippi's southern currents passed through land owned by Spain. For years there would be the question of whether the U.S. government or the Spanish crown could offer these western dwellers the best future. For many years, the U.S. government was not favored in such a contest. Directing domestic affairs was also awkward. The American government's solvency remained uncertain as its revenues dried up while its debt, including a mounting wave of interest, swelled to a crest. The circulating currency was worthless, and many states still stumbled under their equally over-whelming indebtedness.

In short, the Constitution and the government it created did not magi-cally solve the new nation's problems. The greater part of that task fell to ordinary Americans, a motley collection of folk who Europeans rightly concluded were not much to look at. Most of the world's people existed in drudgery, many under fierce oppression, and the bosses who superin-tended that oppression or dictated that drudgery, whether from ornate thrones or rude lairs, were complacent in their power. They watched with attitudes ranging from bemused skepticism to outright hostility as ordi-nary Americans undertook to build a republic so geographically immense and so idealistically principled that there had never been anything like it in the world. The countless names of these Americans would not make it into any history book, nor would any of them ever regard their daily cus-toms as particularly influential. But as individuals independently pursu-ing what turned out to be a collective dream, they were so different from anything before them that they not only conquered their lands but also changed the world beyond them. With callused hands and sweat-soaked clothes, occasionally bloodied by a fight, they proved that courage, tenac-ity, and endurance could secure liberty and court fortune. There had never been anything like it, or them, in the world.

FOUNDATION AND CONFLICT: 1790–1800

Under the Constitution's provisions for selecting a president, the Elec-toral College in 1789 unanimously chose George Washington, greatly admired for his service as general of the Continental Army during the Revolution. Washington remains the only person placed in the presidency honored by such universal accord. Tall for his time at 6'2"—the average height was about 5'7"—Washington was physically imposing but retiring by nature and most reluctant to assume the burdens of the presidency. In his youth, he could be hotheaded and impetuous, but age and experience had steadied him, and though he never claimed great mental agility or pretended to wide learning, his character was as strong as it was stable. His countrymen revered him, and his journey from Mount Vernon to the new temporary capital in New York City showed it. Cannons thundered, bells tolled, and citizens cheered in celebrations that continued even after he took the oath of office on April 30, 1789. Sadly, as virtually all his suc-cessors would discover, there would come a time when the ovations became more subdued.

Rights, Revenues, and Rebellion Persisting in their revolutionary outlook, opponents of the Constitution had criticized it during the ratifica-tion debates for failing to pledge that the new govern-ment would respect freedom of speech, assembly, religion, and other individual rights. Indeed, the Constitution won ratification in part because of the unspoken promise that it would be amended to include such promises. Although theoretically the Constitution could be changed by a new convention at the request of two-thirds of the states, federalist proponents such as Virginia congressman James Madison worried that another convention might thoroughly reverse the work of the first one. Consequently, Madison persuaded the necessary two-thirds majorities in both houses of Congress to authorize the simpler amending process of having changes proposed by Congress and put before the states for approval. Madison also drafted the amendments that he then efficiently steered through Congress.

The prescribed three-fourths of the states approved the first ten amendments to the Constitution in 1791. Known as the Bill of Rights, these measures preserve the most prized American principles of government and society, including freedom of religion, assembly, and speech. They guarantee a press free from government control and a citizenry with the right to bear arms. Citizens are guaranteed trial by jury and can without fear of reprisal petition the government for redress of grievances. The Bill of Rights proscribes cruel and unusual punishment and forbids government seizure of private property without due process.

To prevent such a specific list of guaranteed rights from creating the impression that they were the only ones protected, the Ninth Amendment stated that identifying these particular rights "shall not be construed to deny or disparage others retained by the people." The Tenth Amendment also reserved all rights not explicitly delegated or prohibited by the Constitution "to the States respectively, or to the people." Thus a robust central government spelled out protections for individual liberty and thereby helped to secure not just the grudging consent but the approbation of the Constitution's most vocal opponents.

The first Congress also passed the Judiciary Act of 1789, which organized the Supreme Court to be composed of a chief justice and five associates. New York's John Jay became the first chief justice. The Judiciary Act also established federal district and circuit courts and created the office of attorney general.

President Washington's official circle was small, consisting only of three department heads. Alexander Hamilton was secretary of the treasury, Thomas Jefferson was secretary of state, and Henry Knox secretary of war. Jefferson and Hamilton were arguably the most talented men ever to serve a U.S. administration. Because of the government's dire financial problems, the Treasury was considered the most important of the executive departments, and its first secretary, Alexander Hamilton, assumed the most prominent role in conducting domestic affairs. Only 34 years old, Hamilton had been a boy wonder, but he had his detractors, who distrusted his integrity and suspected his devotion to republican government. Such qualms were intensified when Hamilton unveiled his plan to repair the country's financial situation.

Hamilton's first and foremost job was to restore confidence in the government's credit (known as the public credit), something he intended to do not only by funding the total national debt but by assuming all state debts as well. He insisted that ensuring the financial security of the nation at large would require that the credit of constituent parts of the Union, the states, be restored also. Under his plan, the federal government would retire its debt at face value in addition to about $13 million of accrued interest, a huge sum of more than $54 million. Because many supposed that such a massive debt would never be paid off, government bonds had decreased in value to as little as 10¢ to 15¢ on the dollar. The virtual worthlessness of these securities meant that mostly speculators had bought them, but now those speculators stood to reap incredible profits. Widows and war veterans who had sold their "worthless" government securities for a song felt cheated and betrayed.

The plan to assume state debts—tallied at about $21.5 million—was even more controversial. Hamilton believed that "assumption," as the plan regarding state debts was called, would more thoroughly tie the states to the Union by making their wealthy creditors dependent on the federal government for their money. Although Hamilton also reasonably described the states' debts as part of the national obligation because they had been acquired during the Revolution, the plan appeared to states' rights advocates as a devious way of accomplishing centralization. Naturally Hamilton's plan elated states like Massachusetts that carried large debts, but states that had pinched pennies to stay solvent, like Virginia, believed they were being exploited to assist spendthrifts. Hamilton ultimately overcame these objections by agreeing to place the nation's capital on the Potomac River in exchange for Virginia's support of his economic plan. He was even able to persuade Thomas Jefferson to back the Hamiltonian system and thus secured the necessary majorities to pass it in 1790.

With the country's debt now ballooning to $75 million, Hamilton had to find sources of revenue to pay the continuing interest on it. He chose to rely heavily on tariff duties that would result from a dynamic import trade. Congress had already passed a tariff law in 1789, and the rate of roughly 8 percent on certain imports promised to fill the bill. At the same time, Hamilton hoped to use the tariff as a way of encouraging domestic industries to take root, but he was less successful in this endeavor. Farmers and merchants controlled Congress during the 1790s, and only two small tariff increases were approved in the following eight years.

Excise taxes on domestic products, especially a tax on whiskey, generated additional revenue, but they were by far the most unpopular taxes the government levied. Frontier farmers had been distilling their grains into whiskey for years, a process that made corn less unwieldy as well as more profitable for shipment. In regions where whiskey was used like money—even some preachers were paid with whiskey—the tax was detested, and by 1794, resistance in backwoods Pennsylvania was creating a serious domestic crisis. When "revenoors," as these moonshiners derisively labeled tax collectors, were intimidated into inaction, some by physical assault, President Washington perceived a grave challenge to federal authority. Hamilton agreed. The president mustered militias from surrounding states and personally led about 13,000 men part of the way into Pennsylvania, a gesture that was as significant as it was symbolic. Never much of an insurrection in the first place, the Whiskey Rebellion quickly collapsed before the show of federal force, and Washington pardoned the two offenders later found guilty. Yet the repercussions of the little Whiskey Rebellion were momentous, for the question of whether the central government would have the support of the states in times of crisis was decisively answered. Equally telling, on the other hand, were the rising voices of critics who denounced the large militia demonstration as an overreaction and again pointed to Hamilton as the serpent in Washington's garden.

To Hamilton's thinking, the most important part of his financial system was a national bank, and his efforts to have Congress authorize the establishment of one sharply divided Washington's cabinet and spurred the formation of factions that evolved into political parties. Hamilton modeled his Bank of the United States on the Bank of England, and like the British institution, the American version would be a private establishment with the government acting as a significant stockholder and principal depositor. The bank would print currency to provide a fluid but stable medium of exchange while regulating credit to stimulate business.

The Bank of the United States

Jefferson, who had grudgingly supported Hamilton's funding and assumption plan, balked at the idea of the bank. In fact, in a written opinion produced at Washington's request, Jefferson forcefully argued against it. His main objection, he claimed, was constitutional. The Constitution, he said, contained no explicit sanction for such a financial institution. Furthermore, since the Tenth Amendment (which with the rest of the Bill of Rights was on the verge of being ratified) reserved to the states all powers not specifically granted to the central government, only states had the tacit constitutional authority to establish banks. By interpreting so narrowly the meaning of the Constitution, Jefferson voiced a theory of constitutional understanding called "strict construction."

Washington asked Hamilton for a written opinion as well, in which the secretary of the treasury answered Jefferson's objections. In Hamilton's view, the Constitution granted the authority to exercise necessary powers, not impede them. He specifically cited the constitutional directive that Congress could pass "necessary and proper" laws to empower the government to carry out its duties. Because the government had the explicit power to collect taxes and control trade, the government had the implied power to erect such institutions as would assist those activities, such as a Bank of the United States. In direct contradiction to Jefferson's strict construction, Hamilton used the doctrine of implied powers to interpret the Constitution broadly, a reading of the document called "loose construction."

Ultimately Washington cautiously sided with Hamilton on this issue to sign the bank into law. The Bank of the United States was licensed for 20 years, with its offices in Philadelphia. The institution was capitalized at $10 million, of which 20 percent was held by the federal government, and stock was sold publicly to an enthusiastic response. Yet the congressional debate over the bank had been jarringly venomous on both constitutional and financial grounds. Hamilton had won the day, but Jefferson and his followers, shocked by this defeat, were energized to challenge the secretary on any and all subsequent political fronts.

Factions Become Parties

With relative swiftness, Hamilton's policies restored the government's credit, but they did so at a high political price. Funding the debt, assuming state debts, imposing the unpopular excise taxes that had spurred the Whiskey Rebellion, and establishing the Bank of the United States produced a wide array of enemies and gave them common purpose. Soon enough, systematic resistance grew out of the dispute between Hamilton and Jefferson, and acrimonious political debate became customary.

Americans resisted the idea of political parties, however, because many deemed parties to be pawns of special interests and havens for political corruption. During the colonial and Revolutionary periods, factions formed over specific issues, flourished briefly during fierce debates, and then withered once the issues were resolved or fell from interest. In addition, the hardships of the Revolution had united all but the most incorrigible dissenters, and as the government drew legitimacy from the consent of the governed, those who opposed it seemed intent on thwarting the will of the people.

Jefferson and Madison's organized opposition to Hamilton was not only an innovation; it was close to being perceived as a dangerous one. Yet an energetic press campaign by the Jeffersonians, countered by Hamilton's supporters in newspapers of their own, both informed ordinary people of the debate and compelled them to take sides in it. From these shadowy factions, political parties took shape and gradually transformed into regular organizations that sponsored candidates and pushed programs. Hamilton's faction became the Federalists, and Jefferson's became the Democratic-Republicans, frequently abbreviated to Republicans. Nobody at the time thought this was a helpful development—Jefferson and Madison themselves thought their faction would, like others before them, be a temporary arrangement to meet a passing need—but time would demonstrate otherwise. Despite the bickering and apparent stalemates they frequently engendered, political parties became a crucial element of democratic government. Debate from organized opponents kept in check the political behavior of those in power.

Domestic policies encouraged the formation of fac- **Foreign Problems:**
tions that became parties, but arguments over the U.S. **The French**
response to the French Revolution hardened the divi- **Revolution**
sions and made party formation unavoidable. When the
French Revolution began in 1789, most Americans
applauded what they perceived as a striving for liberty and equality similar
to their own recent revolutionary experience. Yet as Washington's first term
drew to a close, revolutionary idealism in France increasingly gave way to
paranoia and radicalism. Fearful that other European monarchs intended to
restore Louis XVI to complete authority, French revolutionaries inaugurated
what would become an almost uninterrupted quarter century of conflict. In
late 1792, France proclaimed itself a republic, a move greeted with wild
acclaim in the United States, but within months the new republic's most radical elements, styling themselves the Committee of Public Safety, initiated
the Reign of Terror, the program of weeding out supposed counterrevolu-
tionaries. In addition to sending thousands to the guillotine, the radical government abolished Christianity, among other sweeping "reforms."

Such developments deeply divided America opinion. Federalists were
already vaguely suspicious of the extremism early evidenced by some
French revolutionaries, and the Terror confirmed their worst fears. Jeffersonians, however, insisted that the ends of liberty occasionally justified even
the most excessive means. The debate over such diametrically opposite perceptions was disturbing enough, but when Great Britain joined a coalition—
the first of four in the next 20 years—to fight France, the conflict threatened
to involve the United States. Specifically, the possibility that France would
invoke the Franco-American alliance of 1778 cast a long shadow in American
councils. The 1778 alliance had proved indispensable in helping the United
States win independence from Great Britain, and Jefferson and his supporters argued in 1793 that the American debt to France for this assistance
required honoring the treaty. President Washington, however, thought that
impetuous participation in the European war could be catastrophic for the
new nation, and he consequently proclaimed U.S. neutrality. Pro-French Jeffersonians seethed over what they saw as another example of Hamilton's
deceit and unseemly manipulation of the aging Washington.

Neutrality became an even harder pill to swallow when Britain consistently provoked Americans by refusing to relinquish northwestern posts
in U.S. territory, by stirring the Indians to violence on the frontier, and by
assailing American shipping on the high seas. A diplomatic effort to adjust
Anglo-American relations led to the unpopular Jay's Treaty, which only
enraged the Jeffersonians further and even hurt Washington's personal
popularity with the people at large.[1]

President Washington's growing dismay over partisan
strife in the government was matched by his profound sad- **Washington**
ness at being the target of increasingly personal attacks in **Retires**
the press. Extremely dispirited, he chose to retire from office

after his second term, a decision that surprised his foes as well as his friends.[2] Both camps thought that Washington would remain president until his death, and the news of his departure alarmed them. The quarrels that had marred his second term would now be given free and perhaps disastrous rein in a contest for the presidency—the first truly competitive contest for that office. Given the political climate, some thought it might be the last.

Although Alexander Hamilton was the most eminent member of his faction, his unpopularity precluded him as Washington's successor. Virtually by default, the budding Federalist Party chose Washington's vice president, John Adams. Emerging Republicans united behind Thomas Jefferson. The campaign took a nasty turn with searing personal attacks leveled by the opposing camps, and Jeffersonians reminded the country of the vigorous suppression of the freedom-loving Whiskey Boys and the alleged surrender of American honor in the negotiation of the British treaty. Despite such rancor, the election was held without violent incident, and John Adams narrowly claimed victory without his opponents threatening to void the results with revolution. In fact, under the rules of the day, Jefferson, as runner-up, became Adams's vice president.[3]

Hailing from Massachusetts, Adams had a distinguished record as one of the most constant champions of liberty before and during the Revolution, but he was never admired, and though he seemed indifferent to popularity, he nevertheless fretted over his role as Washington's successor. Hamilton intensely disliked him, adding to the uncertainties Adams confronted as the second man to become chief executive of the still-fragile republic. Hamilton had left the Treasury in 1795, but he still exercised considerable control through his lieutenants in Adams's cabinet. For his part, Adams completely reciprocated Hamilton's feelings, which did not bode well for a tranquil time in office.

The Problem of War and Dissent Adams inherited a deteriorating international situation that soon embroiled the United States in an undeclared war with the French. Angry over Jay's Treaty, France began to waylay American shipping and snubbed Adams's diplomatic envoy. Although the country was incensed, President Adams again tried diplomacy by appointing a three-man commission to meet directly with Charles-Maurice de Talleyrand, the French foreign minister. Arriving in Paris in late 1797, the commission discovered that Talleyrand would not meet it unless the United States agreed to substantial bribes and concessions. When news of this behavior reached the United States in 1798, it seemed certain that American anger would lead to war. Overcoming Jeffersonian opposition in Congress, the government expanded the navy and created a sizable army, at least on paper. Meanwhile, shooting broke out on the high seas as U.S. warships clashed with their French counterparts in the West Indies.

At home, the excitement generated by the conflict resulted in instances of appalling legislative excess. Anti-French sentiment allowed Federalists to pass a series of laws designed to shrink their opponents' numbers and suppress their right to political dissent. A new naturalization law raised the residence requirement for citizenship eligibility from 5 to 14 years, and the Alien Act authorized the president to expel foreigners he deemed dangerous.[4] The worst of the lot was the Sedition Act. Under its provisions, anyone who obstructed government policies or wrongly disparaged government officials, including the president, could be prosecuted and, if found guilty, fined and imprisoned.

Despite its clear violation of the First Amendment's protection of free speech, the Sedition Act appeared to Federalists as the only way to contain the violent language that pro-French Jeffersonian newspapers heaped on the government's policies. Scores of editors were charged, and of the 10 who stood trial, all were found guilty by juries frequently badgered by Federalist judges.

Alarmed by these political persecutions, Jefferson secretly drafted a set of resolutions that the Kentucky legislature approved in 1798 and 1799, and James Madison drew up similar though more moderate resolutions that were adopted by the Virginia legislature in 1798. Both sets of resolutions were a skillful statement of the Union from a states' rights perspective, but because no other state would endorse them, they were ineffective in resisting the Alien and Sedition Acts. The Sedition Act expired in March 1801, but before its termination, the measure persuaded many to join the Jeffersonian camp, and the Virginia and Kentucky Resolutions helped to focus opposition to the Federalist Party and rally the Jeffersonians against Federalist "tyranny" in the presidential election of 1800.

In the meantime, full-scale war with France was averted by the happy coincidence that neither Adams, despite his clamoring country, nor Talleyrand, despite his imperious behavior, wanted it. France already had too many enemies to add the United States to the list. And true to his fundamental disdain for easy popularity, Adams resisted the swelling call for war against France because he, like Washington before him, believed that the country was still too weak to play at such a perilous game. His return to diplomacy enraged his own party and did little to endear him to suspicious Republicans, but it did lead to the Convention of 1800, a treaty signed in Paris with the new government of Napoleon Bonaparte.

EXPANSION AND DISCORD: 1800–1810

The presidential election of 1800 sharply defined the formation of the Federalist and Republican parties. Federalists promoted a robust central government that encouraged rather than regulated private enterprise, a stand popular with commercial interests, who generally supported the

Federalists. Because this group saw trade with Great Britain as essential to maintaining the country's economic vitality, Federalist foreign policy favored Britain, especially after the outbreak of the French revolutionary wars, although it was hardly the fawning strategy that Jeffersonians depicted.

On the other side, followers of Thomas Jefferson who crystallized into the Republican Party embraced the notion that the government that governed least governed best. Desirous of a weak central government, Republicans harkened back to the Revolutionary generation's worries by proposing that local control of affairs was the surest safeguard against tyranny. They regarded the national debt as a burden on the backs of the people for the benefit of special interests, and they objected to special considerations given to manufacturing interests. In fact, Jefferson and his followers saw agriculture—and with it the implicit result that citizens would be independent landowners—as the bulwark of purity in the Republic. A man who owned his farm was, in Jefferson's view, beholden to no national politician, no British member of Parliament, or even a French revolutionary. Nevertheless, Republicans favored the French in foreign policy because they sincerely supposed that the liberal ideals of the French Revolution advanced human freedom, while the British response suppressed it.

As might be deduced, Republicans tended to come from agricultural regions, such as the South and Southwest, while Federalist strength was in commercial New England and the mid-Atlantic coastal areas. Such regional differences coalescing into political parties was not seen as a healthy development, and at the end of the 1790s, the Republic's future seemed in ominous jeopardy. The presidential election of 1800 was to be another challenge for the political stability of the nation, and many were not certain the Union possessed the political maturity necessary to survive it.

The Election of 1800

As he had in 1796, Jefferson again challenged John Adams for the presidency in 1800, but this time the Federalists were encumbered by the perception that they had suppressed liberty with the Alien and Sedition Acts and by serious divisions in their own ranks. Hamilton's private attacks on Adams were made public and hopelessly split the party. Beset by harsh criticisms from all quarters, the Federalists responded by lashing out at Jefferson personally, accusing him of everything from adultery to atheism.

Despite such attacks, Jefferson bested Adams in the Electoral College by 73 to 65 votes, largely because of winning New York, but the vote also resulted in a startling stalemate. Ironically, Jefferson had won New York because of his running mate, New Yorker Aaron Burr, but at the same time Burr had received an overall equivalent number of votes as Jefferson in the Electoral College. Voting procedures that did not strictly designate votes for president or vice president caused the difficulty. Article II, Section 1, of the Constitution stipulated that the House of Representatives would resolve such a tie, but the lame-duck Federalist majority in the House was willing to elect Burr over the hated Jefferson. A deadlock ensued in which a frustrating series of ballots rendered no decision until a few Federalists, more fearful of Burr, abstained. Jefferson was finally elected.

Jefferson would refer to this presidential contest as "the Revolution of 1800," but his narrow victory hardly signaled an immense political change. More important and possibly revolutionary in the innovative sense was the orderly transfer of power through a hotly contested and controversial election. Doubts about the growing maturity of the American political system were, at least for the time being, laid to rest.

Less obviously, a great deal had changed, but nobody could have seen it clearly at the time. John Adams would be the last Federalist president, and the Federalist Party itself, once the supreme political statement of the age, would gradually wither and ultimately begin to disappear at the end of the period covered by this book. The party served a vital function in the formation and maintenance of the nation in its early days, but it gradually lost its relevance, especially when it retreated to parochial regionalism and preservation of the status quo. Tending toward elitism, the Federalists became the victims of their own arrogance and were unable to attract the loyalty of ordinary people. That inability, in the changing political and social fortunes of the early Republic, was the surest way to political extinction.

Thomas Jefferson took the presidential oath on March 4, 1801, the first president to do so in the new national capital of Washington, D.C. The setting was more a village than a town, and its pastoral situation seemed to **The Clash with the Judiciary** match the thrift and plainness of the new administration. Indeed, such qualities were mirrored in the simplicity of the new chief executive, who exhibited his connection to ordinary people by strolling to his inauguration. In a famous phrase of his inaugural address—"We are all Republicans," Jefferson said, "we are all Federalists"—he tried to dispel concerns that he would completely overturn the government. Some things, however, were bound to change. Official etiquette was democratized to remove seating arrangements at formal state dinners, and Jefferson adopted surprisingly casual dress for official foreign visitors.

Although determined to preserve continuity in the government, Jefferson was also resolved to reverse intolerable Federalist measures. He pardoned those convicted under the Sedition Act and persuaded Congress to pass a revised Naturalization Act that returned residency requirements to five years. The only part of Hamilton's financial organization that Jefferson touched, however, was the excise taxes, which Congress repealed. Otherwise, he and his secretary of the treasury, Albert Gallatin, did not alter the funding and assumption arrangements or seek to dismantle the Bank of the United States.

Most of all, Jefferson and his party could not abide what they regarded as a dishonest ploy by the retiring Federalist majority in the final days of the Adams presidency. The Judiciary Act of 1801, passed by lame-duck Federalists, established 16 new federal judicial appointments, as well as additional posts, all of which Adams understandably assigned to Federalists. Although virtually all had been dispensed in the light of day, these appointments were scornfully referred to by Republicans as "midnight judges" to emphasize the alleged deceit behind the Federalist scheme to ensconce partisan obstructionists in lifetime posts.

The Republican Congress repealed the Judiciary Act of 1801 and thus legislatively removed 16 judges by abolishing their posts. Republicans, however, were unable to touch the new Federalist chief justice of the Supreme Court, John Marshall, who had also been appointed by Adams in the final months of his presidency. Marshall and the Supreme Court were soon embroiled in the struggle between president and courts in a pivotal incident that ended up establishing judicial independence. Adams had appointed William Marbury a justice of the peace for the District of Columbia, but Jefferson's secretary of state James Madison refused to award the commission. When Marbury requested that the Supreme Court compel Madison to make the appointment, Marshall faced a seemingly insoluble dilemma: the executive branch was empowered to enforce the Court's decisions, so how could one compel the executive branch to enforce a decision against itself?

Marshall's decision in the 1803 case of *Marbury* v. *Madison* was a tour de force, asserting the overarching preeminence of the Court in such a way that the president could not challenge it. Marshall prevented a political confrontation by dismissing Marbury's case, but he did so, he explained, because Marbury's direct application to the Court had been lodged under an unconstitutional federal law, specifically Section 13 of the Judiciary Act of 1789. By altering the original jurisdiction of the Supreme Court, Congress had legislatively modified the Constitution, something that could be accomplished only through the amending process. Therefore, by denying himself the power to challenge the Jefferson administration, Marshall established the Supreme Court as possessing an even higher authority, that of being the final arbiter of the Constitution through judicial review.

The implications of Marshall's decision were immediately apparent to the Jeffersonians. They resolved to tame the independent (or, in their view, obstructionist) Federalist courts by removing obnoxious judges through impeachment. Jefferson urged that Supreme Court justice Samuel Chase, who had been particularly fervent in enforcing the Sedition Act, be the first target. In early 1804, the House of Representatives impeached Chase for "high crimes and misdemeanors" as stipulated in Article I, Section 2, of the Constitution. The attack on Chase filled John Marshall with considerable apprehension because he believed that its success would set the precedent for removing judges on the flimsy grounds of unpopularity, a lethal blow to judicial independence. Yet when the case was heard in the Senate, it became clear that Chase, while unpleasant, had broken no laws.

He was accordingly acquitted, and the precedent was set the other way. The impeachment process would not be an elaborate method of removing judges merely on a vote of no confidence. Judicial independence had survived this serious attack.

Americans traditionally distrusted large standing armies, and Jeffersonian Republicans accommodated those misgivings by reducing the military to a constabulary force of less than three thousand officers and men. Interested in retiring the national debt as quickly a possible, the Jefferson administration also reduced naval expenditures.[5] Yet the world proved too dangerous to allow a sweeping dismantling of the navy. Barbary pirates, so named because they operated off the North African (Barbary) coast, practiced a crude form of ransom and blackmail by preying on merchant shipping in the Mediterranean to extract protection money for their rogue governments. For years, the United States had paid such tribute, but in 1801 the greedy pasha of Tripoli upped the stakes by capturing a U.S. warship and enslaving its crew. Jefferson sent the small American navy to punish these brigands, and over the next few years, U.S. frigates in conjunction with U.S. Marines intrepidly suppressed North African piracy. Aside from taming a barbarous lot in the Mediterranean, the exploits of the U.S. Navy fostered in foreign capitals a grudging admiration of American pluck.

Pirates and Property: The Barbary War and the Louisiana Purchase

More serious and closer to home, the United States faced a grave threat to its security when alarming reports told of a secret bargain in which Spain planned to cede to France vast holdings in the trans-Mississippi region called Louisiana. As if to verify such rumors, in 1802 Spanish authorities in New Orleans revoked the American right of deposit pledged by the 1795 treaty, enraging western farmers who depended on the Mississippi as a way to transport their produce.[6] The domestic upheaval was worrisome, but the possibility of the region passing from weak Spain to the rapacious Napoleon Bonaparte was terrifying. In 1803 the United States mounted a major diplomatic effort to offer France $10 million for at least New Orleans. Indicating the gravity of the American predicament, Jefferson intended to negotiate a British alliance if France would not sell.

Fortunately for the United States, Napoleon's plans for Louisiana abruptly changed when an ongoing slave rebellion in the West Indian French colony of Santo Domingo proved impossible to suppress. He was also cash strapped just as he was contemplating reviving the war with Britain. Consequently, he quickly offered not just New Orleans but the entire Louisiana region to the United States. On April 30, 1803, American envoys James Monroe and Robert R. Livingston signed a treaty with France that ceded Louisiana to the United States for about $15 million. Although Federalists objected that the Constitution did not authorize the president to make such arrangements, and Jefferson's strict constructionist philosophy troubled him about the matter as well, the dazzling prize of Louisiana was too tempting to resist. The Senate quickly ratified the treaty, and public opinion registered overwhelming approval for the arrangement.

The Louisiana Purchase was an astonishing transaction that would profoundly alter American lives for generations to come. It provided a measureless expanse for swelling American settlement while establishing the basis for American power in North America and eventually the world. An expedition led by Meriwether Lewis and William Clark explored the northern reaches of the Purchase all the way to the Pacific coast, and one led by Zebulon Pike traced its contours in the Southwest. They were heralds of a rising tide of American pioneers who were already dreaming of populating Jefferson's "Empire of Liberty."

The Embargo Jefferson easily won reelection in 1804, but his second term was buffeted by the European war that started up again shortly after Napoleon's sale of Louisiana. The conflict, in fact, would outlive Jefferson's presidency, continuing without interruption for the next 11 years. In 1805 Britain and France began campaigns of economic warfare that gradually entangled U.S. neutral shipping, intimidating it with decrees and regulations designed either to prevent American merchantmen from aiding one side or the other or to prevent American merchantmen from showing any profits at all. Added to this injury was the insult of Britain waylaying American merchant vessels to conscript sailors from their crews, a practice called impressment. The Royal Navy claimed it was only retrieving deserters, but it was difficult to determine whether a seaman was an American citizen or a British runaway, and impressment officers did not usually take much trouble to. In 1807 the policy produced a serious crisis when HMS *Leopard* attacked USS *Chesapeake* off the Virginia coast, killing and wounding several of her crew and forcibly removing four of her sailors. American outrage could have meant war, but Jefferson believed a thorough stoppage of all trade with the world would force France as well as Britain to respect American neutral rights. Accordingly, he persuaded Congress to pass the Embargo Act in December 1807, which stopped all exports from the United States whether in American or foreign ships.

Jefferson's grand experiment in economic coercion failed miserably. Rather than injuring France and Britain, the embargo devastated the American economy. As Americans increasingly violated the embargo with smuggling and other deceptions, the government employed increasingly draconian measures to maintain it. Eventually Americans were comparing Jefferson's extreme enforcement of the embargo to the excesses of British policy before the Revolution, and some in New England were discussing disunion. Congress finally abolished the embargo on March 1, 1809, by replacing it with the Non-Intercourse Act, a measure that banned trade with only England and France. Beginning with this modification of the embargo, both Congress and Jefferson's successor, James Madison, searched for an effective form of economic coercion for the next three years as they tried to protect American interests and rights with peaceful gestures rather than belligerent ones. Ultimately, they failed.

WAR AND RESURGENCE: 1810–1820

Coping with the European war dominated James Madison's presidency. Madison was more of a scholar than a politician, and he lacked the magnetism that Jefferson had used to lead the Republican Party. Even Jefferson's ability to beguile the nation had waned at the close of his administration. Madison did not fare any better at the start of his.

When James Madison took office on March 4, 1809, the Non-Intercourse Act was less than a week old and would never prove effective during the year of its existence. Congress replaced the act with Macon's Bill No. 2 in 1810, an even less effective measure that merely encouraged Napoleon Bonaparte to hoodwink Madison into believing that France alone was ending its depredations against U.S. shipping. Ignoring evidence that Napoleon was continuing his rapacious policies, Madison exclusively targeted Britain, a move that had momentous consequences. The administration's anti-British policy was not necessarily pro-French, but it essentially inclined America toward France and therefore made war with Britain more likely.

The 12th Congress, which convened in late 1811, contained a number of firebrands, mostly from the West and the South, **The War** whose passionate calls for war against Britain would earn them **of 1812** the name "War Hawks." They were young men who not only chaffed under the insults of British depredations against U.S. neutral rights but also were convinced that Britain was responsible for Indian uprisings on the western frontiers. With the cry of "Free Trade and Sailors' Rights," the War Hawk faction was instrumental in forcing the reluctant Madison to a moment of decision with Britain. Finally the president sent a war message to Congress in June 1812, and after a heated and divisive debate, the United States declared war on Great Britain at the end of the month.

From the outset, it was an unpopular war, especially in New England, where public displays of dissent gradually evolved into a serious anti-administration movement among New England Federalists. Although the war's main support was from agrarian sections, it was truly fought for seafaring rights, seen by farmers as imperative for protecting the honor and preserving the credibility of the flag. Yet the war disrupted the New England economy, and its origins struck many Federalists, who regarded Napoleon's France as the greater enemy of liberty, as shrouded in Republican duplicity. As a consequence, New England militias frequently refused to serve outside their state boundaries, hobbling the prosecution of the war.

Indeed, the War of 1812 was badly fought from the outset. The populace was never enthusiastic about it; therefore the country was at best largely indifferent and was at worst divided by serious political disagreements. The country was also unprepared for the conflict. Its economy was weak, its regular army was meager and undisciplined, commanded by aging fossils, and its militia was inadequately trained and occasionally spineless. Laboring under such disadvantages, the government in 1812 sought to mount aggressive campaigns on the Canadian border, but each effort proved predictably ineffective. British and Canadian forces, aided by Indian allies, met American invasions with vigorous defenses. Only scanty British numbers and London's preoccupation with the war against Napoleon prevented the affair from becoming an American disaster.

Meanwhile, heavy frigates in the small U.S. Navy bested British counterparts in several single-ship engagements that so disturbed the British Admiralty that it ordered captains to avoid individual actions against Americans. The boost to American morale was brief, though, for in 1813 the Royal Navy arrived off North America in such force as to blockade the American coast and bottle up the U.S. frigates. The British also carried out raids on Chesapeake Bay and by 1814 had extended their blockade from New England to Georgia while seizing parts of Maine.

Americans fared better on the Great Lakes. In 1813 Oliver Hazard Perry's Lake Erie squadron defeated a British flotilla off Put-in-Bay on September 10, 1813, and opened the way for American land forces to shatter the Anglo-Indian alliance in the region. Also in 1813, war erupted in the South between Creek Indian nativists (called Red Sticks) and U.S. forces, but in the following year, Andrew Jackson ended the Creek War by crushing the Red Sticks at the Battle of Horseshoe Bend on March 27. Such military successes were alloyed by the occurrence of atrocities and reprisals directed against civilians. In late 1813, retreating U.S. forces destroyed the village of Newark on the Niagara Peninsula, and the British response was a harsh campaign of devastation on the New York frontier. Likewise, the British cited the American destruction of York (present-day Toronto) in 1813 as justifying their capture of Washington on August 24, 1814, during which they burned several public buildings, including the Capitol and the Executive Mansion.[7]

It was Napoleon's defeat in 1814 that freed up British forces in Europe to prosecute the war in America with greater vigor. In addition to the assault on Washington, a veteran British army invaded upstate New York but was repulsed after the U.S. Navy defeated a British squadron on Plattsburgh Bay on September 11, 1814. In the same month, a combined British naval and army assault on Baltimore failed when American defenders withstood the naval bombardment of Fort McHenry and held off a land attack on the city's outskirts. An American lawyer named Francis Scott Key commemorated the U.S. victory in his poem "The Star-Spangled Banner." As British forces left Chesapeake Bay to mount an operation against New Orleans on the American Gulf Coast, New England Federalists, unable to contain their anger about the war any longer, gathered at Hartford, Connecticut, to consider ways of remedying their complaints. The Hartford Convention met from December 15, 1814, to January 5, 1815, approving a set of relatively modest resolutions. Yet the convention's actions prompted the rest of the country to suspect the Federalists' patriotism, suspicions that eventually doomed the party as a viable political force.

Although the British had refused Russian mediation offers immediately after the war broke out, their initial attempts to secure an armistice were telling. The overarching concern of the British government was always to defeat Napoleon, and London viewed the American conflict as a distraction from that primary task. After some protracted diplomatic maneuvering, peace talks between American and British envoys commenced at Ghent in August 1814, but the timing persuaded the British diplomats to stall the negotiations. Napoleon's defeat in the previous spring and the corresponding expansion of the British military in North America made decisive victories against the United States more likely. Yet news of British setbacks at Plattsburgh and Baltimore chilled those hopes. In addition, the nearly quarter century it had taken to defeat France had fatigued both the British public and its government. The longing for peace was reinforced when Britain's premier military hero, the Duke of Wellington, advised London to make arrangements quickly with the Americans on the best terms possible.

The talks in Ghent subsequently sped to a conclusion. Because the end of the war in Europe removed the practical necessity for impressment, Americans were able to discard their demand for its formal renunciation. In a similar gesture of practical conciliation, the British gave up their plans to alter the U.S.-Canadian border and set up a northwestern Indian barrier state between the United States and Canada. With the removal of these mutually unacceptable conditions, a treaty was signed on December 24, 1814, based simply on the *status quo antebellum,* the state of affairs before the war. Although hostilities closed with virtually all of the war's official causes unresolved, both time and circumstances had made those issues less relevant. Moreover, by the time the treaty arrived in the United States for Senate deliberation and ratification, a significant event persuaded many Americans that the United States had won the war. Unaware of the close of negotiations two weeks earlier, the British had assaulted New Orleans on January 8, 1815, and had been crushed by a makeshift force mainly composed of frontiersmen under Andrew Jackson. Raucous celebrations of this astonishing battlefield success accompanied unanimous Senate ratification of the Treaty of Ghent, convincing many that the two events were related and hence indications of U.S. victory.

The United States thus emerged from the War of 1812 surprisingly energized by the experience. The controversy and angry debate that had impeded the war effort, the political alienation of New England, and the generally miserable showing of U.S. forces in the field were quickly forgotten as swelling patriotism and pride inspired Americans to pursue expansive national aspirations. The removal of British power in the Northwest and the defeat of the region's Indians during the war accelerated settlement on that frontier. Similarly, Jackson's devastation of Red Stick Creeks in the South encouraged rapid settlement of that frontier as well. Americans thus looked westward, and pioneering again became a foremost part of the national philosophy.

The Indomitable American   Amplified American nationalism was the most obvious result of the war, and it worked a palpable change on American life. The unexpected triumphs at the end of the War of 1812 were a factor in the creation of this new nationalistic spirit, but there was more to it than simply a visceral pride over presumably besting Britain. For the first time since the Revolution, the United States could assert a real economic and political independence from European powers. Literature and art began to focus more exclusively on American settings, depicting admirable American characters and celebrating fabulous American landscapes.

Napoleon Bonaparte once said, "There is only one step from the sublime to the ridiculous."[8] The observation was particularly but differently applicable both to him and to the United States in 1815. Refusing to accept defeat, Bonaparte had tried to recapture his imperial throne in France, escaping from exile on the cloistered little Mediterranean isle of Elba. But his fortunes collapsed at Waterloo in June, and he was permanently banished to the forlorn Saint Helena, a South Atlantic island half a world away from Europe. Meanwhile, across the Atlantic in the fall of 1814, the third session of the 13th Congress could not meet in the Capitol because the British had gutted it in August. Instead, representatives and senators crowded into the Patent Office, one of the few public buildings the British had spared. Congress thought about moving the nation's capital from Washington but finally decided to keep the government there and restore its buildings on the Potomac. As a testament to this faith in the future, Congress also voted to reestablish its library. Thomas Jefferson's massive private collection of books, purchased from the former president, formed the basis for this new Library of Congress, a repository that eventually dwarfed those of ancient Alexandria and Athens. Bonaparte would likely have sneered at such a gesture. Yet those congressmen had actually reversed Napoleon's aphorism, just as the advent of the United States had reversed the era's ugly tendency to despotism manifested, for one, in people like Napoleon Bonaparte. Neither Napoleon nor the succession of autocrats in various lands who followed him down through the twentieth century ever understood why those Americans in the ridiculous setting of their smoldering capital could, with one small step, envision a sublime tomorrow framed by new buildings and informed by old books.

The government chartered another Bank of the United States in 1816. Antibank sentiment had allowed the first bank to lapse in 1811, but the clear requirements of financing the conflict with Britain turned the opposition of Jeffersonian **A New Economy** Republicans, who had been harshly tutored by the war, into support for the new national bank.

Americans also had a growing manufacturing capability after the war, partly boosted by the U.S. policy of commercial restriction in the years before the conflict. When British merchants tried to muscle in on the American market after 1815, they cut their prices so drastically that American factories could not compete, and Congress responded by passing a protective tariff. Rather than having as its main purpose the raising of revenue, the Tariff of 1816 was designed to shield American manufacturers from foreign competition by placing as much as a 25 percent duty on imports. The move was extremely popular in manufacturing regions, for obvious reasons, but southerners also supported the tariff in the interest of promoting American economic independence. Parts of New England, however, opposed it because of qualms that it would hinder their shipping trade. Ironically, these regional attitudes would be reversed in a few years as the agrarian South caviled over having to purchase northern manufactured goods made more expensive by protectionism. New England would increasingly move toward manufacturing as the famous textile mills sprouted in the years after the war and would accordingly call for increasing levels of protection.

After the war, Kentuckian Henry Clay, the most prominent War Hawk in the 1812 Congress, hatched a plan of interlocking initiatives designed to accelerate and sustain American economic independence. Dubbed the American System, Clay's plan would protect American industry with high protective tariffs, whose revenues would be managed by the national bank to fund the construction of an elaborate transportation system of roads and canals. Debate over the viability, fairness, and constitutionality of Clay's tripartite system of tariffs, national bank, and internal improvements would frame the American economic conversation for a generation. In the short term, Republican presidents James Madison and his successor James Monroe drew back from wholeheartedly endorsing the use of federal money for projects within a single state, occasionally wielding their veto to cancel undertakings that would do so.

Beneath the exhilaration and confidence of the Era of Good Feelings, then, were signs of brewing trouble. Arguments over Clay's American System unsettled political discourse, and the new Bank of the United States (known as the BUS) was increasingly at the center of the quarrel. Ultimately an attack on the BUS by a state government came before the Supreme Court in the 1819 case of *McCullough* v. *Maryland*. The case involved the constitutionality of a tax that Maryland had imposed on the BUS and by extension the constitutionality of the bank itself. Chief Justice

John Marshall, who had bolstered the central authority of the government in previous key decisions, spoke for a unanimous Supreme Court. He ruled that the BUS was constitutional on the basis of implied powers that sanctioned the central government's employing "necessary and proper" means to promote the public welfare. Furthermore, the Court ruled that Maryland (and by extension all the states) had no authority to tax federal institutions. Marshall observed in one of his most famous pronouncements that "the power to tax involves the power to destroy" and rejected the notion that the people of the United States would consent to grant individual states with such power.[9]

Marshall's decision could make the BUS legitimate (at least for the time being), but it could not make it popular.[10] In 1819, the same year as the McCullough case, a severe financial panic littered the economic landscape with failed banks, mushrooming unemployment, and ruined investors. Part of the cause for the disaster was an overexuberant speculation in western lands and other speculative projects, a bubble that was bound to burst sooner or later. Yet the early policies of the BUS, which encouraged rather than restrained reckless credit ventures, were also to blame, and the central bank's efforts to control irresponsible local banks in the wake of the crash worsened hardship by forcing foreclosures and bankruptcies. The years of heady boom had suddenly turned to catastrophic bust, and the many who blamed the BUS would not forget the hard times.

Expanding America   James Monroe, elected to the presidency in 1816, enjoyed a brief period of national unity and goodwill prompted by heightened patriotism and economic optimism. During his presidential tour of New England in 1817, a Boston newspaper giddily announced the dawning of a new age in American politics and auspiciously, if somewhat awkwardly, christened it the "Era of Good Feelings."[11]

During the years after the War of 1812, the United States also exhibited a more aggressive foreign policy. Monroe was fortunate to have John Quincy Adams as his secretary of state, for the erudite son of the second president was an extraordinary statesman and a match for any diplomatic adversary. Under Adams's stewardship, the United States finalized an important treaty with Britain in 1818 that settled the U.S.-Canadian border westward to the Rocky Mountains and arranged for mutual access to the Oregon country in the Pacific Northwest.

The status of Spanish Florida proved even more challenging for the Monroe administration, especially when Latin American revolutions threatened to collapse the Spanish Empire. As Madrid tried to summon the resources to suppress revolts in Argentina, Venezuela, and Chile, the Spanish drastically reduced garrisons in Florida, with the result that lawless anarchy became the prevailing condition on the Georgia border. When Florida's Seminole Indians took to raiding into Georgia, Monroe authorized Andrew Jackson to pursue them into Florida. Jackson was under orders to steer clear of any Spaniards, but his 1818 campaign completely disregarded the government's instructions for restraint. He executed two prominent Indians without a hearing and summarily put to death two British subjects after a quick court-martial. He marched on and seized two Spanish posts, including the Spanish capital of West Florida at Pensacola.

Several factors complicated framing a response to Jackson's flagrant violation of his orders. The most prominent was his great popularity—he was routinely referred to as the Hero of New Orleans—but another equally significant point was his obvious disregard for constitutional restrictions that made declaring war the exclusive prerogative of Congress. As Congress investigated the matter, the Monroe administration debated behind closed doors about the proper stand to take. Almost everyone wanted either to repudiate Jackson's behavior or to chastise him, but Adams persuaded the president to use Jackson's precipitous invasion as a way to pry Florida from Spain. Presented with the stark alternative of possibly losing Florida to the United States through military fiat or negotiating its cession through diplomatic procedure, Madrid chose the latter. The result was the 1819 Florida Purchase Treaty, somewhat misnamed because Spain also consented to draw a transcontinental line from Louisiana westward to the Rockies and then up to the 42nd parallel, extending to the Pacific coast. By separating American and Spanish possessions in the whole of North America, the 1819 treaty not only presented the United States with Florida but also bolstered American claims to the vast Oregon country in the Pacific Northwest. Congress consented to this arrangement, and the essential illegality of Andrew Jackson's conduct was brushed away by his immense popularity and the success of the mission.

Heated quarrels over slavery and its future made their debut during the Era of Good Feelings. The introduction of slavery **Slavery** early in the colonial period had been one of the most troubling developments of English colonization. The revolutionary generation struggled with the inconsistency of fighting for liberty while holding people in bondage, but southern economic dependence on slaves compelled the Founders to compromise on this most fundamental principle of human freedom. The result was an elemental inconsistency in the American social and political structure that could not be ignored forever. As slavery was ultimately confined to the agrarian South, the budding controversy became a sectional issue that would increasingly pit the South against the North, especially concerning the possible extension of slavery into the West.

In 1819 the Missouri Territory sought admission to the Union as a slave state and set off a furious debate. It had become clear that the South was falling behind the North in population, as the growing northern majority in the House of Representatives showed. With free and slave states each numbering 11, southern equality in the Senate would be jeopardized if

Missouri became free, but such cold calculations of political power struck antislavery advocates as amoral at best. In 1820 the Missouri Compromise finally broke the congressional stalemate by admitting Maine as a free state to balance Missouri's admission as a slave state. In an effort to forestall future disagreements, the southern boundary of Missouri, the line of 36°30′, was designated as the northern boundary of slavery for the rest of the Louisiana Purchase.

In this episode, the country had its first taste of the controversy that would eventually split the Union and plunge its people into the Civil War. Events leading to that cataclysm would unfold in the four decades following 1820, evolving so gradually that those living through them did not altogether grasp their ominous significance. It is not surprising, then, that most Americans in 1820 only vaguely comprehended the dreadful potential of the slavery debate. In fact, most were relieved that the difficult question of Missouri had been politically resolved with such an orderly solution. The moral inconsistency of slavery in a free republic, however, remained, and the debate that contemplated that moral question was a monster that in 1819 had stirred but not completely awakened. It would not slumber forever.

CONCLUSION

The Republic's first three decades saw both remarkable change and admirable stability. The country experienced incredibly divisive political debates during the 1790s but successfully managed a real transition of power without succumbing to violent passions that could undermine the government and weaken the constitutional framework. Instead, the United States was strong enough to withstand threats from abroad and tolerate dissent at home. Economic misfortunes, some quite serious, and even war with powerful Britain did not corrode the American spirit or daunt the American purpose. At the end of the War of 1812, a renewed sense of determination accompanied a surging patriotism to promote nationalism and unity. Pioneers trekked westward while back East, surveyors, engineers, and architects cut roads, dug canals, and raised cities along them. Thoughtful men penned stories and narratives celebrating the American spirit, and artists depicted the boundless optimism of a land without limits and a people eager to populate it.

By 1820, many of the problems of the so-called Era of Good Feelings seemed solvable, and it appeared that extraordinary accord would be the order of the new day dawning. Yet as the Federalist Party fell victim to charges of disloyalty and saw its program co-opted by the opposition, Republicans saw less a need for unity and more a reason to argue with each other. Southerners still grumbled over what they perceived as a shifty assault on slavery in the Missouri debates, while antislavery forces muttered that the resulting compromise revealed the nation's moral compass as badly askew. The economic crash in 1819 and subsequent depression replaced prosperity with poverty, substituted empty storefronts for bustling emporiums, and made eager workers into idle debtors.

The American experience of the day, contrasting periods of glowing confidence suddenly overshadowed by the appearance of hardships and uncertainties, is both sobering and inspiring. Despite the real bounty of the American land, it required great toil and considerable sacrifice to develop it. The native populations who inhabited the land posed an impediment to white settlement, and the resolution of that issue became a moral dilemma of considerable importance. Although the wide happiness of human liberty was truly extraordinary, the legions of slaves exposed the fact that liberty was imperfectly realized and incompletely enjoyed. The great promise of financial security could prove fleeting, an ephemeral dream knocked into reality by events far from one's home and unfathomable to one's imagination. And through it all, the ordinary man, woman, and child moved with the same clumsy gestures of hesitation and ambiguity that mark any people's advance into the future, a place that is always dark, dimly lit by hope at best, and only illuminated when it becomes the past. These were and are the timeless and sobering uncertainties of life. It is inspiring that the Americans who lived through them did not just survive. They also frequently triumphed.

NOTES

1. This widely reviled agreement was informally named after John Jay, who had negotiated it. Despite its unpopularity, Jay's Treaty led to a felicitous arrangement with Spain. The mere fact of its existence so alarmed Madrid that Spain hurriedly granted the United States free navigation of the Mississippi and abandoned claims to a large stretch of territory in the U.S. Southeast.

2. Washington's decision established the tradition for American presidents of limiting their service to two terms until 1940, when Franklin D. Roosevelt ran for an unprecedented third term. In 1951 the Twenty-second Amendment to the Constitution institutionalized the two-term limit for the presidency.

3. In 1804 the Twelfth Amendment to the Constitution changed the process to prevent such a politically awkward situation from recurring.

4. An additional Enemy Alien Act carried similar provisions in the event of formal hostilities but was never invoked because Congress never declared war. In any case, President Adams never used the Alien Act.

5. The departing Federalist majority in Congress had provided for naval reduction when the French war scare waned; therefore Jefferson was able to implement an extant policy.

6. Although it appeared that the revocation of the right of deposit was in concert with the imminent cession to France, the Spanish action in New Orleans was coincidental rather than concerted with the French arrangement.

7. The president's residence was not even informally called the White House until after the War of 1812, when it was whitewashed as part of its renovation after the British burning. It would not be known officially as the White House until Theodore Roosevelt so designated it at the beginning of the twentieth century.

8. "Du sublime au ridicule il n'y a qu'un pas." See M. Dominique Georges Frédéric de Pradt, *Histoire de l'ambassade dans le grand duché de Varsovie en 1812*, 4th ed. (Paris: Chez Pillet, 1815), 215.

9. Kermit L. Hall, William Wiecek, and Paul Finkleman, *American Legal History: Cases and Materials* (New York: Oxford University Press, 1991), 131.

10. The BUS came under fire again during the presidency of Andrew Jackson when in 1832 he vetoed its early recharter, in part because of its dubious constitutionality.

11. George Dangerfield, *The Reawakening of American Nationalism, 1815–1828* (New York: Harper Torchbooks, 1965), 35.

2

FROM CRADLE TO GRAVE: RITUALS OF LIFE, LOVE, AND DEATH

COURTSHIP AND MARRIAGE

Most marriages during the colonial period were arrangements whose primary goal was to benefit the families involved, a practice that emulated European traditions colonists had brought with them to America. For instance, it was not unheard of for a father to withhold the inheritance of a son who married against the family's wishes. By the end of the eighteenth century, however, courting couples themselves increasingly decided whom to marry and when. And just as the philosophy of marriage changed to deem the happiness of the couple as most important, so a couple's affection for each other became the crucial factor for starting a courtship and sustaining it to the altar. Parents then as now, especially fathers, continued to express opinions about the suitability of suitors or prospective brides, but their children more and more made their own decisions of the heart. The new emphasis on affection as the basis for marriage also afforded young people more freedom during courtship rituals. Unchaperoned couples took strolls to steal kisses and attended parties where dancing allowed a degree of public intimacy. Not until later, in the mid- to late nineteenth century, did the Victorian era become so preoccupied with public appearance and private morality that middle- and upper-class couples had little time alone before marriage. The early Republic, on the contrary, was more broad-minded and less prudish. Without chaperones, for instance, premarital sex certainly occurred on occasion, but young women during these years were certainly not sexually reckless, and promiscuity was almost unheard of.

Given more say about whom they married, couples waited longer to wed. Part of the delay was born of caution, for given the freedom to choose a mate, they tended to be more deliberate and less impetuous. Women married between their late teens to mid-twenties and men usually in their mid-twenties.

After a couple decided to marry, few family obstacles stood in their way. During the colonial period, fathers rarely allowed a daughter to marry before her older sisters because doing so could dissuade possible suitors from calling on them. In the new climate, older sisters still tended to marry first, but only because they reached marriageable age earlier. Their weddings were no longer required before the family's younger girls could be courted.

Marriage ceremonies in the early Republic were simple and unpretentious. They usually took place at the bride's home. Couples wore their best clothes, but only the wealthy bought special attire for the occasion. Neighbors treated weddings as a chance to socialize and made the events more celebratory than serious. Newlyweds made merry with the guests before retiring at the home of either the bride's or the groom's parents. During the night, tipsy wedding guests often serenaded them with both ribald and romantic songs.

Married Life   Because of the difficulty of travel and the need to earn a living, wedding trips were a thing of the future and even then generally only enjoyed by the wealthy. Instead, most couples quickly settled into a routine after the wedding. At most, newlyweds might briefly visit nearby friends before embarking on the hard work of setting up a household. Most people believed marriage should bring happiness and fulfillment to husband and wife alike, a relatively new idea that differed from prevailing attitudes during earlier times. Couples in the early Republic sought loving companionship and affectionate devotion, a sentiment reflected by literature, letters, and diaries that spoke of romantic love as the most important factor in a blissful and gratifying marriage. Changing expectations likewise brought changes in behavior. A marriage that emphasized affectionate friendship tended to be happier and thus reduced incidents of infidelity, especially by husbands, and married life exhibited new habits of demonstrative familiarity that would have been unthinkable in former years. Couples openly expressed their feelings, calling each other by first or even pet names, and frequently disclosed to each other in intimate letters their sexual yearnings, especially when apart.

The hope for happiness also meant that its absence was something to be corrected. Couples who found themselves mismatched were able to seek remedies that at best had been extremely rare for earlier unhappy marriages. Divorce was certainly not widespread, but neither was it unimaginable, especially when its emotional liberation was likened to the political liberation that resulted from the Revolution. Women no longer had to tolerate in silence their husbands' adultery, and men whose wives had deserted them no longer had to live like widowers to preserve the fiction of the union. New England and Pennsylvania made significant changes in their divorce laws to allow easier dissolution of marriages, and though several decades passed before laws were similarly liberalized in other parts of the country, attitudes about this difficult and previously forbidden subject were changing everywhere.

Despite the emphasis on companionship in marriage, sharply defined gender roles described differing responsibilities both to society and within the family. In both urban and rural settings, women took the primary part in nurturing the family's children. Unlike in earlier times, couples seldom toiled together to produce or acquire the family's basic material needs, especially in villages and towns, where men left the home to work at day jobs while their wives cared for the children. A mother's task included the cultivation of her children's talents and their preparation for adult responsibilities.

During the early Republic, most people got married and had children. Though families were usually smaller **Sexual Relations** than during the colonial period, numbering about four **and Childbirth** children and two parents, they were still larger than the average western European family. Ignoring increase through immigration, a healthy American appetite for sexual activity is indicated by the considerable population growth between 1790 and 1820. A comparison of birth and marriage records also shows that in some parts of the country, a third of brides were already pregnant when they went to the altar. Premarital sex has always occurred, of course, but the greater freedom for courting couples everywhere and the persistence of bundling in rural areas likely contributed to this large number. In any case, bundling was an eccentric custom, especially for New England, where it had been most prevalent, and by the early nineteenth century, it was in disfavor, for obvious reasons. A suitor who stayed late was spared a long trip home in the dark by sharing his girl's bed, sometimes with a board between them or some other equally ineffective method, such as remaining clothed, to prohibit sexual intimacy.

Illegitimacy was quite rare, but it did occur. Growing cities meant an increase in the vices encouraged by the anonymity of large populations and the corresponding absence of social constraints. Prostitution consequently increased the number of illegitimate children in urban areas.

Childbirth everywhere was usually looked on as a hallowed and celebratory event, but it was also an occasion for great anxiety. Complications were common and could be deadly for both mother and infant, and the absence of routine antiseptic medical practices imperiled even the most robust newborns. A local midwife—in the South, she was often a female slave—usually presided over the delivery with other women from the community and family assisting. The protracted nature of labor, the shared purpose of the midwife and her assistants, and their expectations for a happy result often imparted the flavor of a party to the occasion. It was hardly a merry event for the prospective mother, however. Rather than reclining on a bed, she squatted on a midwife's stool to facilitate the birth and prayed that her trust in tradition was not misplaced. Midwives varied greatly in their skill levels. An older practitioner in the community usually trained apprentices, a form of mentoring that was not as detailed, of course, but otherwise resembled that for most physicians. Late in the period, some urban areas boasted deliveries performed by doctors, but their skill levels often varied as much as those of midwives. In addition, a male doctor not only deprived childbirth of the shared joviality of bustling women but in some ways increased the risks of the actual delivery. A male doctor was bound by canons of modesty that severely hindered any special proficiency he brought to the task. The woman was cloaked in such way that the doctor, unlike a midwife, could not watch the progress of delivery but could only feel it with his hands and instruments.

In farming communities, most births occurred in early spring, indicating that conception took place in early summer. Slaves, however, tended to conceive in the fall and had their babies in mid- to late summer. With the exception of women on the western frontier, women in the early Republic had fewer children during their most fertile years. In earlier times, married women usually were pregnant every other year, but between 1790 and 1820, the birthrate dropped steadily, particularly among the middle and upper classes, as many couples consciously used birth control to limit the size of their families. The decision was partly an economic one—raising and educating children has always been expensive—and was partly motivated by the belief that fewer children allowed the mother more time for individual nurturing. Even farmers ceased to view a large family as the blessing it had been before labor-saving implements reduced the need for many hands in the fields.

The decline in birthrate indicated a greater degree of cooperation between husbands and wives over the most intimate matters of their relationship. It certainly pointed to the wife's developing importance in making essential family decisions, even in the face of the traditional view that a woman's primary duty was bearing children. Only a minority of the medical community sanctioned birth control, and most doctors actively discouraged it as unnatural. In any case, all methods of contraception were unpredictable at best. The primary method was male withdrawal before ejaculation, a technique called coitus interruptus. It was not a sure guard against pregnancy, however, and some doctors warned that the practice could be psychologically harmful and in some case physically injurious by leaving the woman sexually unfulfilled. Condoms made from animal bladders were available but unpopular because they dulled penile sensation. Couples might attempt a pseudoscientific version of the rhythm method, but nobody really understood how a woman's menstrual cycle influenced fertility, the mechanics of conception not being discovered until 1827.

Unintended pregnancy was consequently a likely possibility. Most women who became unexpectedly pregnant either greeted their condition as a happy accident or grimly reconciled themselves to the duties of expectant motherhood. Very few resorted to abortion, a practice that ironically increased dramatically during the later Victorian era. The early Republic had no specific laws against abortion, but most states recognized English common law, which made it illegal to kill a fetus after it quickened, meaning after its movements indicated life in the womb. The first state laws prohibiting abortion did not come until after 1820, so it is not clear why the early Republic essentially rejected abortion as a method of birth control. Perhaps the Second Great Awakening, a widespread revival of evangelical Christianity in which women played a major role, restrained the practice on moral grounds. In addition, surgical abortions were extremely dangerous procedures that could trigger hemorrhaging and frequently caused serious infections. Abortions induced by drugs were also risky and always painful. In this case, as in all instances of regulating human behavior, moral compunction and physical fear were far more powerful curbs than legislation.

Most wives became mothers within a year and a half of marriage and usually nursed their babies for about one year.[1] In some cases, particularly in the plantation South, wet nurses, frequently slaves who had infants of their own, **Republican Mothers** nursed the baby. During these years, however, the use of wet nurses was in decline. Most new mothers were allowed a period of rest or "confinement" for about one month. This period varied, depending on how much the new mother was needed for work around the home or business. Slave women were given much less time to recuperate from childbirth.

Before the Revolution, women led lives of relative isolation. Restricted by poor transportation and saddled with never-ending chores, most women cooked, cleaned, bore and raised children, and finally died without having set foot much beyond sight of their modest homes. Then dramatic changes loomed. In one respect, the American Revolution's exhilarating rhetoric of liberty was not limited to the political arena, as women made considerable contributions to the drive for independence. Many women enthusiastically sustained boycotts of British goods during the growing tensions before the war, and women provided significant moral and material support to patriot armies after the war began. Afterward few people seriously considered giving women any role, let alone an important one, in the running of the government, but perceptions nonetheless dramatically changed about women's responsibility to preserve what the Revolution had achieved. In sharp contrast to earlier views of women as morally fragile, spiritually delicate, intellectually anemic, and physically weak, women were now described as the morally superior sex and therefore uniquely competent to mold the next generation of Americans, the one that would either sustain the brittle experiment in liberty or lose the Republic to tyranny. The concept of "republican motherhood" that exhorted women to impart their superior virtues to their children was more than a plan to create good citizens; it was a way to fashion a great nation. While the men of the new republic supported their families, the nation's women would prepare their little boys to maintain democratic government and teach their little girls how to become "republican mothers" themselves. For years, tradition had dictated that women almost exclusively rear their children because men were busy doing more important things. Now, for many, there was the realization that "the formation of the moral and intellectual character of the young is committed mainly to the female hand."[2] In the early Republic, raising a child to meet the nation's challenging and uncertain future became the most important job in the world, one far too vital to entrust to the workaday practicality of men.

At least, that was the theory. In application, it lost some of the luster. In preparing for their key role in shaping society, young American women enjoyed more opportunities for education and relations outside the home than their European counterparts, but the education was of a sort and the relationships were of a type calculated to promote a specific purpose. Because men still viewed women as intellectually unqualified to absorb political theory, girls' curricula consisted of texts that celebrated the virtuous life and guided them to cultivate a pure heart. They were to pass on these virtues to their offspring. Such as they were, even these tedious educational experiences usually vanished after a woman married and had children. Republican mothers were too busy for much else besides motherhood. It would be wrong to suppose, however, that all women felt trapped by their place in life or deprived because of the distinctive burdens that station placed on them. Contentment in family and a sense of making important contributions to society by raising good children seems to have fulfilled all but the most restless women of the early Republic.

Fatherhood Fatherhood did not so much involve power and authority over wife and children as it did a duty to provide for them.

Like mothers, fathers were expected to be more nurturing than authoritative in meeting their responsibilities. The father had an obligation to ensure the family's material comfort, support his wife's efforts to instill republican values in the children, and serve as an example of upright behavior. Since work usually took him away from home during the day, his family became a refuge from the routines of his job, and children, who in earlier times had represented a source of income or labor, now became a solace. Farmers taught their sons horticulture, and artisans in towns and villages trained their sons in trade.

FAMILY LIFE

By the early nineteenth century, the urban family no longer acted like an economic enterprise for which all members except the youngest children worked. Even on many farms, this significant change evolved as the family became less self-contained and began purchasing goods rather than making them. Parents bought cloth rather than weaving it and even shopped for ready-to-wear clothes. Items such as candles, soap, and shoes, previously produced by tedious labor, were becoming available at stores and freed family members to spend more time together in leisure and recreational pursuits. Almost all families read the Bible aloud, and particularly pious homes featured morning and evening prayers. More secular readings included novels and periodicals. Sunday morning church attendance was customary, with families always sitting together during services.

The family spent most of its time together at home. The average house was larger than most colonial homes, but still **Dwellings** small by modern standards. An ordinary farmer or his urban counterpart, the artisan or laborer, seldom had more than two or three rooms in his house. The front or public room served as the cooking area, the sitting and eating area, and usually the sleeping area for younger children. Only parents had a private bedroom. Children slept several to a bed, segregated by gender, usually in the public room or a loft. If prosperous, the family might have separate bedrooms for girls and boys, but even the wealthiest households seldom boasted private bedrooms for children. Except for the cradle, beds were sized for adults and could accommodate several children.

Bedrooms were functional sleeping quarters rather than aesthetic retreats, containing only those items of furniture needed for a night's rest. Beds were valued as among the most precious furnishings in a house—people often specifically bequeathed them along with other household treasures—while other fine furniture was kept in the house's public areas. A straw-stuffed mattress was the usual bedding for the poor, while the affluent had feather beds. Only the wealthiest people used more than one room for entertaining visitors, and even middle-class homes generally lacked a separate dining area. Most people ate in the kitchen. In the South, wealthy planters placed kitchens in separate buildings to reduce heat and avoid fire dangers in the main house. As a result, the convention evolved of having a room set aside especially for dining.

Most houses were decorated quite simply, with few if any floor coverings and no artwork or decorations on the walls. Instead, walls served as a place to hang utensils, clothes, or guns. The public area had only enough chairs, stools, and benches to seat the family and a few guests. Clocks and mirrors were luxuries until late in the period, when better manufacturing methods made them affordable. Until then, only the affluent possessed a clock, usually placed on the mantel, and mirrors were quite rare.

Nearly all houses were constructed simply. They were framed with mortise-and-tenon joints and covered with whatever material was locally available, such as boards, clapboards, stone, or brick. Log houses were built only on the frontier. In rural areas, the community might pitch in to build a neighbor's house; otherwise local carpenters fashioned and assembled most dwellings.[3] Though each region of the country had its own distinctive style, some features were common to all. Except in the cities, for instance, houses rarely sat parallel to the closest road. Instead, they were situated to take advantage of the angle of the sun. In the North, most houses faced east so that the morning sun would warm them quickly.

For most Americans, houses were functional and reasonably comfortable dwellings that seldom featured fashionable architecture or pointless frills. Only the wealthy painted their houses or landscaped their grounds, and the area around ordinary houses was usually cluttered with debris and rubbish. Animals roamed the yard, their droppings remaining where they fell, and garbage was simply tossed out of windows and remained on the ground until a sizable accumulation signaled the time to bury it. Gardens were for vegetables rather than scenery, and no one but the affluent ever considered the wasteful practice of planting a lawn. Most wives worked at keeping the inside of their houses tidy and fairly clean, but even the most fastidious housekeeper lost the battle to dust, especially in the summer, when windows always remained open. By the end of the period, manufactured brooms were making housekeeping a bit easier, a sign that cleanliness in general was becoming more important.

The rich in both cities and countryside, however, set the standard to which many lower- and middle-class families aspired. Their affinity for Georgian architecture imported from Britain created the popular Federal style, a uniquely American version of the Georgian motif widely displayed in mansions that celebrated order and symmetry. Only a privileged few ever lived in such homes, but the middle class began to emulate the habits of the affluent in dining, leisure, and child rearing. By the end of the period, people saw the home as the place where the family should be most comfortable, better to enjoy each other's company.

Relationships
During the early Republic, the family changed from an economic unit into a social refuge whose leisure time was increasingly separate from the outside world. Some historians have argued that this transformation was a result of the period's developing market economy, which made both work and economic transactions less personal than in previous times. Others have suggested, however, that this type of family not only predated an industrial economy but also made the transition to it easier. For whatever reason, the family became less an economic entity whose main purpose was the material

security of its members and more an emotional support system whose primary goal was preparing the next generation of citizens. The Enlightenment played a part in promoting the change, especially because of its emphasis on individual rights, an idea conveyed in popular novels, poems, and other texts that appeared throughout the period. Such works described parental love and obligations as more important than patriarchal authority while celebrating marriage as a union based on love and respect rather than an arrangement for economic benefit.

Modern conceptions of how families lived years ago frequently suppose that they were usually extended families, meaning that they included relatives beyond the so-called nuclear family of parents and children. The extended family of grandparents, aunts, uncles, and cousins certainly existed and in some instances resided in some form under one roof. In the rural South and on the frontier, the extended support network provided by such a wide number of relations remained important for survival and companionship. Yet the nuclear family became far more common during the early Republic.

As children became the center of the loving family, some observers noted that the family became preoccupied with child rearing. In middle- and upper-class homes, the parents no longer kept the cradle in the home's public area but instead placed it in the parents' bedroom or in a separate nursery. Particular home furnishings exclusively designed to meet the needs of small people also appeared during this period. For example, the forerunner of the modern high chair was introduced to help mothers feed toddlers, and craftsmen began making small chairs and tables specifically for children.

Possibly as a result of a rising middle class and its emphasis on democratic values, many saw the family's real purpose as properly molding children. Declining birthrates made children more emotionally precious as parents came to know them better as people rather than unformed family adjuncts. A child's death marked both the loss of a loved one for the family and an unfulfilled potential for the world at large. Unquestionably, children became a much more important part of American society during these years, more so than they had at any previous time.

Children grew up quickly during the colonial period. They were expected to make a real contribution to the household **Childhood** by no later than age seven. A physical manifestation of this abrupt and premature end to childhood was the practice of dressing children like miniature adults, usually beginning in their seventh year. After the Revolution, though, parents of middle- and upper-class children increasingly deferred both the trappings and obligations of adulthood. Children in poor families remained destined to take up labor quite early, particularly by hiring out to craftsmen or formally becoming apprenticed to them. The rising middle class, however, embraced childhood as essential for a person's proper development.

During the colonial period, parents believed that they had to control the bad urges of inherently wicked children while compelling them to acquire basic skills such as walking and talking. Told that their children were potential vessels for Satan and that only strict supervision and constant useful activity would shield little souls from evil, mothers often became martinets, taking to heart the idea that idle hands were the devil's workshop. Conversely, late-eighteenth-century parents strove to develop their children's potential instead of merely fashioning them into obedient workers. Children learned to make decisions for themselves to enable them to live independently as adults. Children were also viewed as innocents whose boundless potential needed only correct guidance, not relentless correction, to reach its fulfillment. Poignant signs of this changing perception of children were their grave markers during the period. Whereas a common symbol on such headstones in earlier years was a death's head, these later gravestones often depicted angels or cherubs.

The new belief in childhood innocence prompted some experts to discourage strict forms of punishment, but not all parents agreed. A persistent view of human nature as intrinsically evil held that children were just as iniquitous as anyone else and to rear a child properly required the subjugation of his or her will. Despite the similarity of this attitude to that of earlier periods, the motive was nonetheless different. Rather than disciplining children as merely a higher form of domestication—in essence, why we housebreak dogs—people believed that strict discipline was crucial to make children better people by improving their characters. Experts even counseled that guilt and embarrassment, rather than spankings, were more effective for altering unruly behavior. Many parents refused to abandon the maxim that sparing the rod spoiled the child, though, and corporal punishment continued as the most widely used penalty for misbehavior, especially for young children.

Authors of child care books during the early Republic aimed their message at mothers rather than fathers and advocated a more natural approach to skill development. Mothers were encouraged to allow children to learn to walk and talk at their own pace. Enlightenment thought defined natural law as a set of patterns in which human behavior was a normal part of the universe's routine mechanics. As one intellectual of the period noted, "the first seven years of life are a period of greater importance, in the business of education, than is generally imagined."[4] Childhood, with all its tempers and silliness, was merely one of the natural stages of life, an idea reinforced by the growing awareness that childhood experiences shaped the adult character. Raising a child should thus be done according to natural laws, expected developments, and steady progressions. In this philosophy, children were actual people with individual personalities and distinct temperaments. Rarely in their diaries and letters had parents of earlier times referred to the gender of newborn babies or even noted them by name, but early-nineteenth-century parents did.

Rather than depict children in portraits as diminutive adults complete with coiffures and mature attire, painters of the early Republic dressed them as children and set them among toys and other trappings of childhood. These children were seldom named after a dead older sibling, a practice that suggested parents were merely replacing one unformed person with another. Rather, children were deemed people in their own right whose unique qualities merited their own names.

Changes in how children were clothed also reflected the natural Enlightenment approach. Responding to warnings from physicians that swaddling infants could physically deform them, many parents abandoned the practice and dressed babies in loose smocks. (Immigrants, especially those from Germany, nevertheless tightly wrapped their babies well into the nineteenth century.) Careful mothers still placed a band of cloth around the baby's middle for back support and tended to overdress infants, even in the summertime. When child care books criticized the custom, however, a reaction set in against layering children with heavy clothes, and the pendulum swung to the opposite pole. Experts believed that "a new-born infant cannot be too cool and loose in its dress."[5] Mothers came to believe that constantly shielding babies from cold air made them susceptible to its ill effects as adults, an old idea that John Locke had endorsed a century before. At the end of the eighteenth century, parents gradually but avidly embraced it. The belief that cold temperatures made babies robust fostered the cruel and absurd notion that bathing children in cold water was good for them, a practice that could most charitably be described as misguided, more correctly characterized as unintentionally abusive.

The way that older children were treated also began to change. Children's clothes, for example, became more practical for active little people. Upper- and middle-class boys of toddler age still wore a sort of gown, but it looked far less like a woman's dress than before. After a boy reached the age of four or five, he could wear long trousers and short coats over simple shirts, an outfit sometimes called a skeleton suit. At age 10, he began wearing a less formal version of his father's clothes. Prepubescent girls usually wore a loose-fitting frock, and after they reached the age of 12 or 13, they wore dresses more like their mother's. They were even fitted with stays to shape their developing figures according to the current fashion. Even after American women adopted in the early nineteenth century the looser Empire style of dress, stays remained an essential part of a woman's ensemble. Until puberty, children of both sexes wore their hair very simply. Upon reaching their teens, they sported the adult hairstyles appropriate to their sex.

The simplicity and practicality of dress and haircuts was partly to accommodate play. The colonial period regarded child's play as something to occupy those too young to work while parents and older children went about their labors. In contrast, the early Republic judged play as essential for a child's natural development. Again, children's portraits from the era tell a tale wherein the presence of toys for both genders exemplified this changed thinking about the importance of play. Because play was seen as key to the physical and mental preparation for adulthood, children beyond the toddler stage were separated for play by gender. Girls played with toys and pretended at games that prepared them for marriage and motherhood. Their main toys accordingly were dolls. Boys, on the other hand, were expected to develop physical strength and mental agility. Their games were livelier, and their toys were balls, hoops, and marbles—the kind of playthings that were generally used out of doors.

The new emphasis on play sadly did not affect the lives of poor children or the children of slaves. The poor often apprenticed their children to craftsmen, sometimes as early as their sixth birthday. The custom removed hungry mouths from meager larders or provided a way for a community to deal with orphans while preparing them for a trade. The arrangement was a formal one, delineated by a contract called an indenture, which spelled out the obligations of both parties. In exchange for room, board, and instruction in the arts and mysteries of a particular trade, the apprentice pledged to labor in his master's service for a specified number of years, usually at least four, or until reaching 21 years of age. Many masters treated their apprentices with kindness, but some simply exploited them for their labor while ignoring the obligation to teach them anything at all. The apprentice had a difficult life in either case, and many fled out of homesickness; they were quickly returned to their masters. Masters were legally bound to provide adequate food, clothing, shelter, and training, but a child's chances of successfully challenging violations of his indenture were less than slim. If placed with a negligent, indifferent, or malevolent master, the apprentice donned his shabby clothing to work from sunup to sundown, ate unpalatable food, and finally bedded down in crowded, unheated quarters. Given enough of such treatment, many apprentices simply ran away. If they were clever enough to stay clear of their parents, they were hard to catch. Cities, especially in the Northeast, attracted relatively large numbers of such runaway boys. They quickly became indigent and usually joined roving gangs that staked out streets as their territory in the poorer sections of the city.

Slave children went to work at a very early age. By the time they were six, they were expected to perform light labor around the plantation or farm, such as feeding chickens or watching after younger children. A slave child's mother returned to regular tasks within a few weeks of childbirth, and the elderly women who cared for her child during the day usually left constant supervision to older children, usually under the age of 10. Slaves not much older than 10 were expected to help in the fields. On cotton plantations, they trailed behind adult slave gangs to pluck stray bits of cotton from stalks.

These unfortunate children, whether from impoverished families or as part of a slave community, suffered in varying degrees from inadequate diets and negligible child care, deprivations that along with a regimen of grueling work made them much more susceptible to disease and accidents than their counterparts in the middle and upper classes. Yet moderately prosperous and even affluent children died in startling numbers. Part of the cause was an incongruous combination of avid attention and casual neglect at all levels of society. Wealthy mothers certainly supervised the rearing of their children, but servants or slaves often tended to their daily care. In middle- or lower-class homes, mothers were normally too busy to watch over young children all the time and left the chore to their older children, a circumstance fraught with potential calamity in any century. Childhood accidents that resulted in serious injury or death were numerous.

The relatively primitive state of the medical arts meant that any disease had the potential to be fatal for child and adult alike. Efforts to reduce infant mortality focused on prevention more than cures. During colonial days, infants were literally strapped into cradles constructed from solid pieces of wood to promote straight bone growth. Parents in the early Republic tried to preserve air circulation around sleeping infants by employing new cradle designs featuring slats or spindles on the sides. Nonetheless, children sickened and sometimes died from a variety of ailments. They were most susceptible in their first 10 years. About one in six babies died in the first year. Approximately 10 percent of children died before reaching adulthood. High infant mortality rates paradoxically made even doting parents wary of becoming too attached to newborns, and some did not name children until they were at least a few months old.

Children were especially vulnerable to intestinal diseases, but respiratory infections were the most lethal. Whooping cough, diphtheria, scarlet fever, and secondary infections from measles and chicken pox killed countless children during the period. Few effective treatments existed, and parents generally relied on traditional remedies such as potions laced with alcohol or opiates. Mothers regarded alcohol as preventive medicine and routinely dosed their children, including infants, with it at the earliest sign of illness. It was the rare child, in fact, who had not been introduced to some sort of alcohol from the time it was weaned. The growing influence of temperance movements after 1810 persuaded mothers to use a variety of syrups purportedly designed for children, but most still contained alcohol or other drugs. Children were thus treated for illnesses in the same manner as adults. As a result, the cure was almost as likely to kill them as the disease.

EDUCATION

The role of education in forming an intelligent citizenry became an important concern in the early Republic. During the colonial period, education had been an academic exercise carried out by "Latin" schools, primarily in New England, whose principal purpose was to put boys on the path to universities that would prepare them for the pulpit, the classroom, or the courtroom. Curricula were inflexibly limited to subjects inherited from the classical educational tradition in Europe, courses that focused on language, philosophy, and rhetoric rather than matters of practical utility. In part, this was a reflection of the old British idea that education was the special preserve of the upper classes.

In colonial New England, which was heavily influenced by Congregationalists, another purpose of primary education was to make people godly. The ferment of revolution, however, helped change these attitudes, and the years following American independence were to see marked transformations in beliefs about the purpose of education. "Speaking generally, it may be said that every New Englander receives the elements of education," a British visitor said several years after this period.[6]

In addition to leveling tendencies that dismantled British notions of aristocratic privilege, new ideas about the utility of education appeared. Book learning for some became a viable alternative to apprenticeship, providing a way to get ahead in a competitive world while simultaneously promoting solid principles of patriotism. Yet ordinary Americans were basically of two minds about education, and the early Republic was illustrative of that ambivalence. On the one hand, they were suspicious about education as simply an impractical pretension offering little of practical value for the great bulk of the population, those young men who would have to make their way behind plows and workbenches, or those young women who would spend their days at cradles and cookstoves. On the other hand, people intuitively believed that both the future welfare of the country and the prospects of enlarged opportunity for their children required an education. "Larning is of the gratest importance to the seport of a free government," conceded William Manning, a marginally literate Massachusetts farmer, who nevertheless noted that "costly collages, national acadimyes & grammar schools" were merely ways for the powerful "to make places for men to live without work."[7]

Such mixed assessments about the worth of education resulted in mixed applications in the establishment of schools. Popular nostalgia imperfectly recalls that rural areas boasted the little one-room schoolhouse whose prim schoolmarm presided over students ranging in age from very young children to relatively mature young adults. The myth of avid learners and enthusiastic teachers frames this picture, but the reality was not as ideal. The building was typically makeshift and dark, the pupils were unruly, and the teacher was usually a marginally skilled young man whose primary qualification for the job was an ability to maintain order, often with brute force. As to education, at most he could impart the rudiments of the three Rs—readin', writin', and 'rithmetic. The emphasis was on routine and drill, with a heavy reliance on recitation from worn and tedious texts, a pedagogical method that rightfully earned these common schools the informal name "blab schools." The school day was also long, usually beginning at first light. Breakfast was at eight o'clock, followed by several hours of recitation until lunch. Several more hours of study and recitation followed lunch, and the day finally ended at five o'clock with prayers. These schools were privately and therefore inadequately supported, either through affiliation with the church or by modest tuition fees paid by parents, sometimes with something as simple as room and board for the teacher. Because older children were needed for chores on the farm during the growing season, their attendance tended to be spotty during those months.[8]

Urban schools likewise relied on rote memorization and ceaseless drill, but they also attempted innovations necessitated by rapidly increasing populations of students. Desiring to impart moral virtue and mental discipline, some urban schools experimented with a teaching method invented by Englishman Joseph Lancaster, a Quaker convert troubled by the plight of the ignorant poor. Using teaching assistants called monitors, the Lancastrian system sought to increase class size to promote efficiency without diminishing the quality of instruction. A master teacher first taught the monitors, typically older students themselves, who then simultaneously ran pupils seated in groups through their drills. Nine different recitations could be conducted at the same time. In the morning, students gathered under the watchful eye of their monitor to recite their lessons in reading and spelling and progressed to advanced levels based on their rate of learning. Quakers established the first Lancastrian school as a charitable organization in New York City in 1801 and later opened a similar school in Philadelphia. In Virginia, Norfolk and Richmond also adopted the Lancastrian model in schools supported by a mixture of private donations and city taxes.

The apparent efficiency of such schools appealed to communities who resisted taxation for even the most basic city services. There was also the fascination of applying the concept of the factory to the education of children, especially for an age impressed with the wonders of mechanized routines. Yet the Lancastrian method was in the end more a fad than a lasting solution to the problems of mass education. In the first New York schools, for example, the classrooms were designed to accommodate as many as 500 students, certainly a tribute to economy of effort, but ultimately too great a sacrifice to the real business of instruction. In short, the Lancastrian system's methods were superficial, and its results increasingly unsatisfactory. It was eventually abandoned in all but a few places.

As a matter of tradition, all but elementary schooling was aimed at educating males. During the period, though, schools for girls were founded, and some exclusively male schools began admitting girls as well. Accordingly, literacy among women increased during the early Republic. Women were not encouraged to pursue significant intellectual endeavors, but the increasing number of educated women gradually opened the way for new careers. In New England, women began teaching younger children the rudiments of reading and writing, especially because such jobs were often seen as too unprofitable for men. The practice began in so-called summer schools while boys were working on farms. These schools admitted girls, who were instructed by the young women of the community. Gradually it became more acceptable for women to teach full-time, and educated single women thus had a respectable way of earning a living. It would have been unheard of, however, for a woman to remain employed in such a position after she married. Motherhood was considered her natural calling.

Throughout the period, primary schools supported by taxes—what became known as free public schools—were quite rare. Where they did exist, they were largely philanthropic enterprises established to educate impoverished children and were consequently considered inappropriate for middle- and upper-class children, who either attended private academies or, if sufficiently wealthy, were instructed by tutors. In this, as in many other aspects, the early Republic was a time of transition. The rise of common folk in the 1820s with the advent of Jacksonian Democracy persuaded the upper classes that educating the American masses was necessary in their eyes to preserve the country from mob rule. In the decades that followed, reformers and activists argued that society had an obligation to educate the people for the health of the country as well as their own well-being. Free public education was slow in coming and often sectional in nature, but the chance for its realization was born during the early Republic.

HEALTH AND MEDICINE

The constant threat of disease and the chances for contracting a serious illness cut across all ethnic groups and economic classes during these years. Most diseases were not fatal, but the scarcity of reliable medicine meant that they could be debilitating. Because sickness was omnipresent and its effects were possibly dire, Americans seemed almost obsessed with the topic of health, whether that of family or friends. Letter writers almost always opened with, and sometimes repeated in closing, news detailing the good or bad health of family members. Americans suffered pain, bowel ailments, and breathing problems with stoic resignation because they had little choice but to accept these events as normal and expected parts of life.

Diseases   Americans of the early Republic suffered from intestinal complaints with disconcerting frequency, and such illnesses could be dangerous, especially when they caused dysentery, a debilitating inflammation of the bowels that causes bloody diarrhea. Adults were better able than children to ward off the potentially fatal effects of intestinal ailments, and they more or less expected them to be part of life. Poor sanitation, bad water, and spoiled food caused most out-breaks, especially when these circumstances occurred in conjunction with lax personal hygiene. People on farms usually wore grimy clothes and grubby shoes that created an unhealthy mix of dirt, animal manure, and perspiration. The stench of privies, chamber pots, and soiled diapers per-vaded towns and farms alike.

Americans also suffered from a wide range of respiratory complaints that ranged from common colds to serious influenza. Flu had not yet mutated to produce the deadly strains that would appear in the later nine-teenth century and the early twentieth, but pneumonia and tuberculosis could kill and frequently did. Tuberculosis, often called consumption by the people of the time, was especially virulent in crowded cities and in homes where large families suffered from poor ventilation. In fact, inci-dents of tuberculosis mounted so rapidly in the United States that it was the leading cause of death by disease among adult Americans. Some stud-ies estimate that 23 percent of New Yorkers who died in 1804 did so of tuberculosis or its related maladies. Boston and other large cities experi-enced similar ravages. Because tuberculosis is transmitted by saliva, even-tual laws against public expectoration were prompted more by health concerns than by a prim sense of etiquette, but during much of the period, tuberculosis was viewed as a hereditary disease, and so even people who were infected were not isolated from the general population. Many times a person infected with tuberculosis did not immediately develop symp-toms because the dormant bacterium waited until a different illness weak-ened its victim. Several years might pass before tuberculosis finally claimed the sufferer.

Widespread epidemics were relatively rare during the colonial period because most people were young immigrants whose exposure to many diseases in Europe had improved their immunity. Succeeding genera-tions, however, possessed diminishing levels of resistance to what in turn became increasingly uncontainable diseases. Meanwhile, the increasing population and its growing interaction allowed infectious diseases to spread more easily. The result was a greater incidence of epidemics in the later eighteenth century, when diseases like whooping cough and chicken pox were rampant. Why the incidence of some serious illnesses increased, however, remains a mystery. Scarlet fever had rarely been fatal during the colonial period, but it and other diseases might have mutated in the early nineteenth century to become successful killers.

Smallpox was always dangerous, disfiguring its victims, sometimes horribly, when it did not kill them. Colonial Americans lived in dread of it. Yet during the early Republic, smallpox inoculations—the process of injecting a small amount of the disease into a healthy patient—made it much less common. Inoculation was controversial, though, and many people opposed it because it could make an otherwise healthy person seriously ill, and some of those inoculated actually died.[9] The introduction in 1796 of a new type of vaccine using cowpox virus greatly improved inoculation's safety and effectiveness, although risks associated with smallpox inoculation remained, just as they do to this day.

Population growth and trade interaction made yellow fever even more terrifying than smallpox. Because Europeans had limited exposure to yellow fever, it had a higher mortality rate than smallpox, and no one knew how it spread. Not until a century later would scientists determine that people catch the disease from the *Aedes aegypti* mosquito. The unwitting partnership of infected people and carrier mosquitoes could allow the illness to cover astonishing distances with amazing speed. A person with yellow fever who traveled to an area inhabited by the *Aedes aegypti* mosquito or who traveled on a ship with such mosquitoes could trigger an epidemic. Adults of European ancestry were the worst yellow fever cases, while children of any race and those of African ancestry the mildest. Symptoms included jaundice (hence the name), fever, and bloody vomit, often called the black vomit. "Some lost their reason and raged with all the fury madness could produce, and died in strong convulsions."[10] About a quarter of those who contracted yellow fever died, but survivors were protected from its recurrence. Because mosquitoes need warm temperatures to survive, the disease occurred only in summer, and outbreaks did not necessarily take place in consecutive years, because carrier mosquitoes did not convey yellow fever in larvae. Instead, new outbreaks hinged on infected people being bitten by the *Aedes aegypti*.

Philadelphia's yellow fever epidemic of 1793 was the most notorious incidence of the disease during the early Republic. The outbreak probably occurred as a result of the slave uprising on the Caribbean island of Santo Domingo that drove thousands of refugees into Philadelphia during the hot summer of 1793. By August, the disease had reached epidemic proportions. Black men drove carts through deserted city streets dolefully ringing bells for households to bring out their dead for speedy burial. As one observer noted, "the wealthy soon fled; the fearless or indifferent remained from choice, the poor from necessity."[11] More than 5,000 people died, about 10 percent of the population, most of them previously healthy adults. Over the next 30 years, outbreaks of yellow fever ravaged New York, Baltimore, and Boston, areas that were not native habitats of the *Aedes aegypti* mosquito and whose cold winters eventually wiped out mosquito populations that had been brought in by ship. The South, on the other hand, was not so blessed.

In the Deep South, the carrier mosquito is indigenous. Many southerners succumbed to yellow fever and malaria (also a mosquito-borne disease), but the wealthy escaped the worst outbreaks by relocating to higher, interior terrain during the summer, for although yellow fever's cause was unknown, experience had taught that low-lying regions were most at risk. During the first two decades of the nineteenth century, New Orleans alone experienced five yellow fever epidemics, each of them effectively shutting down the city. Shops closed, artisans ceased their trades, wharves fell silent, residents tightly shuttered their windows, and the grim population of mausoleums swelled.[12]

Ailments were treated with a wide range of herbal medications and nostrums dispensed by folk healers, mothers, and wives. Meanwhile, an increasing number of trained physicians used both herbal and pharmaceutical medicines. Doctors of the period were usually educated in their profession in one of two ways. A few went to medical schools, but most went through a process similar to that of any artisan learning the arts and mysteries of any trade, apprenticeship to an older practitioner. No level of government required a license to practice medicine, and quacks could represent themselves as doctors after casually studying only a few books.

The Medical Arts

The medical arts were mainly a static set of skills and knowledge in any case, marked by few innovations and as little understanding about what caused disease and what promoted good health as the ancient world had possessed. The Greek Galen was still a primary authority, for example, and his theory about the four humors of the body was a guiding principle. Keeping the four humors of black bile, bile, phlegm, and blood in deft balance was believed to be imperative for good health. Illness was simply a sign that one of the humors was in excess and required purging. Methods for eradicating excessive humors varied, but they commonly included blistering the bottoms of the feet, the belly, the back, or head with heated goblets. Purgatives were administered to induce diarrhea or vomiting. By far, though, drawing blood was the most universally applied therapy for almost all ailments. Needless to say, these debilitating treatments further weakened an already fragile patient and were almost always the worst course of action.

Doctors employed a wide range of medicines, but many were more harmful than effective. The most commonly used medication was calomel, or mercurous chloride, a chemical compound that in its mildest form could seriously damage gums and teeth when taken with any regularity. Because anesthesia had not yet been invented and infection was almost certain, surgery was a last resort. Tooth extraction and amputations were fairly common, the former because of poor dental practices and the latter because of limb-crushing accidents or rampaging infections from wounds. Such procedures were extremely painful, and amputees often died of shock during the operation if not from the inevitable infection that usually set in days later. Tooth extractions could also lead to acute infections. During the period, advocates for better dental hygiene began with some success to encourage people to brush their teeth regularly, a regimen that could avert painful trips to barbers who frequently doubled as dentists, proving the maxim that an ounce of prevention is worth a pound of cure.

Some American physicians studied in Europe, where advances were being made in the diagnosis and treatment of diseases, but these individuals were few in number and had relatively little influence when they returned to the United States. Some American doctors, particularly those affiliated with the few medical schools in the country, conducted medical research, but most of it was of little value. The majority of Americans remained skeptical about changing the way things had always been done. Even as avid a devotee of science as Thomas Jefferson said, "Some diseases not yet understood may in time be transferred to the table of those known. But were I a physician, *I would rather leave the transfer to…accident,* than hasten it by guilty experiments on those who put their lives into my hands."[13]

Hygiene Overall hygiene generally improved during the early Republic, though baths in which the entire body was immersed in water remained rare. Daily cleaning consisted of splashing cold water from a basin usually situated in the household's kitchen area or, in warmer weather, outside near a well. Most people washed only their face and hands during this daily ritual. Soaps were normally too harsh for skin and were used exclusively for cleaning house and laundering clothes. The most affluent Americans used milder soaps imported from Europe and, by the end of the period, had begun acquiring tubs for soaking the entire body. Even primitive showers were installed in some homes. Convincing most people to bathe on a regular basis, however, proved difficult. One woman wrote after experiencing her first shower that she "bore it better than I expected, not having been wett all over at once, for 28 years past."[14] Ordinary folk had to settle for ceramic basins and pitchers to wash up privately in their bedchambers.

Bathing might have become somewhat more customary, but other sanitation practices promoted rather than discouraged disease. Disposing of garbage and clearing away human and animal waste remained problems. Farm families piled up their garbage and periodically buried it, but urban areas had limited choices. Most towns had large numbers of feral pigs to roam streets and eat garbage tossed there by householders and business owners. Such pigs not only cleared refuse but also provided a food source of sorts for the most impoverished of the community, although the pigs carried more parasites than farm-raised pigs and passed them on to anyone who ate them. Human waste was also more of a problem in cities and towns than in the countryside, where it was buried or given to pigs to eat. Most households in both town and country featured privies placed away from the main residence, hence the "outhouse." Some rural poor simply answered the call of nature in the woods. No matter where privies were placed, they reeked in the summer and afforded ample opportunity for breeding diseases. Affluent city dwellers had their privies empty into a chamber that was periodically cleaned by itinerant laborers. Loading human waste into what was sardonically called a "honey wagon," the workers trundled this "night soil" out of town to sell to farmers for fertilizer. Most people generally used a chamber pot during the night, and only the poorest families did not have at least one chamber pot for use at night or by sick family members, giving rise to the expression "without a pot to piss in." The woman of the house or her servants emptied the home's chamber pots, so it is little wonder that homeowners increasingly sought new ways to make the disposal of human waste more convenient and agreeable.

Even with improvements in hygiene, life expectancy remained fairly stable during the period. Americans did generally live longer than people in other parts of the world, with people in the rural Northeast enjoying the longest life expectancy. Americans who survived childhood could expect to live into their sixties.

DEATH

Dying was as social as it was somber in the early Republic. Embracing the belief that a person should never be alone during the last stages of a terminal illness, family and neighbors took turns sitting at the deathbed, especially at night. In rural areas, neighbors traditionally came to "watch the night" with a dying person, and consequently most deaths occurred at home with the failing person surrounded by loved ones.

A tolling church or courthouse bell announced a person's death if near a town. Nine peals signaled the passing of an adult male, six an adult female, and three a child, followed by one toll for each year of the person's age. By the time the bell **Wakes and Funerals** was ringing, family members would be preparing the body for burial by bathing the corpse, dressing the hair, and finally covering the body in a burial shroud. Women usually prepared bodies for burial, even those of deceased men. In cities, certain women performed burial preparations for pay, making them the forerunners of modern funeral directors. Embalming was not practiced during the early Republic, and therefore the funeral had to be conducted fairly quickly after death, especially during the summer months. During the colonial period, some people were hastily buried by simply wrapping them in cloth and placing them in the ground. Americans of the early Republic, however, were typically buried in wooden coffins that were usually custom made.

A wake was customary, the open coffin sitting in the parlor or front room of the house to allow family and neighbors to pay their respects. Before the growing influence of the temperance movement, alcohol was served to the men during the wake. The house itself was considerably altered for the occasion. Mirrors were covered with a white cloth, and furniture was moved into the public areas to accommodate guests. The funeral service was conducted in the house, and afterward the coffin was sealed and shouldered by pallbearers to a wagon for conveying it to the graveyard; everyone else walked behind. In frontier areas far removed from church graveyards and on plantations with family burial plots, the person would be buried on the property. Slaves, too, were buried on the grounds of the home in a separate slave burial ground. They usually conducted their own services, though the owner and his family might attend. These ceremonies usually occurred just before nightfall.

Most people who attended funerals did not wear black, as became the custom in the later Victorian era. If they could afford a special mourning outfit, close family members wore black, and widows were expected to wear black for at least six months after their husband's funeral. Many women widowed in old age wore black for the rest of their lives. Male mourners wore a black armband.

If the deceased owned a home and property, community leaders or the local court appointed three reputable men to list the household's effects and other property for probate. Probate records are still valuable sources to enhance our understanding of the material culture of the early Republic because these appointed agents recorded everything from each teaspoon in the house to the smallest tool in the barn. The list was then presented to the court, which distributed possessions and property in accordance with the deceased's last will and testament, or if no will existed, according to state law.

CONCLUSION

While some customs of courtship, marriage, family relationships, and death were similar to those of earlier periods, much also changed in the early Republic. The Enlightenment fostered new outlooks about the role of human volition in improving life and consequently changed perceptions about the role of individuals in American society. Husbands saw wives differently, parents saw children differently, and most people benefited from optimism about their potential for fulfillment and the country's chances for success. As in all ages, illness, accidents, disease, and death were a part of everyday life. Most people of the early Republic came into the world, fell in love, raised children, and aged to infirmity well aware that life was fragile but also confident that it was meaningful.

NOTES

1. Historian Linda K. Kerber and others use the term "republican mother" to explain what many men in late-eighteenth- and early-nineteenth-century America viewed as women's ideal role. See Kerber, *Toward an Intellectual History of Women* (Chapel Hill: University of North Carolina Press, 1997), 58.

2. Steven Mintz and Susan Kellogg, *Domestic Revolutions: A Social History of American Family Life* (New York: Free Press, 1988), 57.

3. House construction is discussed in more detail in chapter 4.

4. Karen Calvert, *Children in the House: The Material Culture of Early Childhood, 1600–1900* (Boston: Northeastern University Press, 1992), 61.

5. Ibid., 64.

6. Thomas Hamilton, *Men and Manners in America* (Edinburgh and London: William Blackwood and Sons, 1833), 127.

7. Manning's famous essay "The Key of Libberty" is ably examined in Samuel Elliot Morison, "William Manning's *The Key of Libberty*," *William and Mary Quarterly*, 3rd ser., 13 (April 1956): 202–54.

8. The customary pattern of school years broken by summer holidays is a holdover from the necessity of accommodating an agricultural economy, when children were especially needed for labor in the fields during the summer months.

9. The renowned clergyman Jonathan Edwards died in 1758 from a smallpox inoculation.

10. Gerald N. Grob, *The Deadly Truth: A History of Disease in America* (Cambridge: Harvard University Press, 2002), 75.

11. Albert Bushnell Hart, ed., *American History Told by Contemporaries*, vol. 3 (New York: Macmillan, 1897–1929), 40.

12. A sign of the desperation that yellow fever caused was the practice of perforating letters with small holes to fumigate them with a mixture of diluted carbolic acid or sulfuric acid gas during yellow fever epidemics. See A. Fisk, Watt and Co. to Wesley Bolls, 1 October 1832, Fisk, Watt and Co., Fumigated Letter, Historic New Orleans Collection, New Orleans, Louisiana.

13. Richard Harrison Shryock, *Medicine and Society in America, 1660–1860* (New York: New York University Press, 1960), 73.

14. Ibid., 91.

3

LIFE ON THE LAND

From the beginning, the most urgent human need has been to produce enough food to sustain life. Only in the modern period has abundance made for surpluses of food that permit other human endeavors, for without enough food there can be no cities, no arts, no culture, no progress. The reality of this fundamental human necessity and the relatively recent conquest of it is attested to by the fact that most Americans during the early Republic were farmers. In 1790 approximately 90 percent of the population cultivated the land. Yet the remarkable agricultural advances that would become so much a part of the American story—advances that in the early twenty-first century would have about 3 percent of the American population supplying most of the world's food—were already under way in the years following the American Revolution. In fact, the three decades after 1790 rank among the most extraordinary for agricultural advances. "Agriculture here assumes her most cheerful aspect," a traveler earnestly reported.[1]

By 1820, about 72 percent of Americans were farming, still a remarkably high figure by today's standards, but also marking a sharp decline during the preceding 30 years that would not be matched again until the next century. (During the next 20 years, for instance, progress slowed, so that in 1840, farmers still made up about 70 percent of the population.) The figures reveal that in the early Republic, Americans were employing significant mechanical advances in farming equipment and adopting innovative practices for the use of the land.

GROWING

Plowing
Equipment and innovation aside, wherever and whenever growing things on the land has been practiced, it has always required four clearly defined steps: (1) soil preparation, (2) planting and tending, (3) harvesting, and (4) processing. In the beginning of all farming, there must be broken ground, and hardly anything is so physically demanding and tedious as preparing a field for planting. Changeless for centuries, the plow was the principal tool for turning the earth, and its design as well as the way it was pulled over the ground decided where farms would lie and how extensive they could be. Plows consisted of three basic parts: the blade that cut the earth was called the "plowshare"; the "moldboard" caught the broken soil and turned it away to create a furrow; and the "land side," the flat surface opposite the moldboard, provided the plowshare with a firm grip on the soil. Plowing appeared quite simple—it seemed that one need only direct the blade in a fairly straight line for the length of the field. Actually, though, plowing required considerable skill, and the cruder the plow, the more astute the successful plowman needed to be. Setting too fast a pace caked up the moldboard and spoiled the furrow. Going too slow prevented the share from properly cutting the ground. Old hands claimed, with good reason before the days of standardization, that each plow had a different temperament, requiring a different pace and a different way of handling to work the soil well. Oxen were frequently used as dray animals, but the preferred work animal for plowing was eventually the mule. Mules had long been in North America when, in a famously generous gesture, the Marquis de Lafayette sent George Washington a pack of asses from the Mediterranean island of Malta. Washington bred them to produce mules at Mount Vernon, joining a growing number of farmers who judged the mule superior to any other working animal. Given their tendency to kick, mules could be bad-tempered, but they were generally steadier than horses and rarely ran away. They thrived on the simplest diet of corn husks and straw, while horses could be finicky and preferred a varied menu. Mules were healthy and hardy, did not require much attention, and withstood physical injury with remarkable stoicism.

Agricultural progress was closely tied to advances in plow designs and plowing methods, and important improvements occurred during the late eighteenth century and the early nineteenth. As in many changes of the time, the Enlightenment played an important part in this process, because the Age of Reason did not concern itself only with political philosophy and intellectual inquiry. A strong practical bent emerged from Enlightenment thinkers whose contemplation of how to make the world more efficient encouraged them to apply systematic, mathematical principles to everything from rocking chairs to stovepipes. Thomas Jefferson of Virginia, a true child of the Enlightenment, always regarded himself as a farmer as much as the world marked him a statesman, and many credit him with creating the first improved plow design in America. Though Jefferson's plow was an advance—John Randolph, one of Jefferson's enemies, acidly remarked that his plow was the only worthwhile idea he had ever had—his dream of it being produced on a large scale was never realized.[2]

Instead plows were painstakingly hewn from wood on homesteads or, if the luxury of iron was available, pounded out, glowing red hot, under pinging hammers by leather-clad blacksmiths. Because iron was scarce and therefore costly, wood was used to fashion all but the working parts of plows until the eighteenth century. Plowshares and moldboards, the surfaces that cut and turned the soil, were frequently made of iron or at least had iron straps protecting a wooden base, but after the American Revolution, rising iron production meant the increasing appearance of entirely metal plows. The first U.S. patent for a cast-iron plow was granted in 1797 to Charles Newbold of New Jersey, whose design was a sturdy implement of one piece. Newbold's plow, however, had limited appeal because it was both expensive and difficult to repair. In fact, its one-piece design meant that damage to any part of the plow frequently rendered it useless. Sixteen years later, Baltimore inventor R. B. Chenaworth was selling a cast-iron plow with a removable plowshare, moldboard, and land side, a feature that facilitated replacement when parts were worn or damaged. In 1814 New Yorker Jethro Wood patented a similar plow with several additional improvements including superior and less expensive parts. Eventually Wood's plow set the standard for the implement, and when Edwin Stevens discovered a way to make the plowshare more durable in 1817, Wood integrated the process in his 1819 design.

Widespread use of the iron plow with interchangeable parts revolutionized farming during the early Republic. Like most machines, the plow was designed to allow more work to be accomplished by fewer people. In the South, the use of slave labor discouraged labor-saving innovations, so that hoeing and chopping persisted as the means to prepare soil for planting. Small southern farms tended to employ trowel-hoe plows and shovel plows. The trowel-hoe broke ground by slicing a single trench rather than a furrow. The shovel plow, on the other hand, was a simple device resembling a large spade with handles. It did not so much cut the soil as scratch it to about a three-inch depth, a result that restricted its use to certain types of soil unless it was supplemented with hoe and ax. The shovel plow was popular on poorer farms because it did not require as much animal power or skill as moldboard plows, and cotton planters preferred it because they could use it to cross-plow while not producing the large chunks of earth the moldboard plow did.

Even in the North, the American plow was lighter than its European counterpart. In part the difference stemmed from the American practice of regarding all innovations as temporary milestones on a path to something better. Utility was more important than sturdiness, and the lower cost of today's less durable product was appealing when gauged against the belief that clever improvements would make something superior available tomorrow. In addition, American farmers only rarely needed heavy plows in soils that gave fine yields with shallow cuts and small furrows. Labor saving was the main object of improved plows, which were able to accomplish half again as much work as their predecessors using half the number of animals. As the size of farms increased and the need for animal power and human labor lessened, the limitations on production ceased to be a problem during the planting phase and instead emerged during the harvest season. Not until the advent of mechanical reapers in the 1840s would the harvesting problem be mastered, but the road to an amazing increase in food production began in these years with these humble but important American innovations to one of the world's oldest farm implements.

Planting and Cultivation   Moldboards slowly drawn over fields tended to leave large lumps of soil unsuitable for planting, so plowing was only the first stage in preparing the ground for seeding.

Horses or mules then pulled a harrow over the ground to produce the right soil consistency. The harrow was simply a wooden frame with attached spikes or metal disks that could break up large clods. Occasionally farmers hitched heavy round logs on axles behind a horse to squash down furrows and break up small earthen chunks.

How one planted or seeded depended on the type of crop. Many plants require space for proper growth and to ease cultivation once they take form, but some general procedures applied to all. Using a hoe or a similar implement, the farmer opened holes in plowed furrows and placed seeds in them. Grass, grain, and some vegetable seeds were usually broadcast, literally strewn by hand in sweeping motions over broken ground and then later thinned or transplanted. Tobacco was planted this way in seedbeds for transplanting, a tedious and backbreaking chore.

Corn planting went faster with two workers, one to work the hoe and the other to place a half-dozen seeds in the hole and close it with his heel to make a small hill. Hand corn planting devices—tubes that dispensed a measured amount of seeds—were occasionally used, but they did not solve the problem of covering the seed, so they were mainly employed in gardens rather than large open fields. Nonetheless the relatively large seeds in corn planting made them tempting candidates for mechanizing the seeding process, usually through the use of drills, which were in limited use after the Revolution. Jefferson, for example, experimented with seed drills in his fields at Monticello. Seed drills could be quirky tools, though, because they had to place a certain number of seeds in consistent patterns along set intervals. The slightest irregularity in the ground could disorder the machinery, and the occasional rock could damage it. The advantages of mechanical seeders were obvious in the diminished wastage and larger yields they produced, but during the early years of the Republic, farmers found them expensive and temperamental experiments rather than useful tools.

Cultivation commenced once plants sprouted. It took different forms depending on the crop. Wheat, for instance, required little attention, while almost all other crops needed some degree of thinning and weeding. Depending on the availability of labor and the method of planting, weeding was done with hoes or plows during the growing season. The era knew nothing of pesticides, so insects were removed by hand. Some larger farms employed irrigation if near a source of water, but for most, rainfall was the main irrigator, and droughts could devastate a crop; several years of drought could destroy a farm.

By far the greatest enemy of the American farm during the period was soil exhaustion caused by repeated overplanting. Fields worn out by such a practice were frequently deserted and allowed to return to native grasses. Farmers would put in "Mays [corn] as long as it will grow, perhaps to two or three crops: the land is then left to nature, and fresh land resorted to and worn out in its turn."[3]

Conscientious farmers let fields lie fallow for one or two years and sometimes as long as four years. By the late eighteenth century, some were planting clover, a restorative plant, to refurbish fallow fields while providing pasturage for livestock. Most livestock roamed free, however, and manure was not widely used for fertilizer. Near coastal regions, diligent farmers applied fish and seaweed. Indian lore prescribed one fish per maize mound; seaweed was spread at a ratio of 10 loads per acre, usually every third year. In the South, the repeated planting of tobacco and cotton so rapidly depleted the soil that when yields declined, people tended to move west to settle on relatively cheap, fertile land. These migrations resulted in tobacco culture spreading to the piedmonts of Virginia and North Carolina and cotton into the piedmont regions of South Carolina, Georgia, Alabama, and Mississippi. Writers like John Taylor of Caroline County, Virginia, encouraged soil conservation during this period, and some began early efforts at it, but the most important writings on the subject came after 1820. Meanwhile a few farmers experimented with lime, marl, and gypsum, but the abundance of land to the west and the ease of migration away from depleted farmsteads discouraged systematic and widespread efforts to sustain and replenish the soil.[4]

Climate, weather, and pests dictate farming techniques as much as soil conditions, and the natural rhythm of seasonal   **Harvesting** change made farming a strange mixture of the routine occasionally interrupted by the disagreeable and unexpected. The routines of spring planting, summer cultivation, and fall harvest were the constants, but sometimes things went awry. Wheat farmers in the mid-Atlantic states and New England were devastated by the invasion of the Hessian fly in 1797. In 1816 the weather turned bitterly cold and remained subnormal for several years afterward. People who lived through this peculiar chill referred to 1816 as the year without summer or, more colorfully, "eighteen hundred and froze to death." Rather than merely diminishing the growing season, the climatic change almost eliminated it in New England when even the summer months experienced killing frosts. The consequences rippled out like waves from a stone tossed in a pond: food shortages resulted, some farmers were ruined, and a westward exodus commenced to what migrants hoped would be more temperate climes. The cause for the abnormal cold was unknown to those afflicted by it, but we now know that a violent volcanic eruption in Indonesia in 1815 hurled so much debris into the air that the Earth cooled noticeably in the years following.

All this is to say that farmers have always been hostages of fate even as they have always been reassured by the regularity of seasonal change. Just as the farmer can be sure that the sun will rise each day, he knows that the approach of autumn will require him to harvest and handle his crops, and much of his labor all year long is directed to that final, key process.

Harvesting requires speed, and new tools for reaping grain that appeared after the Revolution helped. For years, farmers had used sickles or scythes to cut grain. The sickle, with its dramatic arc and sharp blade, could cut grain stalks close to their tops, but the scythe's tendency to smash grain usually restricted it to grass and hay cutting. Whatever the case, wielding these tools was difficult and exceedingly time-consuming work. Near the end of the Revolutionary War, American farmers began harvesting grain with a device called the cradle. An imported European invention, the cradle was a scythe fastened to a wooden frame from which extended curved metal fingers set just above and back from the blade. Competently swept, or "thrown," the implement sheared the wheat stalks into the fingers (hence "cradle"), from which the reaper could toss them to the ground for bundling into sheaves. Americans could "mow *four acres* of *oats, wheat, rye,* or *barley* in a day," marveled one observer, possibly with some exaggeration.[5] Harvesting with a cradle was physically demanding but relatively fast, allowing a strong and experienced reaper to cut twice as much acreage in the same amount of time as someone wielding a sickle. Cradles, undergoing various improvements in design, would persist well into the nineteenth century as the preferred implement for reaping, until mechanical harvesters gradually began replacing them in the 1840s and 1850s.

Cutting the grain was only the first step in harvesting. As the reaper threw the cradle, another worker followed with a hand rake to bind the stalks into sheaves that were in turn bundled together into shocks for drying in the field. The grain then had to be removed from husks by threshing. As the name indicates, threshing was long accomplished by simply beating (thrashing) the husks, and New England farmers who grew grain for their own food stores usually threshed it by striking it with flails. Commercial growers in the mid-Atlantic region threshed their larger quantities by trampling it with livestock, a process called treading. Because the ground considerably dirtied treaded wheat, a better quality resulted from treading on platforms to produce cleaner and more expensive grain. The process used depended on the intended market, with southern farmers, whose wheat would be locally sold, using less costly ground treading. Large commercial operations aimed at international markets always used platforms.

The corn shock of stacked stalks with fat pumpkins resting in between has been emblematic of harvest season in America since the beginning of agriculture. Indians were planting pumpkins and corn to ripen together long before the first white settlers arrived. Corn's high yield in proportion to acreage had always made it a staple of human and animal diets in America, yet planting, harvesting, and processing corn required considerable effort because everything had to be done by hand. Expensive and unreliable seed drills obliged the farmer to put in seeds by hand; at harvest time, he had to remove the ears from their stalks, husk their thick shucks, and remove their kernels, all by hand.

Different techniques for harvesting corn either had harvesters shearing cornstalks or pulling the entire stalk from the ground, but whatever the method, the cornstalks had to be bunched into shocks in the open field for ripening and drying. When using corn for fodder, the farmer could pulverize the cob and the kernels together, but ideally corn was shelled from the cob. Some writers have suggested that the early use of seashells to scrape kernels from corncobs was the origin of "shelling" to describe the procedure. In the South, shucked corn was sometimes shelled by setting it on gapped shelving and flailing it with poles to beat the kernels from the cobs, but the method wasted a considerable amount of corn. Hand shellers used metal scrapers to rasp corn kernels from ears, a slow and tiresome chore that encouraged Americans to invent machinery for the job. The simplest mechanical sheller was also the most enduring basic design. It comprised a set of drums with spiral teeth through which the ear was cranked, stripping off the corn along the way. Mechanical shellers tended to miss a portion of the corn by leaving the tapered ends of the cob untouched, but improved designs gradually diminished the waste, and shellers were slowly introduced in all parts of the country.

Farmers in all regions made whiskey by distilling grains. Corn or rye in liquid form was frequently easier to transport across difficult terrain and fetched better prices. In remote western Pennsylvania, farmers even used whiskey as currency and thus were especially resentful when the new federal government levied a tax on it in the 1790s. The result was the notorious Whiskey Rebellion, which quickly dissolved when George Washington summoned militia to suppress the uprising. The Whiskey Rebellion indicated, however, how widespread and important personal whiskey making was in the early Republic. The availability of West Indies molasses in New England ports encouraged rum making, and farmers everywhere distilled whiskey, gin, and brandy. An avid taste for spirits led to the creation of factory distilleries that provided an important market for farm commodities as well, as commercial distillers needed countless wagonloads of grain, potatoes, and apples. Distilleries could also profit by selling grain residue for animal fodder. By the same token, brewers created a demand for barley and hops that led some farmers in various parts of the country to devote extensive tracts to these crops.

Livestock and Dairying   For most of the colonial period, livestock on farms were a marginally domesticated lot of free-roaming animals that foraged for themselves. They were fenced out of crop-producing fields and were periodically rounded up from open woods for slaughter. Pigs, for instance, ran free and were largely feral, such as the razorbacks that came to be associated with western areas. A traveler in Kentucky noted that "of all domestic animals, hogs are the most numerous."[6] Even large towns had marginally tame pig populations that roamed muddy streets and scavenged garbage-strewn back alleys, and it was true that the most omnipresent farm animals were pigs. Pork rather than beef was the much more prevalent dietary meat. Pigs ate anything, making them easy to sustain, but they were runty and stringy unless the farmer took care in feeding and finishing them. Successful pig growers supplemented garbage with beans, fruits, vegetables, and cornmeal. Beechnuts were said to improve the taste of pork noticeably.

Everyone grew poultry of all sorts, both for home consumption and for market. The woman of the house generally tended the poultry, and the so-called egg money she earned at the local farmers' market helped meet household expenses. Chickens were most numerous, but geese and turkeys were plentiful also. Several times a year, women plucked goose feathers to stuff in bedding and mattresses and to sell for fashioning quill pens.

Improving roads saw the colonial oxcart gradually replaced by horse-drawn carriages and wagons. New England in the 1790s was the origin of a particular breed of horse whose short, muscular legs and fast gait made it especially desirable. Named after Justin Morgan, the owner of the breed's progenitor, a stallion named Figure, Morgan horses were sought out in New England and, with westward migrations, moved to newly settled regions as well. In due course, Kentucky, with its ample expanse of bluegrass, would establish itself as the premier horse-producing region in the country.

Many New England farmers began raising sheep when they found they could no longer compete with the longer growing seasons and more fertile soils of western settlements. Sheep supplied both wool for local textile mills and mutton for the table. At the turn of the century, the introduction from Spain of long-staple Merino sheep rapidly transformed New England sheepherding into a major enterprise that encouraged investment in textile factories and contributed to making the region the nerve center of American manufacturing.

Eighteenth-century agricultural advances in fodder crops and the better understanding of how animal manure replenishes the soil promoted more vigilant animal husbandry, especially for sheep and dairy cattle. When properly tended, sheep could yield two to three pounds of wool per animal. Farmers in all regions began to pasture their cattle during the summer. The South's warm climate allowed farmers to graze their animals in pastures throughout the winter as well, but by 1810, many southerners were emulating their northern neighbors in feeding their animals fodder in the colder months. Dairy farmers took care to shelter their animals in stables, where they fed them hay, corn, and oats. As western migration increased after the War of 1812, newer and more fertile wheat-growing areas in the West encouraged eastern farmers to emphasize animal husbandry and boost dairy farming. As a consequence, hay production to increase stores of winter fodder became important. Farmers planted large stands of hay and rapidly harvested it in autumn with scythes, clearing as much as two acres per day. After drying on the ground, hay was raked up for use in the winter. Better grades of fodder produced better milk, so care went into the feeding of livestock, a routine called "finishing." Farmers forked fodder into feedlots or brought it into barns on carts to toss into stalls. It was commonly pitched onto the ground in both barns and stockyards, a practice that both wasted fodder and undernourished animals, but the custom remained in force through the middle of the nineteenth century.

Virtually all dairy products were processed on farmsteads during the early Republic. Cows' milk, drawn by hand, was transferred into tubs and stored in a relatively cool place, such as a cellar or an outbuilding called a springhouse, so named because it was situated over or near a stream (or spring). The brick floor of the springhouse usually had several inches of water diverted onto it, where the milk tubs sat while the fatty, lighter portions of the milk (cream) rose to the top. If the farmer desired whole milk, he let the cream sit on the top long enough to sour a little before skimming it off with a ladle; skim milk resulted from ladling off the cream sooner. The springhouse did little more than slow the souring of milk and at best cooled it as a beverage to tepid temperatures.

Butter was produced by churning cream, a laborious and lengthy procedure that was never done to whole milk. Instead farmers skimmed the cream and placed it into a churn, a tall, enclosed wooden vessel where the cream was agitated with a paddle to congeal it into butter. The farmer then placed the butter in a tub or a large cask called a firkin. Because subsequent churnings were added until the firkin was filled, farm butter varied greatly in quality; the oldest layer in the lowest part of the cask would be rancid, while the most recent on the top was relatively sweet. Nothing was wasted, though: rancid butter could be used to coat milk curds as they ripened into cheese. Because the cream had reached some degree of sourness before churning, even the topmost butter had a strong tang that probably would not appeal to today's palates. After 1810, commercial dairy farmers who produced butter for market had pioneered the use of sweet cream churned in large vessels that could hold many gallons at a time. These commercial churns were connected to treadmills or wheels powered by small animals, such as dogs. After the cream had turned to butter, it was set in large tubs or casks and covered, sometimes with cloth but usually with salt, and sealed to produce a consistently sweet butter. Nonetheless butter did not travel well in the absence of refrigeration or pasteurization (the process of heating and rapidly chilling to kill bacteria), and such advances were still decades away in 1820. Consequently butter was a local product, and only places near dairy regions could regularly enjoy it.

Cheese, on the other hand, profits from age and thus could travel far beyond the point of its creation without refrigeration. Cheese traveled so well that communities sometimes offered it in tribute to acclaimed events or people. In one celebrated episode, dairy farmers in the small Massachusetts town of Cheshire commemorated Thomas Jefferson's election to the presidency by combining a single day's milking of their thousand cows to make a giant cheese more than a yard across, almost two feet thick, and weighing about 1,200 pounds. A committee of Cheshire's citizens transported this enormous cheese by wagon and boat to the new capital of Washington, where it was presented to Jefferson on New Year's Day, 1802.

Cheese was sometimes made on farms by simply allowing milk to sour, a bacterial process that produces a thick precipitate (curd) and a watery residue (whey), which was removed. Cheese makers could speed curdling by heating the milk and adding rennet, the lining of a calf's stomach. The curd was then salted, for taste and curing, and ladled into a cheese press, a barrel with a perforated bottom lined with cheesecloth. After weight applied to the top pushed out additional whey, the curd remained for two or three days in the barrel. It was then taken out of the press, placed in molds, smeared over with something to seal it, such as lard or sour butter, and stored in a cool place for ripening. Ripening took anywhere from weeks to several months, during which the curing cheese was occasionally turned. All the cheese types during this period were of European origin; Dutch Edam is said to have been the first.

Life and Labor   Farmhouses were usually extremely simple frame or log cabins. More prosperous farmers might have clapboard houses, but they were rarely painted until later in the period, when the increasing manufacture of linseed oil made paint available as well as affordable. Farms obtained their water from wells with buckets or, if near a spring, from crude aqueducts fashioned by boring holes in logs.

All the tasks of farming were accomplished only by unremitting toil performed by many hands. In the North, if the farm was too large for the family to work, extra hands were hired. As in other trades, young boys could be apprenticed to farmers who would teach them how to farm while providing them with clothing and shelter. The apprentice was usually indentured to work under this arrangement until reaching 21 years of age, when he was released from his obligation, almost always leaving with gifts and money to help him make his start in the world. The apprenticeship system could be cruel and exploitative, depending on the temperament and character of the master, but it could also be instructive and familial. In any case, at most the system prescribed a term of limited service that helped young men get a start rather than ensuring, as southern slavery did, that they would never have a chance. In contrast, bondage in the South not only offset the high labor demands of growing and tending crops but tainted honest labor with the brush of slavery, discouraging whites from working anywhere but on their own land.

When hiring extra labor often proved too difficult or expensive for farmers who needed it only briefly, such as during a hectic season like the fall harvest or for specific chores like raising a barn, neighbors could band together for a "bee," an event that underpinned a festive social gathering with hard work. The men labored, and the women cooked; after the task was completed, jugs were raised and hearty appetites satisfied in a ritual that fostered neighborly cooperation and encouraged reciprocal generosity.

On the less settled, remote frontier and in poorer regions such as the marginal lands of the South, women might work alongside the men at all but the most physically demanding farming chores, although one observer in Kentucky noted that "women seldom assist in the labors of the field."[7] Women in more established farming communities only took to the fields when an emergency required all hands to save the crop. Women toiled at equally demanding jobs, though, such as tending poultry and livestock, especially dairy cows, in addition to concentrating on their principal responsibility, the household. There a woman's days were filled from before dawn to well after dark with cooking, cleaning, spinning thread, weaving cloth, stitching clothes, making candles, molding soap, and raising children, a duty that frequently included their basic education as well as their moral improvement. She was the family's doctor of first and sometimes only resort, its moral arbiter, its chief confessor, and its primary comforter. The old homily about man working from sun to sun but a woman's work never being done persisted because it was so true.

SOUTHERN AGRICULTURE

The South has a growing season with killing frosts in the winter, but unlike the North, the region enjoys much warmer temperatures for a longer period. In the upper South across the region spanning from Maryland through Missouri, the growing season lasts about six months. The region from the Virginia coast south to northern Georgia and east to western Tennessee has a growing season of about seven months, the Piedmont regions of the Carolinas about eight months, and the Carolina Low Country and coastal regions of the Gulf of Mexico a luxurious nine months. The length of those various seasons determined the most prevalent crops in them. Generally speaking, tobacco flourished in the upper South, cotton would come to thrive in the middle regions, and rice, indigo, and sugarcane grew in areas with the longest summers.

Where rice was grown in abundance, such as the Low Country of South Carolina, it was the principal dietary cereal grain. Otherwise corn held pride of place, specifically the variety called "Indian corn." In those early days, yellow corn was almost always used for animal fodder. Southerners prepared corn in a variety of ways, from roasting or boiling whole ears to shelling the kernels and boiling them to a mush, a concoction called hominy. Coarsely ground corn produced grits (always in the plural: there is no such thing as a "grit"), while a finer grind produced cornmeal for corn pone, which was corn bread usually made without eggs. Corn muffins and spoon bread, so named because it remained doughy after baking and required a spoon for eating, were also traditions. Southern corn bread was never sweetened with sugar, as it frequently was in the North. Because Irish potatoes did not store well in the South's hot climate, the southerner's substitute was the yam, which he called a "sweet potato." Sweet potatoes ripened slowly in autumn and were only bested by corn as the main staple of southern diets. Amid their stands of corn, southerners grew cowpeas, a legume that more resembled a lima bean than an English sweet pea, which required cooler weather to prosper. Apples grew in higher regions, and peaches flourished in the hot, humid weather of lower areas. Melons, especially watermelons, thrived throughout the region.

Common but inaccurate conceptions of the Old South have been formed by motion pictures in which opulent homes with white-columned terraces are surrounded by lush gardens and extensive fields of cotton. Actually, the South's large plantations constituted a very small fraction of the land and were lived on by an even smaller portion of the population. A visitor in 1825 to the Georgia frontier noted that the plantation he was visiting, "like all others, is made up of log houses. Through our quarters the wind blew to its heart's content; no light could keep burning, so that we had to see by the flames of the great fireplace. There was no ceiling, only the shingle roof directly above us through which the light penetrated."[8]

In any case, by 1800 the plantation system was not fully developed throughout the South, and cotton had not yet become the region's dominant staple. In 1820 cotton was gaining rapidly in importance, but its days of overarching importance in both the southern and national economies still lay ahead. That said, it should be noted that as the plantation system evolved in the South, small subsistence farms, inhabited by the poor whites of the region, tended to be less prosperous than northern farms. The result was a strangely oligarchic culture, extremely stratified, with a small proportion of wealthy planters at the top, a larger number of middling planters below, and the great majority of the white population in the lower class. That is not to say that the South did not have a middle class, but its members were more likely to be in commerce, banking, and the professions.

Slave labor was used in the South, but its scale was more limited than commonly believed. During this period, only about a **Slavery** quarter of the white population of the South was even indirectly involved in slavery, and a much smaller percentage owned slaves. In addition, most slave owners were not plantation grandees but rather were farmers who owned a few slaves and usually worked with them in the fields.

Wealthy planters constituted a very small minority of the population, and even their homes were usually more practical than splendid. Very few planters had inherited their wealth during this period. Most were self-made men who ran large working farms rather than lavish agricultural showplaces. Generally, the largest houses consisted of two stories divided into 10 to 15 rooms, the lower level serving as a social area with a dining room, parlor, and perhaps a library, the second floor containing the bedrooms. Because of fire danger and to keep the heat of cooking fires away from the main house, the kitchen was a separate building, as was the smokehouse. Stables also sat some distance away. Larger plantations also featured a cotton gin and separate offices to oversee operations.

Rather than exhibiting affluence, the planter was expected to behave as a gentleman with honor and to fill his proper place in society, especially by extending hospitality to strangers and friends alike. A visitor to a crude log plantation in Georgia in the mid-1820s was pleased with the fine meal and "surprised to see the works of Shakespeare" on his host's bookshelves.[9] Yet the plantation culture, for all its intended graciousness, promoted and preserved the degrading institution of human slavery. Immediately after the American Revolution, slavery was actually in decline because the decrease in foreign markets depressed prices for plantation products such as rice, indigo, and tobacco. Consequently, some planters began freeing their slaves, partly for idealistic reasons, but also because economic trends encouraged them to do so. Troubled by the incongruity of slavery in a free republic, southern churches began to question the institution of slavery, and after 1810 many southerners joined the American Colonization Society, a group organized to promote the transport of freed slaves to the west African country optimistically named Liberia. Yet significant changes in southern agriculture regrettably undermined and ultimately destroyed these benevolent impulses. As early as 1803, with the admission of Louisiana to the Union, the need for laborers in the sugarcane fields increased the demand for slaves in that region. By then, more importantly, the cotton gin was revolutionizing cotton growing in the South, and the need for an abundant labor supply to grow and harvest cotton unfortunately solidified slavery as a southern institution.[10]

Tobacco   Grains dominated the agricultural landscape of the North, and while corn and wheat were obviously grown in the South, they were rarely grown commercially. The exception was in northern Virginia, where a fading tobacco culture was gradually replaced late in the period by wheat farming on a scale comparable to that in the North. In the main, though, tobacco, cotton, rice, indigo, and sugarcane were the prevailing southern crops.

Tobacco was the principal crop during most of the colonial period because it enjoyed the best market, especially because cotton was difficult to process until the invention of the cotton gin in the 1790s. Tobacco, on the other hand, posed special difficulties in planting because its seeds are minuscule: about 10,000 will fill a teaspoon. Because sowing such small seeds in an open field was a pointless exercise, they were mixed with sand or ash and broadcast in seedbeds prepared by mixing in cinders, both to enrich the soil and hinder the growth of competing plants, weeds, and grasses. Planting was done near the end of winter to give the small plants the best chance of surviving relocation to open fields during spring rains. As the plants germinated in the seedbeds, growing fields were plowed and then fashioned into small mounds at three-foot intervals. At the first rain, slaves worked frantically to move the small plants from the seedbeds to the muddy fields, the best receptacle to prevent transplant shock. When the fields went dry, the transplanting ceased to await the next rain. A cycle of idleness and frenzied activity continued until the entire crop was transplanted. As the plant leafed out during the summer, considerable care had to be exercised in tending it. Those with experienced eyes knew just the right time to cut off the uppermost section of the stalk to promote sizable leaf growth. Shoots that sprouted between leaf and stalk—called suckers because they literally sucked out the plant's vitality and inhibited large leaf formation—were immediately pinched off throughout the growing season. Both the tops and undersides of leaves were regularly inspected for voracious hornworms, which could strip every plant in the field if left alone.

In early autumn, yellowing leaves signaled harvest time. Stalks were cut and laid in the fields for wilting before being strung on racks to dry. Prosperous planters could dry tobacco by hanging it from the rafters of tall barns. Outdoor curing was sometimes accelerated with low fires. Cured leaves became brittle and crumbled if handled too much, so the dried plants were left alone for the bulk of the winter. The return of humid weather in early spring made the leaves pliable and ready for final processing. Stalks were taken down and piled to preserve foliage texture as leaves were stripped and sorted into three grades of quality: the prime bright leaf, the less desirable darker leaves, and lugs from the lowest part of the plant. Bundling took place in wet weather for prizing, the packing of the bundles into casks called hogsheads. Weights and presses ensured that a hogshead was packed tightly to weigh about a thousand pounds when sealed off. The hogsheads' considerable weight meant that their transport was most easily accomplished by rolling them to river landings that served as shipping depots, a trip almost always undertaken in summer because roads were driest then. As this was taking place, the new crop had already been seeded, transplanted, and was under cultivation. It was all hard work with little idle time, since last year's crop was being processed while the current year's was being tended in the fields. Harvesting was backbreaking, curing required skill, and sorting and packing were arduous. "Nothing but a great crop, and the total abnegation of every comfort, to which the Negroes are condemned," wrote one traveler in 1788, "can compensate for the cost of raising this product and getting it to market."[11]

Rice

Rice was grown only where a large supply of water was readily available and fields could be designed to dam it and drain it away, a procedure that required elaborate levees and networks of ditches. Consequently, rice was grown in the coastal regions of South Carolina and Georgia. Brooks or swamps were the ideal location for this thirsty crop. Certain other necessities were required as well. Fields had to be situated in freshwater tidal floodplains to facilitate flooding and draining. Considerable ingenuity and vigilant maintenance were always necessary, and almost everything that could go wrong usually did. River creatures often damaged the dams, unexpectedly draining the crop and sometimes ruining it. Too much water was just as bad as none at all. Bad weather could bring freshets that scoured the fields, and coastal hurricanes could shove the ocean far up estuaries to turn freshwater tides brackish.

After the fields were broken, broad hills about a foot apart received broadcast rice seeds. If the hills were already muddy, they were covered; if dry, the field was flooded (or flowed) to promote sprouts. A set pattern of flowing and draining the rice fields could vary, but generally fields were flowed after the plant's first appearance, again in midseason, and finally when the mature stalks needed support to keep from breaking under the weight of the grain. Flows were interspersed with drainings for cultivation to remove weeds and grass with hoes. Upon draining the final flow, harvesting commenced as the stalks were cut with a sickle and put aside for sheaving and drying. As with wheat, threshing was done by flailing or animal treading in preparation for milling. Unlike the grinding of wheat, which is meant to separate the chaff and break the kernel, rice milling seeks only to remove the husk. Rice mills thus resembled great mortars and pestles, with larger timbers mechanically raised and dropped to hammer the rice rather than smash it. After milling, the rice was winnowed, sifted, polished, and packed into barrels, the whole grain for market and broken kernels for the farmer's family. The chaff was either sold to brewers or fed to livestock.

Indigo

       Although planted and cultivated in the same way as cereal grains are, indigo is actually a legume. Because it was a valuable source of dye and ink—its leaves yield a dark blue resin when fermented—the whole object of indigo growing was the reclamation of this dyestuff. After the plants bloomed, they were carefully harvested to preserve the leaves intact. The whole leaves were soaked in vats of water to produce a slurry that fermented in another vat while being violently agitated. At just the right moment, fermentation was halted with a stop agent, such as limewater. When the suspension settled, the water was drained off, leaving a solid, foul-smelling residue that was scooped, strained, pressed into cubes, and dried for market. Indigo was a demanding crop whose yields were relatively light—frequently less than a hundred pounds of dyestuff per acre. In its heyday, however, it offered a moderately good return for the investment of time and labor. In due course, West Indies indigo supplanted the American variety, especially because British bounties for growing it ended with the Revolution. By the late 1790s, some indigo growers were turning to long staple cotton.

Sugarcane

       Sugarcane grows only in regions with long summers. Cane fields did exist as far north as middle Georgia, but southern Louisiana had the best growing conditions. Despite its demanding cultivation requirements and difficult characteristics, sugarcane could be a lucrative crop. Some plantations by the late 1790s were producing a high grade of sugar that netted as much as $12,000 per season, the modern equivalent of almost $200,000.

Cane growers planted their crop in deep, parallel furrows as early as possible in the year to take advantage of a long growing season. Even so, cultivation would not seriously commence until late summer. Because frost ruined the crop, cane was reaped anytime after reaching some level of maturity. Harvesting occurred in two stages. The first consisted of cutting a portion of the crop for seed cane that would remain in the field for reseeding in the following year. The second stage consisted of stripping and cutting the cane stalk by swinging a large machete in four rhythmic swipes: two to remove leaves, one to chop off the stalk at its base, and the final to remove its top. Gathered up on carts and taken to the plantation's mill, the cane was run between heavy rollers that mashed the stalks to squeeze out a clear liquid-sugar solution. Harvesting and milling could take place simultaneously, but a threat of frost focused all attention on clearing the fields. The necessity for speed at harvest made for a relentless schedule of virtually nonstop labor, especially at the mill.

Extraction was a wasteful business because the spongy stalks tended to reabsorb some of the liquid sugar as they exited the rollers. The smashed stalk also released impurities that had to be removed to permit the sugar to crystallize. Boiling the solution in a series of cauldrons brought up this residue as a scum that was repeatedly skimmed off to clarify the solution. The boiling also reduced the mixture to create a concentrated slurry that, when cooled and drained, became a mass of crystals, tinted brown because of the high molasses content. During the first 20 years of the nineteenth century, improvements in beet processing, especially in France, were successfully used to process sugarcane. Pressure cookers and condensers allowed for higher temperatures that increased clarification and reduced molasses to produce a higher-quality, whiter sugar. Also, by 1817, new types of sugarcane, such as rapidly ripening variegated ribbon cane, shortened the growing season and increased yields. Despite such advances, though, American sugarcane was never able to match West Indies varieties, which reseeded with little trouble and flourished in the much longer growing season. Sugarcane in the West Indies was so abundant, in fact, that much of it was only partly processed to extract a heavy molasses for making rum, one of the ingredients in the infamous triangular slave trade. Slave traders bartered West Africans for West Indies molasses, which they sold to New Englanders at significant profits. In contrast, the relative smallness of the Louisiana crop, the considerable domestic demand for refined sugar, and the competition of Kentucky and Ohio corn and rye whiskey meant that Louisiana cane was rarely used to make rum.

There are many varieties of cotton, but only two grew in the American South. The most common was short staple cotton, pro-   **Cotton** duced from green seeds with a velvet covering that clung tightly to the short fibers in the boll. Short staple cotton thrived in the uplands, while the other variety, long staple cotton, flourished only in the special climate and high moisture provided by coastal regions. It was frequently called Sea Island cotton because it was best grown on the islands off the South Carolina and Georgia coasts. Grown from shiny black seeds, long staple cotton was relatively new to the continent in the 1790s. When indigo was waning as a lucrative crop, farmers in the coastal regions sought to replace it by importing seeds from the Bahamas, by most accounts beginning in 1786. Sea Island cotton was noted for its long, silky fiber that was ideal for lace or fine linens; short staple cotton was more suited for coarser fabrics.

Carefully nurtured, long staple cotton could yield as much as three-quarters of a million pounds in one season, valued at more than $300,000, the equivalent of about $4 million today. Despite its great value, however, long staple cotton posed special difficulties. It could flourish only in the special conditions along the coast, limiting the amount of acreage the crop could occupy. Planters preferred to prepare the ground for Sea Island cotton by hoeing rather than plowing because they claimed that even shovel plows clumped the soil. After harvest, seeds could be removed with relative ease by hand, and that practice continued even after the invention of the cotton gin. Ginning tended to break the long fibers and robbed the lint of its most desirable characteristic. Sea Island cotton required cleaning by hand.

Until Eli Whitney invented the cotton gin in 1793, cotton of the more abundant short staple variety stood little chance of becoming a viable cash crop. Whitney's cotton gin had a profound impact on southern culture, but it also had a significant influence on national and international finances. Cotton became profitable as its more efficient processing coincided with the advent of textile mills in the North and in Great Britain. Over the next few decades, cotton production and export grew at a slow but steady pace, and the insatiable search for new places to plant cotton was one of the reasons for the rapid settlement of Mississippi and Alabama, which became states in 1817 and 1819.

Although planting, tending, and harvesting cotton was extremely hard work, the greater problem had always been processing it. Short staple cotton's green seed clung tenaciously to the fibers in the boll, and removing it by hand was so time-consuming that progress was measured in ounces rather than pounds. Whitney, a northerner who had been a mechanic in his youth, was visiting a Georgia plantation when he set out to conquer the age-old problem of removing seeds from short staple cotton. The device he contrived was remarkably simple but remarkably effective. Two cylinders sat in a box, one bristling with fine wires, the other covered with brushes. The bristles protruded through a slotted side of the box against which the cotton was pressed. As the bristles rotated, they pulled cotton lint through the slots but left its thick seeds behind. The brush cylinder removed the clean cotton from the wires. His original design "required the labor of one man to turn it and with which one man will clean ten times as much cotton as he can in any other way before now, and also cleanse it much better than in the usual mode."[12] Based on this prototype, large gins (short for "engine") could clean enormous amounts of cotton, making it profitable and hastening the transformation of what had been predominantly a tobacco-growing culture into the eventual Cotton Kingdom of the antebellum South.

Economics drove the change. In 1799, South Carolina planter Wade Hampton produced 600 bales that sold for about $90,000, a result that was at first tempting and then irresistible. As more planters and farmers planted increasing acres of cotton, the market fluctuated annually, occasionally falling precipitously when bad news from foreign markets suppressed demand. Such an event occurred in 1812, when the news of war with Britain saw the price plummet a whopping five cents per pound in one day. In addition, cotton made for other maladies. In spite of appeals for farmers to raise corn and other food grains, cotton continued to dominate southern agriculture for the rest of the nineteenth century.

The problems of processing solved, cotton nonetheless remained a demanding crop to plant and harvest, requiring prodigious labor from start to finish. The usual planting routine was to prepare fields with shallow-draft shovel plows that were driven over fields twice to break the ground more thoroughly. Then, moving single file over the tilled ground, one slave shaped a hill with a hoe and opened a hole in it, a second seeded, and a third scraped the soil to cover the seed. The process was carried out simultaneously by slave trios working in tandem across large acreages, moving side by side along lengthy rows from dawn to twilight. To keep down weeds, fields required backbreaking hoeing during the high heat of summer, and in the autumn, cotton was harvested by hand. Picking cotton was simply grueling because the low plants bent backs and the tough fibers of the cotton boll cracked all but the most callused hands.

Cotton rapidly depletes the soil, but drives for replenishment through fertilization were slow in coming. Instead there was a tendency for centers of high cotton production to move west, with new settlements established in the search for fruitful soil. By 1820, the richer earth of Alabama and Mississippi had already made the region, known as the Old Southwest, much more important for cotton growing than the eastern areas of the South. Southwestern planters could rely on the westward-spreading wheat boom in the North for food and could thus focus exclusively on cotton production. Slaves spent relatively little time producing food on these plantations, and planters worked these slaves intensely to swell production. Most crucial in cotton growing was assessing how much the labor force could harvest, for planting and tending a crop grown exclusively for commercial outlets was pointless if it could not be brought to market.

Small farmers took their cotton to gins throughout the South, and large planters frequently installed their own to clean their cotton and that of neighbors for a fee. During the 1790s, ginned cotton was stuffed by hand into hemp or burlap sacks and tamped down for baling, a slow process that could take a laborer a full day to fill one sack. Many planters used a lever press to pack their cotton, but gradually the more powerful screw press replaced it and by the early 1800s was the most prevalent method of sacking. Usually worked by two men and a mule team, the screw press could produce about 15 bales a day. Even so, planters rarely packed their cotton compactly enough to suit cotton brokers, whose shipping costs were determined by weight instead of volume. Consequently, southern ports featured large presses that further compressed the cotton before shipment, ideally to a standard weight of 500 pounds per bale. Brokers also erected fireproof cotton houses to store bales safely before they were shipped. Once the cotton was sold for shipment, slaves would roll the 500-pound bales to docks where stevedores, wielding hooks and tugging on block-and-tackle rigs, hoisted the bales into the ships' holds, their destination northern or British ports. Planters commanded prices for their cotton according to quality determined by the excellence and length of its fibers.

BUYING AND SELLING

Isolated farmers bought many goods from peddlers, the fabled traveling salesmen of so many ribald jokes featuring farmers' comely daughters. More established farming communities had access to the general store, which stocked everything from barreled pickles to shiny plow-shares. Farmers were almost always cash poor, with prospects heavily reliant on a good crop, so transactions with rural merchants usually resorted to barter or credit with crops or the expected profit from them as collateral. Small farmers sold produce, eggs, butter, and cheese beyond what they did not need for their own larders at village farmers' markets not unlike those that can be found in small towns and cities today.

Brokers and Factors   Larger commercial farmers and southern planters placed their produce in larger markets, either in urban areas or for shipment abroad, a design that usually required middle-men, for even the most prosperous farmers lacked the con-tacts and expertise to exploit fluctuating profits and vague markets. Middlemen took the form of jobbers, brokers, or factors and could be expensive. Brokers acted as buyers' agents and could charge commissions as high as 20 percent; factors were sellers' agents who usually handled both the sale of the agricultural commodities and the financial affairs of their clients, such as securing loans and making purchases of goods in urban markets. Middlemen frequently owned warehouses in transporta-tion hubs, such as cities along major roads, river towns, or coastal ports. Goods destined for shipment abroad would be purchased by middlemen from the farmer at wholesale and stored for sale to retailers or for oceanic delivery. The middleman could also serve as a central hub gathering diverse types of farm products to distribute to specialized sellers. Jobbers rarely owned storage facilities and most often focused on selling goods directly to the public, at auctions, for example. The exception to reliance on a broker-factor system was the case of small farmers. Wool growers also frequently sold directly to local textile plants in New England. In any case, because the undeveloped transportation network of the early Repub-lic made markets regional for most farm products, the broker-factor sys-tem was in its infancy throughout the period.

Livestock marketing was a case in point. Farmers infrequently put their own livestock in retail markets because of the expense and complexity of doing so. Instead drovers bought livestock from farmers and herded the animals into towns or cities, a difficult chore fraught with risks because the journey usually killed some animals and wore down the rest. Before going on the auction block, animals had to recuperate from the journey with ample feed and water, an additional expense for the drover.

Crops such as grains, cotton, and tobacco enjoyed much wider markets. Grain farmers sold their product to middlemen who stored it in sacks in large warehouses. Corn was usually sacked, while wheat was occasionally kept in barrels. Grain middlemen were frequently mill owners who would sell flour locally. Wheat shipped abroad was always unmilled and was simply poured into the ship's hold. In any case, the considerable expense and labor necessary to turn wheat into flour made specialization a necessity. Wheat grains had to be lifted to a mill top, dropped into chutes, and funneled between the grinding stones, a labor-intensive job made potentially easier by a chained series of buckets invented by Oliver Evans in 1785. Yet even this first, crude grain elevator did not come into wide usage until the 1840s.

Southern planters who grew tobacco, rice, or cotton were completely at the mercy of the broker-factor system. Because most capital originated in Europe, for years the main brokerage houses were in London, but gradually Americans took over these transactions. American brokers and factors would station themselves in southern ports, but they usually had ties to banks in the North. Certain cities became the centers for the large cash crops associated with their regions. Richmond was the center for tobacco, for instance, Charleston and Savannah for cotton and rice, and New Orleans for cotton and sugar.

While the undeveloped transportation system of the early Republic meant that most farm products were marketed regionally, there were some notable exceptions. In 1787, South Carolina watermelons and sweet **Perishables and Preservation** potatoes, carried by ship, were marketed in Boston. Nonetheless, perishable items such as produce and fruit were always unavailable out of season. Farmers tried to overcome the problems of perishables with a variety of ingenious solutions. Orchard tenders sun-dried apples, pickers pulled green corn from stalks and parched it, women of the house piled potatoes, carrots, and cabbages in cool root cellars and corn in cribs. Yet things simply did not keep for long, and such simple methods of preservation only slightly retarded spoliation. Meat was pickled, salted, or smoked (methods designed to remove excess moisture, the great accelerant of decay), but pickling altered the taste, and salting the texture. The art of curing meat in smokehouses is now regarded as a way of producing an appetizing delicacy; in the early Republic, it was a necessary process to prevent spoilage. Because city dwellers lacked an effective way to store food or dry meat, most perishable food remained on farms, even if destined for urban markets, until it was to be consumed.

Meanwhile the period's inventive minds tackled the problem of food preservation. When Napoleon Bonaparte sponsored a contest for a method to preserve food for armies on the march, Nicolas Appert devised a process to vacuum-seal food in glass jars. Because the detection of bacteria, let alone their role in food spoilage, was decades away, nobody was sure why the simple application of high temperatures to containers that then sealed themselves upon cooling resulted in extending the life of fresh food. Yet by performing the relatively easy procedure of "canning" food, summer fruits and vegetables could be enjoyed in January. By 1819, transplanted Englishman William Underwood was canning seafood in a

Boston factory, sealing his jars with tar, and another British immigrant, Thomas Kensett, was establishing a similar plant in New York, an establishment that in a few years would substitute tin cans for glass jars.

Self-Sufficiency Self-reliance was the custom of farm life, and remote farmsteads were by necessity self-sufficient. Although the practice varied depending on the locality, even southern plantations preoccupied with tobacco or cotton growing set aside a certain portion of their fields to grow food. Meanwhile the South Carolina Low Country, which primarily produced rice and sweet potatoes, became dependent on other areas for corn. Nothing went to waste, and everything had a use. Extra grain was distilled into whiskey or fruit into brandy by countless stills; at hearthsides, women pumped spinning wheels to spindle thread from wool or cotton and weave it into cloth, creating aptly named homespun clothes. Tallow from animal fat was extracted during slaughtering to make candles and soap.

CONCLUSION

"Nothing was more evident" to foreign observers "than the general esteem in which the farmer was held and the important part he played in public life."[13] The spirit of self-reliance and the custom of autonomy made the American farm family of the early Republic remarkably durable. By the end of the period, farmers had weathered the economic dislocations of trade restrictions, the disorder of war, the uncertainties of a depressed and occasionally panicked economy, all the while clearing their land, raising their houses, tending their livestock, educating their children, and nurturing their crops. They discovered new horticultural methods and applied ingenious inventions to increase productivity that lessened labor and improved life. In the predawn darkness on countless farmsteads of the early Republic, these ordinary Americans stiffly moved through countless cold mornings to begin their chores, their children trudging toward barns with milk pails swinging at their sides as their mothers braced themselves for another day of endless labors and their fathers hitched plows to scratch furrows into American ground, slowly but inevitably to move the world, one acre at a time.

NOTES

1. France Wright, *Views of Society and Manners in America,* ed. Paul R. Baker (Cambridge: Belknap Press of Harvard University Press, 1963), 99.

2. For Randolph's remark and the circumstances that prompted it, see David S. Heidler, *Pulling the Temple Down: The Fire-Eaters and the Destruction of the Union* (Mechanicsburg, Pa.: Stackpole Books, 1994), 6.

3. William Strickland, *Journal of a Tour in the United States of America, 1794–1795,* ed. Reverend J. E. Strickland, with a facsimile edition of William Strick-

land's "Observations on the Agriculture of the United States of America" (New York: New York Historical Society, 1971), 126.

4. "Gypsum costs about 3 Dolls [dollars]," noted William Strickland, but he also remarked that "frauds are imputed to the dealers in Gypsum, as some barrels are found to have little or no effect when compared with others, it is supposed that they grind chalk, or some sort of limestone along with the Gypsum" (ibid., 108).

5. William Cobbett, *A Year's Residence in the United States of America: Treating of the Face of the Country, the Climate, the Soil, the Products, the Mode of Cultivating the Land, the Prices of Land, of Labour, of Food, of Raiment; of the Expenses of House-Keeping and of the Usual Manner of Living; of the Manners and Customs of the People; and, of the Institutions of the Country, Civil, Political and Religious. In Three Parts* (New York: Clayton and Kingsland, 1818), 190.

6. Francois André Michaux, quoted in Reuben Gold Thwaites, ed., *Early Western Travels, 1748–1846* (Cleveland: Arthur H. Clark, 1906), 245.

7. Michaux, quoted in Gold Thwaites, *Early Western Travels*, 250.

8. Bernard Karl, Duke of Saxe-Weimer-Eisenach, in Oscar Handlin, ed., *This Was America: True Accounts of People and Places, Manners and Customs, as Recorded by European Travelers to the Western Shore in the Eighteenth, Nineteenth, and Twentieth Centuries* (Cambridge: Harvard University Press, 1949), 161. The planters of Alabama by this time were more prosperous, and only slave cabins were made of logs.

9. Bernard Karl, in Handlin, *This Was America*, 161.

10. The lives of slaves are discussed in chapter 7.

11. Jean Pierre Brissot, in Handlin, *This Was America*, 86.

12. Eli Whitney wrote these observations to his father in September 1793. The letter is printed, in part, in *The Annals of America: Volume 3, 1784–1796, Organizing the New Nation* (Chicago: Encyclopaedia Britannica, 1968), 551–52.

13. Jane Louise Mesick, *The English Traveller in America, 1785–1835* (New York: Columbia University Press, 1922), 151.

4

A CHANGING ECONOMY: ARTISANS, FACTORIES, AND MONEY

Part of America's revolutionary legacy included the fundamental belief that work was a noble enterprise. The Puritan work ethic, which extolled the busy life and warned against idleness, reinforced the repudiation of languid European aristocrats as part of America's revolutionary philosophy. Work was decent in itself. Americans of the early Republic embraced gainful employment as another mark of good citizenship, and political and social leaders endorsed work as essential for the free exercise and proper appreciation of political liberty. In that regard, the American Revolution was truly innovative, as it profoundly revised the customs of old Europe. Aristocrats might be better educated and more grounded in the theories of government, but they were so far removed from working people that they were not suitable to govern them. From Benjamin Franklin's homely advice about work building character to the realities of men like Washington and Jefferson being gentleman farmers, the Republic was steeped in the belief that work not only informed citizens but ennobled them. Historians have noted how Americans developed a uniquely heightened sense that labor carried its own worth, evidence of which was the belief that hard work justified private property much more than mere birthright did. The bitter arguments over Alexander Hamilton's plans to fund the national debt were rooted in these attitudes (see chapter 1). Not only did it seem unfair that speculators would profit from Hamilton's plan, but the plan itself seemed to run counter to fundamental beliefs about fairness and equality in the American setting. The claims of original bearers of government securities were more legitimate because their motives for purchasing them were purer. Original bearers had supported the country, while speculators merely wanted to make money. Original bearers had worked for the money they had invested in the country; speculators preferred the leisure of cunning to accumulate their profits.

Those who worked with their hands—be they artisans, mechanics, or farmers—were not inclined to show much deference to anyone in any case, whether in matters of political leadership or social status. The attitude of an apprentice carpenter in rural Massachusetts is instructive. As part of a program of cultural improvement, he attended a literary club's debate on the question of who had more benefited society, lawyers or mechanics. He was pleased that mechanics won the day.[1] The 1790s saw the formation of the country's first working-class associations, the forerunners of labor unions. Primarily aimed at promoting the interests of skilled artisans, these associations were also the symbol of the working class's new political and social independence from the landed gentry. More than coincidence had working-class associations appearing at the same time as Democratic Societies, the political action groups that protested political elitism in general and such measures as the whiskey tax specifically. The 1792 association of Connecticut artisans stretched across craft lines and was formed primarily to protest burdensome taxation. Mechanics with soiled hands, village artisans in leather aprons, and distilling farmers in the Pennsylvania backwoods foreshadowed Jacksonian Democracy, eventually to win voting rights for all adult white males during the 1820s. During the early Republic, the clanging hammer in small workshops throughout the country amounted to a death knell for the old ways of doing things socially as well as politically.

Yet such gains did not occur overnight. Before the American Revolution, Pennsylvania abolished property qualifications for holding office, but other states not only sustained them; in some instances they increased them. The influence of the Revolution, however, was as telling in this regard as in others. Towns and cities saw growing working-class participation in political affairs, and legislative representatives from the working class gradually increased in number throughout the country. It marked a dramatic change from colonial times, when legislative assemblies were almost exclusively preserves of the landed elite.

More immediate was the disappearance of a class consciousness inherited from England that gauged artisans and mechanics as socially inferior. Instead, little distinction marked highly skilled laborers from people in the professions. Work meant economic independence, and economic independence meant status as well as freedom. It cannot be stressed enough how uniquely American this new reality was to the development of modern life. So universal was this understanding that by the end of the period, the federal census included a query about occupation.

Work not only had the appeal of functioning as a civic virtue; it provided practical benefits of material progress. America's promise was as apparent as it was abundant for the young man willing to learn a craft and work hard at it. Cities were growing at extraordinary rates, and the economy was expanding to include financial interactions that were more complex. Family enterprises of small scope became embryonic factories of ever-widening reach. And some changes foreshadowed modern problems. The old system of skilled craftsmen and their relations with apprentices rapidly unraveled. Instead of craftsmen acting as masters to apprentices, they became employers of wage earners, reflecting the new realities of a market economy in the dawning industrial age. The breakdown of the craft-guild system removed traditional controls on young men by hierarchical authority. The system that for ages had substituted for patriarchy simply disappeared as apprentices became employees. They enjoyed larger measures of economic freedom, but they also were socially untethered, often too soon for their own good, and became denizens of the streets, creating unforeseen social problems similar to those that trouble our own time.

ARTISANS

In the preindustrial economy of the early Republic, the artisan's special skills distinguished him from ordinary laborers and made him an important member of the community. He was an independent craftsman with liberty to work where and how he wished. He attained his station through a ritualized form of promotion in his craft, a system that was as old as the venerable guilds of the Middle Ages. The arrangement featured the process whereby one learned the "arts and mysteries" of a craft, a specific wording that denoted the importance of both expertise in workmanship and gratification in craftsmanship. The artisan did not merely produce material goods; he maintained an ethos of excellence imperative for his community to function properly.

The early Republic saw the last days of an arrangement that had dictated the relationship between, and responsibilities of, masters toward journeymen and apprentices. Derived from time-tested practices, the system was supposed to provide for the needs of pupils while they learned skills of a craft at the hands of an expert. The process was lengthy because acquiring proficiency with tools and materials took time, but it also sought to season young men by imparting an appreciation for the worth of good work. The good and conscientious master was not only charged with teaching his charges about how to make a living. He was also responsible for teaching them how to make a life.

The path to becoming a skilled craftsman followed one well marked by European tradition. Fathers taught **Apprenticeship** their sons while accepting other promising young men to help in the shop in exchange for instruction. The understanding was framed by a legal agreement negotiated by the boy's parents, who paid the craftsman a small fee for his pledge to care for and teach his new apprentice. The contract establishing this relationship was, in fact, an indenture with clearly outlined responsibilities for both parties. The artisan would supply the apprentice with food, shelter, and instruction, including a basic education in reading and mathematics in addition to his craft work. In exchange, the boy would labor in his master's shop for a stipulated time, typically at least four years, sometimes seven. In any case, the indenture expired when the apprentice reached age 21. While in service, the apprentice was expected to preserve the mysteries of the master's trade, protect the privacy of his home, respect his property, and maintain a good moral character. What little courtship that might be allowed was closely supervised and could not in any case result in marriage until the expiration of the indenture. In fact, virtually all activities of the apprentice fell under the watchful eye of his master, who in theory had the authority to know where his charges were at all times of the day or night. The apprentice, for example, had to secure permission to leave the shop during the day and the premises during the evening. Many did not have the energy for mischief after workdays that could easily stretch into 14 hours.

Even under benign tutelage and benevolent regulation, apprentices were in for long, difficult, and tedious years, made especially unhappy by a system that denied them the open enjoyment of even the most harmless enthusiasms of youth. In addition, as earlier noted, some masters worsened this already despondent existence with inexcusable negligence or deliberate cruelty. Although the legal system tried to protect badly treated apprentices, haphazard and infrequent efforts at intervention were at best imperfect remedies. Apprentices frequently sought their own salvation by running away.

As the early Republic absorbed and implemented the lessons of the American Revolution, reformers increasingly criticized the apprentice system not just for these occasional barbarities but also as a vestige of medievalism out of place in the new nation. The absolute authority enjoyed by artisans under the terms of indenture was compared to a kind of quasi slavery even as doubts arose about the artisan's exclusive ability to teach his craft, especially in a literate society whose youth could consult handbooks with greater ease and less trouble than toiling for years in a dark workshop. The indenture became less common, and the mutual obligations of master and apprentice transformed into the duties of employer and employee. The change carried advantages, but as with any change, it also was alloyed. Just as the apprentice no longer owed unconditional loyalty to his master, so the security afforded by careful masters who fed and clothed their apprentices was gone as well. Some prospered in the new, evolving system. Others fell through its cracks.

Journeymen   Nothing illustrated the troublesome aspects of this dying system better than the example of the journeyman. Under the old system, the apprentice's goal was to acquire skills sufficient to allow him to seek employment as a journeyman for wages. In that position, he could count pennies and through heroic frugality save enough money to set up his own shop and assume the role of master. Accordingly, the journeyman was better than an apprentice in both skill and situation, but he was not a self-sufficient craftsman. He was paid for his work, but he also usually lodged in quarters provided by his employer.

During the early Republic, a trend that had been developing during the colonial period continued. A noticeable disparity had become apparent that increasingly separated the master and the journeyman in social and economic standing. The system of labor ensured that masters rose on the backs of journeymen as well as apprentices, accumulating personal property and economic security while the apprentices who toiled in their shops were exploited and journeymen were frozen in place. In part, this was a function of the age-old economic reality that scarceness enhances value: the few skilled craftsmen who owned shops could obviously claim the lion's share of profits, while the partially skilled and more numerous journeymen had to pay their dues while accepting modest wages. Yet the system promoted and then sustained this arrangement into an artificial stagnancy in which masters deliberately kept their numbers low to enhance their worth. The result was that journeymen found their situations increasingly immobile.

The lucky journeyman became a master. Most stayed put in their social and economic place, if not their jobs, as they became permanent itinerants (hence the name "journeyman") searching for work. They coped with competition from immigrants and apprentices who would often work for food and lodging in the North and watched talented slave artisans do the same thing for the same compensation in the South. During the early Republic, this unformed army of luckless laborers began to form associations that at first filled the role of benevolent clubs by aiding sick members and looking after the families of dead ones. Eventually, though, these groups encouraged journeymen to adopt tactics familiar to modern labor organizers, including public relations initiatives and strikes (what were then called "turnouts") against a specific trade. A host of difficulties, however, frustrated the formation of an influential labor movement during these years and for decades afterward. Workers found it difficult to cohere in large numbers across different skill levels, the pride of competent craftsmen a conceit that was impossible to shake. They stumbled over other differences as well, such as gender, race, and nationality. Hard economic times made immediate employment more important than farsighted ideals. Therefore their efforts were small, insignificant, and unsuccessful throughout the period. The day would come, though, when that changed as well.

The development of modern labor relations flew in the face of the traditional system in which masters defended their trades **Masters** from overproduction by limiting apprenticeship and the dissemination of purportedly arcane expertise. In response to these changes, masters continued to establish their own trade organizations, a practice that for them dated from the early eighteenth century. In addition, they began to fulfill roles normally associated with entrepreneurs and middlemen. They haggled with suppliers, bargained with journeymen, and adjusted the way they sold their products, sometimes eliminating themselves from retail operations altogether to have their operations perform only production chores similar to those of a modern manufacturing plant. They became politically active as well, especially to prevent statutory regulations and to encourage the adoption of protective tariffs.

Yet their time as master artisans was waning, a circumstance over which they ultimately had little control. They inherently opposed factories as directly contrary to their ancient codes of craftsmanship. In thus opposing mass production, they were on the wrong side of economic history, for the dawning market economy of the nineteenth century would clamor for more things made more affordable for more people. Opposed to upward social mobility for their workshop employees, they were behind the changing times in social awareness as well, no matter their ongoing but threadbare attempts to disguise economic self-interest as compassionate paternalism. The years of this period were the beginning of this dramatic shift, and sometimes its advance was marked more in stalling fits than starts, but it was a shift inevitable in any case. Its acceleration in the latter part of the nineteenth century would make the master craftsman a nearly extinct species of worker. The artisan as artist, surrounded in his workshop by racks of tools passed down through the generations of his family, would be at best a quaint remnant of a time when the nation was new and its promise of explosive economic energy yet unrealized.

Preindustrial Work Ethics Machines produced a few products during the early Republic, but craftsmen working in shops with uncomplicated tools made most things during most of the period.

The pace of work was hardly constant. Visits from fellow craftsmen and customers frequently interrupted work, and pauses for conversation and refreshments were regular. In any case, a craftsman took his time, often varying his tasks, sometimes according to nothing more pressing than his mood. The craftsman measured his progress by the quality of the work rather than the time it took to complete it. Consequently, the particular days of the week held little importance for him. Mondays, for example, did not necessarily require steady labor, for he could always accelerate his pace during the balance of the week to finish a pending project.

A typical week of work for an artisan and his shop might pass as follows. Monday was frequently a day of preparation for the real work of the following days, and there were practical reasons for this. What were called "blue Mondays" saw the artisan and his charges tending their tools, collecting materials, and arranging for work to begin in earnest on Tuesday. The rest of week would pass in labor at the pace already described. Journeymen were paid on Saturdays, and they frequently did not put in much effort that day, especially when kegs of beer might be brought into the shop to celebrate the end of the workweek. The journeymen's celebration continued on Saturday night, in the town and in saloons, with rollicking merriment that stretched into Sunday, making the shop on blue Monday a sluggish and listless place.

What appears to modern eyes as a languid work rhythm should not be confused with idleness, though. People generally accepted the Puritan work ethic that extolled labor as virtuous. They also accepted the idea that an industrious people were an imperative ingredient for the maintenance of republican liberty. Moreover, artisans firmly embraced the notion that economic independence through discipline and self-sufficiency was the surest path to individual freedom.

In an ideal world, such noble sentiments would have been uniform, contributing to a high standard of behavior and an infallible quality of workmanship. But the early years of the American nation were no more ideal than those of our own time. Shoddy craftsmen did exist then who produced inferior goods, and government tried to install regulations to ensure that such shady characters did not bilk unwary buyers with sub-standard materials and slapdash workmanship.

In an ideal world, too, the honest, hardworking craftsman would have made a success of his trade, but events and fate sometimes made that impossible. The challenge of operating a shop, laying aside capital to keep tools current, paying for the repair of those that broke, tutoring appren-tices, managing journeyman, taking commissions, and fulfilling those commissions in a timely manner with excellent products was a tall order for the most talented and diligent of artisans. Many were not capable of meeting the varied demands of the shop while ensuring the happiness and safety of a household, and shop failures were more the routine than the exception, especially in risky economic times.

Moreover, the work ethic of the day was simply running out of time. A workweek that at best consisted of four days could not survive the scrutiny of the reform-minded nineteenth century, with its temperance movements and clanging factory bells. Teetotalers frowned on the Satur-day beer and Sunday revels as sinful; manufacturing managers scowled at employees who showed up late to run machines that were never late, and at workers who rested to leave idle machines that were never weary. The transition that began in the early Republic from the artisan economy to the industrial one had a profound impact on the sense of how work was done as well as what work meant for Americans.

FACTORIES

The clanging hammer of the artisan's workshop sounded a knell for the old politics of class and privilege, but it was also the sound of a dying system gradually passing from the scene. The early Republic was mainly a preindustrial society of farms and workshops, but the seeds of a factory system were planted in the earliest years of the period. "It may be worth observing," said a visitor in 1819, "that there is something in the character of the American population, as well as in the diverse products of the soil, which seems favorable to the growth of manufactures."[2]

In 1787, investors founded the Pennsylvania Society for the Encouragement of Manufactures and the Useful Arts, which established a textile factory in that city. When it burned down, the charitable Guardians of the Poor replaced it with another plant that operated until 1812 as a way to employ the impoverished. Both of these "manufactories" foretold the future of labor in an industrial setting: weavers gathered in one building where their labor was supervised and scrutinized in a way that would have been unimaginable to the average craftsmen in the average workshop. In this new world, traditional permanent wage labor would virtually eliminate apprenticeship. Conversely, master craftsmen would become less definable as an economic and laboring class as they combined shop ownership with administrative functions associated with management rather than production.

All this was happening more rapidly than the misleadingly unhurried pace of the times might have suggested. The accomplished political economist Tench Coxe prepared a telling report that detailed the progress of manufacturing in the United States from 1787 to 1804, a snapshot of the remarkable variety already embraced in what was becoming a vigorous transformation of the American economy. Coxe noted that Americans had "invented or acquired the machinery for freeing cotton wool from the seed, the spinning jenny, the spinning mule, the roving, twisting and carding machinery, the perpetual carding and spinning water mill, the flying shuttle with its appropriate loom, the machinery for coining or stamping metals, leather, &c., that for cutting cardwire and nails, for reducing old woolen cloths or rags to the state of wool, for boring cannon which have been solidly cast, for pressing, packing and lading cotton, for spinning flax, hemp and combed wool, for various operations in the staining and printing of cotton and linen cloths, for rolling the finer metals, for plating the coarser metals with silver, for steam-engines, for grinding, in quantities, optical lenses, for fine turning in wood, metal, stone and other substances."[3] In 1810, Secretary of the Treasury Albert Gallatin issued another report that was even more enlightening about the rapid progress of American industrialism. Gallatin detailed the production of everything from soap and tallow candles to pottery and windowpanes.[4]

Much manufacturing during this transitional time was the result of the "putting-out" system, an early form of factory labor that had been in use for decades. Merchants provided materials to workers, primarily women, who labored in their homes to make a variety of products for which the merchant paid them by the piece. The regions near American cities became busy scenes of household manufacturing, providing work for thousands of people who made everything from straw hats to tallow candles.

Just as in England, though, it was in the production of textiles that the emerging American factory system recorded its greatest gains. The first spinning mill was erected in Rhode Island in the year 1791, and others quickly followed. At the end of 1809 alone, 87 new mills were either put in operation or were being established, making the number of additional whirring spindles at the start of 1811 an astonishing 80,000.

The unique concept of the factory consisted of placing machinery and workers into a building or collection of buildings to create constant production. Modern conceptions of factories always picture workers in orderly arrangements stationed at points along an assembly line. Early factories, however, were simply large workshops where artisans worked independently. As new machines increasingly mechanized textile processes such as spinning and weaving, artisanship became unnecessary. Unskilled machine operators with a minimum of training produced cloth quickly and cheaply on equipment too costly for any place but a heavily capitalized factory.

The Factory System

For the United States, the main impediment to establishing factories was Great Britain's prohibition on the export of both machines and the plans for them. The enterprising Briton Samuel Slater solved the problem of acquiring machinery. Slater had been an apprentice to a partner of British inventor Sir Richard Arkwright and had carefully committed to memory Arkwright's designs for textile machinery. When the fledgling United States offered bounties to prospective inventors, Slater leaped at the opportunity, immigrating to America and, at the request of wealthy investors, opening a profitable spinning mill at Pawtucket, Rhode Island, in 1791. Soon merchant investors eagerly founded additional mills under New England's new laws of incorporation.

Finding ways to power machinery was a predicament, and its solution ironically made it difficult to find a ready supply of laborers. New England boasted an abundance of running streams and rivers that could supply power to textile mills, but these rural settings were relatively far from population centers. Booming job markets in cities made it difficult to entice laborers to countryside factories. Samuel Slater solved part of the problem by hiring entire families to work in his mills, but male laborers were increasingly difficult to come by, leading the large-scale mills of Francis Cabot Lowell's textile empire to employ farm girls from the surrounding countryside. Dexterity rather than strength was important to operate the increasingly complex machinery, and most women brought a basic knowledge of spinning and weaving to the task. In 1812, 87 cotton mills employed 3,500 women and children and only 500 men. With minimal training, women performed the tasks in Lowell's mills, working a six-day week, 12 to 13 hours a day. They were supervised by matrons, housed in dormitories, and forbidden to marry. For most of them, employment in a mill was a temporary state of affairs that ended when marriage removed them from the workforce. They were consequently a passive body of laborers with little interest in long-term labor improvements such as better wages or shorter hours, at least at first. Eventually, mill owners would face growing complaints about working conditions and poor pay that actually resulted in a few strikes by angry women workers, but those occurred in the decades following our period.

The Spread of Factories

The embargo of 1807 and subsequent nonimportation measures passed by Congress quickened the pace of American industrial growth as domestic manufacturers tried to fill the gap left by absent British imports. That situation continued and the tempo of industrialization even accelerated after the War of 1812. Labor shortages forced American manufacturers to use machines for as many tasks as possible, but the unexpected industrial dynamic meant that the greater number of machines required a greater number of operators, increasing rather than diminishing the problem of the inadequate labor supply. Not until the widespread application of steam power would factory development become less dependent on natural sources of power, allowing for the placement of factories at the manufacturer's convenience.

Designing machines that could be repaired easily by relatively unskilled mechanics was necessary if factories were to branch out from the textile industry and move beyond the status of glorified workshops. The development of new machinery and techniques for building machines gradually made it possible for the factory system to extend to other industries. American inventor Eli Whitney, who invented the cotton gin in 1793, made an essential contribution to the factory system with his experiments in the use of interchangeable parts. Beginning in 1798, Whitney established an armory whose production of firearms attempted to use this novel concept, one that eventually eliminated custom work, later made possible the modern assembly line, and prepared the way for mass production. Machine tools—machines that made other machines—became more precise, and as the jig (a guide that allowed precise replications of the same part) came to be used extensively, the use of interchangeable parts spread to other manufacturing processes. Jethro Wood's iron plows featured interchangeable parts. By 1820, the application of interchangeable parts to the manufacture of timepieces led to standardized production techniques that made clocks more affordable.

Roads and Rivers

A better transportation network was a crucial ingredient for the development of a healthy, diversified economy. In 1790 primitive methods of travel were the norm, with commerce on the coast or on rivers dependent on wind, weather, currents, and tides. Wagons lurched and bounced on rutted roads that when dry slowed an already slow pace and when muddy stopped it. "The road to Baltimore is frightful, built over clay soil, full of deep ruts, always in the midst of forests, and frequently obstructed by trees uprooted by the wind," a French traveler complained in 1788.[5]

Finding inexpensive and reliable ways to transport raw materials to factories and finished products to markets was essential. The cutting of better roads, often by private investors who charged tolls to cover expenses and make a profit, was a major development of the 1790s. These all-weather roads were called turnpikes because their tollgates bristled with pointed pikes that were opened, or turned aside, only after travelers paid a fee. Turnpikes were profitable investments, promoted brisk commerce wherever they appeared, and were a key venture for the next two decades, helping to speed western settlement. In 1811 the federal government began constructing the National Road, which started in Cumberland, Maryland, and eventually stretched to Vandalia, Illinois, but the project spanned decades and was not completed until 1852. Instead, the later years of the period stretching into the 1820s would see canal building as a popular trend, beginning with the fantastically successful Erie Canal that linked Albany to Buffalo.

Steamboats made their first appearance during the period. In 1787, inventor John Fitch's makeshift steam-powered vessel *Perseverance* had chuffed slowly along on the Delaware River. Experiments and improvements by Fitch and others made steamboats less a novelty and, by the turn of the century, something of a fad. The real turning point came in 1807 when artist-turned-engineer Robert Fulton displayed the prowess of his *Clermont*. The *Clermont* huffed and puffed up the Hudson River from New York City to Albany, completing the 150-mile trip against the Hudson's current in less than two days, half the time it took a sailing vessel. Derisively dubbed "Fulton's Folly" by skeptics, the modest *Clermont* with her noisy boiler and ungainly paddlewheels had actually achieved a fabulous milestone. In fact, steamboats were nothing short of breathtaking in the difference they made in river travel. With the backing of wealthy investors and his own unwavering resolve, Fulton led the way in turning America's navigable inland waters into busy avenues of thriving commerce. Fulton died in 1815, but the transportation system he had helped develop and the steam technology that drove it continued unabated. By 1820, more than 50 steamboats churned the waters of the Mississippi River, besting swift currents at the phenomenal speed of 10 miles per hour. There and on other rivers of the country, populations spread along their banks, farmers to ship out their produce and merchants to ship in the products of the growing eastern factory system.

An unfortunate consequence of the developing factory system was an increasingly serious problem with labor. The putting-out **Labor** system had made manufacturing an extension of household rhythms, and the artisan's small shop had promoted congenial relationships between masters, journeymen, and apprentices. Factories, however, were places with unapproachable owners whose expectations about diligent attendance and workplace discipline ran counter to the traditions of preindustrial America. Increasingly as urban workers labored for long hours that left little time for relaxation and recreation of any sort, there was a sense of social dislocation and emotional dissatisfaction. Many workers could vividly recall when they had been artisans working for themselves at their own pace. Working for someone else was hard enough, but to accept an employer's belief that he owned your time was virtually impossible. In response, workers labored at their own pace and took time off when they needed a rest. Unauthorized absenteeism in early American factories was common, and it is easy to understand why. Workers toiled long hours for low wages in poorly ventilated, badly lighted, and barely heated buildings. Laws kept them from forming associations that could collectively negotiate for better conditions and pay, the courts having judged such associations to be criminal conspiracies.

In Samuel Slater's Pawtucket mill, the first workers were seven boys and two girls, all under 12 years of age. As we have noted, children had always worked, but the factory system exploited them shamelessly. Tending machines that never rested was mind-numbing, and for small children, it was always dangerous and occasionally lethal. Slater realized the potential for abuse and tried to alleviate it, establishing Sunday schools for his child laborers to teach them basic skills as well as provide them with moral instruction. Lowell never used young children in his mills. Other owners and managers, however, were neither that benevolent nor fastidious. In 1820, one-half of the nation's industrial labor force consisted of children younger than 10 years old, many of them fated to remain in dreadful ignorance, psychologically damaged and physically ruined. Some factories had whipping rooms that were the scenes of dreadful cruelties. Unfortunately, child labor conditions in America's factories would not materially improve until the elimination of child labor itself became a reformist cause in the early twentieth century.

The Industrial Work Ethic The people who ran mills and factories expected laborers to show up every day on time, prepared to devote their full energies to at least 12 hours of work, often 14. The length of the workday became a major point of contention, especially as workers accustomed to the more measured pace of the workshop struggled to adjust to the relentless march of machinery in factories. Accordingly, workplace discipline was another point of conflict, as laborers took unscheduled breaks, chatted with fellow workers, paused for refreshments, and generally asserted an independence learned in the simpler workshops of America's preindustrial culture. The most successful practitioners of the old ways in the new factory setting were skilled artisans. The relative simplicity of certain machinery made them indispensable for performing necessary tasks. For others, managers tried to break old habits with punishments that ranged from fines to firings, but

American workers have rarely submitted to such treatment. In later times, they would form unions. In the early Republic, they were apt to quit. In good economic times, quitting was easier, as it was in certain seasons, such as spring and fall, when the demands of planting, harvesting, and processing agricultural goods could absorb the unemployed. Americans were a restless bunch, anyway, and a factory laborer might quit over nothing more tangible than the whimsical impulse to try his luck elsewhere.

BUILDERS

A factory could not build a house, and artisans in the construction trades were immune to the changes that industrialism portended. Construction techniques were less sophisticated than those used in today's buildings, but they were not so simple as to permit anyone to build his own house. Construction of a proper house required specialized skills and tools limited to a variety of craftsman who contributed to the creation of a correctly built structure. Focusing on a specific craft was partly a tradition, but the sizable investment in tools and the years of training necessary to acquire adequate expertise virtually dictated specialization. The proverbial jack-of-all-trades was at best a rarity and probably a myth because few men possessed the time, capital, and acumen to assume such a role. In populous areas, there were brick makers, brick masons, carpenters, joiners, painters, glaziers, plasterers, and stonemasons. In less established regions, some men might ply closely related trades, such as carpentry and joinery, but even that level of general skill had limits. A mason would not have made bricks, for example, nor would a carpenter have forged his nails.

These were happier years at least in the fact that agreements between tradesmen and customers were usually quite simple and entirely straightforward. Typically consisting of a single page, a contract stipulated the dimensions of the house and contained the master builder's pledge that the work would meet expectations regarding workmanlike standards and practices and would be completed by a specified date. The prospective owner agreed to purchase materials and to ensure that the builder would be paid, even if the owner's death required his heirs and estate to meet the obligation.

In the absence of an architect, a talented carpenter acted as master builder. Beyond the predetermined dimensions of the structure, the master builder was largely responsible for the design of the house and was in charge of securing the services of other specialized artisans, such as painters. In that regard, the master builder performed the functions of today's contractor. To formulate estimates, he consulted "price books" that provided extremely detailed labor costs of artisans by trade. Artisans agreed to adhere to these as maximum charges to ensure their employability and to attest to their integrity. During hard economic times or in remote areas, the master builder might have employed some craftsmen at cheaper rates, but never for more than listed in the price books. Payment by the owner normally called for installments at the beginning, middle, and conclusion of the project. The contract also spelled out penalties for breaches.

Construction   Before construction began, the site was cleared and graded in preparation for digging a foundation. Unskilled day laborers toiled at these tasks with picks, shovels, and wheelbarrows. Following this initial excavation, a stonemason began the work of laying the foundation, the first and most crucial part of the construction process, for without a good foundation, everything that followed would be defective.

Carpenters then framed the house, a task that usually required the expertise of several different types of woodworkers. One might be employed to join large pieces into joists and studs, another made roof shingles, another carefully carved and finished tongues and grooves to join floor planking, and another finished interior walls or prepared them with laths for a plasterer. Affluent house builders might secure the services of a master carpenter called a joiner who fashioned items that had to fit precisely, such as door frames, windows, and stairs. The joiner was also responsible for aesthetically important details, such as crown molding.

Pegged joints, a remarkably sound construction method, were used to fasten the house's frame, but nails were available during the period. Before 1790, nails were made by hand in a laborious process that required the flattening out of their heads with a hammer and pounding them to taper on four sides. After 1790, cheaper nails were produced by machines and were tapered only on two sides. Forged wood screws before 1812 had irregular threads, but afterward machined screws came into use, the slots in their heads a bit off center from a hacksaw cut.

Brick Making and Masonry   Wooden houses required bricks for fireplaces and chimneys, and a wealthy owner might contract for a complete brick house, an expensive proposition because the bricks were made by hand. The process, in fact, required considerable ability to produce anything other than an inferior result. The practiced eye of the artisan brick maker could spot good clay, combine it with the proper amount of sand, add just the right quantity of water, and blend the whole for the correct length of time. He and his journeymen and apprentices then pressed the clay into wooden molds for drying in the sun. The final step involved stacking the bricks in a kiln, where they were fired at a temperature of nearly 2,000 degrees for several days. After they cooled, they were ready for laying. This work was usually done at the building site, where an expert brick maker with experienced help could turn out an astonishing number of bricks in a relatively short time. Though they proved remarkably durable, bricks were almost never uniform in appearance because of uncontrollable variations in clay, water, sand, and the heat of the kiln, something evident in the interestingly inconsistent character of brick buildings and houses erected during the period.

Combining sand, clay, and lime with some sort of bonding agent like cow hair made the mortar for bricklaying. The most difficult ingredient to come by was the lime, which had to be produced by firing limestone or burning shells to extract calcium oxide, or what is called quicklime. The quicklime was mixed with water in a sand pit to produce a chemical reaction so intense that the concoction boiled itself down to a powdery mass of calcium hydroxide, which, when mixed with water, became the bricklayer's mortar.

Bricklayers turned different sides of the bricks to set patterns for a pleasing visual configuration but mainly to create a strong structure, because a durable, solid bond required the alternation of bricks in some fashion. The most common patterns were English bond and Flemish bond. English bond placed the long side of bricks (the courses) in layers that alternated with layers of the end of bricks (the headers). All stretcher layers were aligned vertically, and header layers were placed to center on the stretchers above and below and the mortar joints between them. The Flemish bond alternated stretchers and headers in the same layer to produce what many considered a more elegant appearance, but with the disadvantage of being not quite as stable as English bond. The bricklayer used a trowel, a short-handled hand tool with a pointed blade, to spread, shape, and smooth the mortar. The trowel, a hammer, and a saw were used to cut the bricks to size, and a level and carpenter's square helped ensure that the work was plumb, straight, level, and to specifications.

Fine window glass from Europe was of the best quality, but American glassblowers could produce serviceable panes through a simple process that created "crown glass." The artisan superheated sand in a kiln, rolled it onto a hollow rod, and blew the molten material into a bubble that he then pressed into the form of a flat disk. The glassblower then tapped the disk off the rod and allowed it to cool before scoring it to crack into rectangular panels. Crown glass was relatively bulky and had swirling patterns that affected its transparency. It was called crown glass because one pane in each batch contained a noticeable blister from the blowpipe. Green glass (because of the mineral content of the sand), sometimes called German glass, was considered inferior for windows. Cylinder glass gradually replaced crown glass because it was both cheaper to make and of better quality. Molten sand was blown into a tube or cylinder. While the glass was still pliable, the cylinder was cut open and the contents pressed into a thin, clear pane absent of swirls and blisters. Panes were a standard size and put in window sashes by a glazier, a job so simple that an artisan painter often did glazing as well. The glazier mixed white lead and linseed oil to make supple putty that rigidly set to hold panes firmly in the sash. Painters had apprentices mix pigments with linseed oil and white lead to produce one of the period's popular colors for interior trim and plastered walls.

THE ECONOMY

Uniform currency, ready credit, and a sound central banking system that supported currency and credit were important components in the changing economy of the early Republic. Nothing had the potential to affect the daily life of Americans more directly than these fundamental issues relating to their pocketbooks. During the period, they went through several distinct stages, starting with the extremely unstable economy of the post-Revolutionary years that the first Bank of the United States helped to repair and put on a firmer footing. The uncertainties leading up to the War of 1812 were compounded by the high cost of that conflict. Finally, the mismanagement of the Second Bank of the United States in its early years was to contribute to the volatile economy that crashed precipitously in 1819, causing dire hardship across all sectors of society.

Money and Currency
Fundamental to an understanding of the problems confronting the country's young economy is the distinction between money and a circulating medium that represents money. Money has an intrinsic value. That value can derive from several factors, but traditionally it had resulted from the material from which money was made. Coins (or specie) were valuable because they were usually made of a precious metal such as gold, and they had value regardless of who minted them or what was engraved on them. They operated as money in its simplest definition, but even that simplicity was fraught with confusion. The profusion of various types of money in the early Republic gives us an idea of the problem. Coins from every nation were jumbled together in countless transactions throughout the cash-starved country. Even the nomenclature for money was muddled. Westerners called a Spanish reale a "bit," while New Yorkers called it a "shilling."[6]

Because it circulated in the economy, however imperfectly, money was always currency. Yet currency was not always money, because items that merely represented money could circulate in the economy as well. That sort of currency had no intrinsic value but derived its worth from external sources. Currency in the form of paper notes could be valuable, for instance, because it represented money in the form of specie, either gold or silver coins. More intangibly, but no less effectively, currency could be valuable if people had confidence in it to function as a medium of exchange for goods and services. As long as someone accepted it to satisfy debt, it had value. The more people who accepted the currency, the higher the level of confidence in it, and the more functional it became as a substitute for money. The opposite was also unfortunately true. The paper currency issued by the Continental Congress during the Revolution offered a sorry example of how such specimens, not backed by gold, could turn worthless after losing public confidence. By the end of the war, what was colloquially called the "continental" was not worth the paper it was printed on, and the term actually entered the vernacular as a synonym for anything worthless. The experience colored an entire generation's perception of paper money and resulted in general and enduring suspicions about it.

Money had a great advantage in that it would always spend. As the wretched "continental" showed, under certain circumstances, currency would not spend at all, or it would not spend as effectively as money. Yet the advantage of currency was that its quantity could be artificially increased or decreased according to the needs and condition of the economy. Because an expanding (or inflated) currency was more abundant, its buying power was reduced, and prices rose to reflect the lower purchasing power. Inflationary cycles, however, usually promoted easier credit, because inflation typically stimulated buying and spending. A diminished amount of currency increased in value, but it also slowed economic activity and usually resulted in tighter credit. Achieving a balance between the two extremes of inflation and deflation was imperative, for that was how healthy economies expanded with reasonable credit while avoiding the hazards of spiraling prices. A key component was creating and sustaining public confidence, as Alexander Hamilton insisted in his plan to restore faith in the public credit. Confidence in currency for many years was founded on a reasonable ratio of currency to gold. A certain amount of currency represented a certain amount of gold and could be exchanged for it in that ratio.

Of course, this simple definition belies the considerable complexity of all but the most rudimentary economic systems, but the basic principles are sufficient to understand the largely undeveloped but nonetheless turbulent economy of the years following the Revolution. In the first place, many parts of the country had neither money nor currency and conducted transactions through barter. Observers in remote areas of America remarked that one never heard the words "buy" or "sell" but instead heard about "trades."[7]

Where it existed, currency was uniform only in relatively small localities. Currency in the form of bank notes was only as valuable as the reputations of the issuing institution. States chartered banks during the 1780s primarily to issue bank notes to supplement the small amount of money in circulation, but also to accept deposits and make loans. These banks had no requirements to hold a percentage of deposits in reserve; therefore there was virtually no curb on a bank's capacity to make loans. The soundness of a bank's notes, however, was controlled by its reliability in exchanging them for money, for the bank thus gave a rough indication of its money reserves (liquidity). Every bank would theoretically honor its own notes, and a trustworthy bank would have a sufficiently good reputation in a community and its environs to have the public honor those notes as well, accepting them for goods and services. Yet in distant locales, unfamiliar bank notes could make merchants wary. At the least, notes would be discounted at a rate commensurate with the cost of redeeming them. For example, someone with a note for $10 from a highly regarded bank in Boston would have no trouble using it to purchase $10 worth of goods and services in most of Massachusetts; the farther one took the note from Boston, though, the less valuable it became. Cashing a Boston bank note in Savannah, Georgia, might result in a discount rate of 10 to 20 percent, making the $10 note only worth $8. The balance of the discount rate was the levy for the trouble of cashing it at its distant, originating institution. Bank notes from an unfamiliar institution would likely merit an even larger discount, and some would be worthless.

Obviously, the local nature of currency was troublesome and expensive, and the establishment of a national currency that would be as valuable in Savannah as in Boston was most desirable. Regional efforts to set up central banking systems were an indication of this need, and a truly central bank was the answer. A central bank was essentially a bank used by, and exerting control over, other banks. For instance, small banks in rural areas usually had accounts at a large bank in a nearby city to smooth the progress of their transactions over a wider region. Yet a national central bank required government sanction to control the money supply, whether through specie or currency, and thereby promote economic stability.

The Bank of the United States   In 1791 the federal government chartered a central bank, the Bank of the United States. The bank, as a repository of government funds and a source of loans for individuals as well as federal and state governments, was the source of great controversy because many thought it nothing more than a servant of special interests. State banks were especially critical of its operations because notes on the Bank of the United States were redeemable at face value throughout much of the country, making it difficult for state banks to compete for customers.

The bank's most important public function was to regulate the amount of notes that state banks could issue by distributing money reserves to different parts of the country. Because it was the depository for the U.S. Treasury, it could exert enormous influence in this regard, and economic historians generally praise its operations as sound, profitable, and stabilizing. Several potential panics were averted when the Bank of the United States transferred funds to prop up endangered banks on the verge of failure, and it went quite far in establishing a uniform currency. In 1811 its approximately $5 million in notes amounted to 20 percent of the nation's circulating currency. Yet, as said, its operations were extremely unpopular with state banks constrained by its control and disadvantaged by its issuance of reliable notes. Currency issued by the bank was never discounted, whereas notes from state banks could be subject to discounts ranging from 1 to 100 percent. Finally, political pressure from state banking interests and widespread misgivings among the public about a national bank caused the bank's demise in 1811.

For the five years that followed, the American economy operated without the stabilizing influence of a central fiscal institution. State banks in this vacuum greatly inflated the currency with extravagant issues of bank notes. Unfortunately, legislatures chartered additional state banks that worsened the inflationary situation even as the economy was being generally assailed by the war with England. As should have been expected, the extraordinary rate of inflation had a corresponding effect on prices, pushing them up more than 13 percent a year. In response to this mess, Congress chartered the Second Bank of the United States (BUS) in 1816 as an exact duplicate of its predecessor. In its early years, though, a mediocre administration and occasional forays into fraud too often described the new national bank's activities, and it failed in its primary responsibilities to the average American citizen. The BUS did not maintain a stable currency ratio, nor did it exert much effort to control an explosive postwar economic boom. Finally, its attempts to restrict credit in 1819 contributed to a financial panic that turned into a major depression. Banks across the country failed, people lost their savings, foreclosures of farms rose, thousands of small business folded, and large firms cut payrolls, increasing unemployment. "Instability seems more common to Americans than to the youth of other countries," noted a perceptive observer even before these events unfolded. "They frequently have the misfortune to see the finest hopes betrayed by tragic changes."[8]

The Second Bank of the United States

The BUS would eventually rebound under responsible management and the resumption of steadying policies, but for farmers, small merchants, and artisans who had felt the hard consequences of the economic downturn, the damage to the bank's reputation was resonant and permanent. As the country moved into the 1820s, anger over the presumed role that the BUS had played in wrecking the economy coalesced into the new political movement of Jacksonian Democracy, a movement that would play an important role in shaping the lives of working people in the decades that followed.

CONCLUSION

The changing economy of the early Republic accelerated its transition in the 1820s and the decades that followed, hurrying commerce in America's cities and extending it along a developing transportation system. The transition was in part the result of countless innovations, decisions, and risks taken by merchants, workers, investors, and farmers. Intent on improving their material lot and social status, they embraced the concepts of upward social and economic mobility as certainly realizable goals for their children, if for the moment beyond their own attainment. Some emerged from these pivotal years as the beneficiaries of changing patterns, while others were to see their lives altered in dramatic and permanent ways, the casualties of new markets and changing times. Innovators like Samuel Slater and Francis Lowell, and inventors like John Fitch, Eli Whitney, and Robert Fulton, were conspicuous examples of a new, fresh American energy in entrepreneurial originality and technological improvement, but countless others whose names would never be recorded in the chronicles of American progress also made their contributions. The workers whose spirit of craft artisanship survived even the necessary adjustment to the manufactory made their own innovations to improve work and the products it produced, doing so out of a traditional pride of craft. Such extraordinary material creativity was a reflection of the amazing political creativity of the American experience. It was also evidence of ingenuity and inspiration that opened the way to new challenges even as it solved old problems.

NOTES

1. Michael W. Bell, "Apprenticeship: An Example from Rural Massachusetts," *Tennessee Historical Quarterly* 62, no. 1 (spring 2003): 97–99.

2. Frances Wright, *Views of Society and Manners in America,* ed. Paul R. Baker (Cambridge: Belknap Press of Harvard University Press, 1963), 200.

3. Tench Coxe, *A Communication from the Pennsylvania Society for the Encouragement of Manufactures and the Useful Arts* (Philadelphia: Printed for the Society by Samuel Akerman, 1804), 23–24.

4. 11th Congress, 2nd Session, House Report 325.

5. Jean Pierre Brissot, quoted in Oscar Handlin, ed., *This Was America: True Accounts of People and Places, Manners and Customs, as Recorded by European Travelers to the Western Shore in the Eighteenth, Nineteenth, and Twentieth Centuries* (Cambridge: Harvard University Press, 1949), 82.

6. The reale was worth about 12.5¢. Two bits totaled a quarter, four bits a half dollar, and eight bits a full dollar. According to some sources, the term "bit" originated with the curious practice of making change for transactions by physically breaking a dollar coin into eight wedges, or bits.

7. Everett Dick, *The Dixie Frontier: A Social History of the Southern Frontier from the First Transmontane Beginnings to the Civil War* (New York: Capricorn Books, 1964), 117.

8. The quote is from Giovanni Antonio Grassi, an Italian Jesuit who was president of Georgetown College from June 1812 through 1817, in Handlin, *This Was America,* 143.

Baltimore, 1792. The United States was a rural country, but cities sprang up along the eastern seaboard, and some became great ports. Blessed with a fine harbor, Baltimore was destined to grow into a center of commerce and international trade. (Library of Congress)

TO BE SOLD on board the Ship *Bance-Ifland*, on tuefday the 6th of *May* next, at *Afhley-Ferry*, a choice cargo of about 250 fine healthy

NEGROES,

juft arrived from the Windward & Rice Coaft. —The utmoft care hàs already been taken, and fhall be continued, to keep them free from the leaft danger of being infected with the SMALL-POX, no boat having been on board, and all other communication with people from *Charles-Town* prevented.

Auftin, Laurens, & Appleby.

N. B. Full one Half of the above Negroes have had the SMALL-POX in their own Country.

Slavery and Liberty. The early years of the new nation regularly featured events such as the one advertised here, a circumstance that clearly discomfited the revolutionary generation enough to have it abolish the foreign slave trade in 1808. Americans were a freedom-loving people, as the 1796 depiction of Lady Liberty shows. The inconsistency of slavery existing under the gaze of that kind mistress grew more troubling each year. (Library of Congress)

Above:
Washington, D.C., circa 1812. The nation's capital had been the seat of government for the new republic for little more than a decade when this illustration appeared. The capital was and would remain for many years more a village than a city, with unpaved streets and a rustic character its most conspicuous traits. (Library of Congress)

Right:
The *Western Review,* 1820. Although some foreign visitors sniffed that America was devoid of culture and its citizens unfamiliar with learning, journals such as the *Western Review,* which featured literary criticism, original fiction, and poetry, indicated otherwise. Moreover, such publications appeared in such far-flung outposts as Lexington, Kentucky, a town that in 1820 boasted a population of about 5,000 people. (Library of Congress)

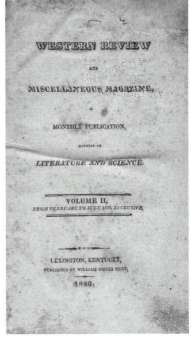

WESTERN REVIEW

AND

MISCELLANEOUS MAGAZINE,

MONTHLY PUBLICATION,

DEVOTED TO

LITERATURE AND SCIENCE.

VOLUME II,
FROM FEBRUARY TO JULY, 1820, INCLUSIVE.

LEXINGTON, KENTUCKY,
PUBLISHED BY WILLIAM GIBBES HUNT,
1820.

Blacksmith's Shop. One could find workshops such as this in villages, towns, and cities throughout the country, for in them was fashioned and repaired the hardware of daily life under the hands and watchful direction of the blacksmith, his apprentices, and journeymen. (Library of Congress)

Camp Meeting. The Second Great Awakening stirred an unprecedented religious revival on the western frontier, where thousands attended massive, multidenominational services held in the open air. (Library of Congress)

Shakers. Visitors frequently commented on what they regarded as the peculiar method of worship by the Shakers in their meetings. An offshoot of Quakerism, Shakers practiced celibate marriage and observed, as this illustration shows, a symbolic as well as tangible gender separation in their services. (Library of Congress)

Stagecoach. Rutted roads and jolting conveyances characterized travel in the early Republic. A well-maintained stagecoach was not merely necessary for relatively reliable transportation. Safety concerns often were the most important consideration. Surveying the poor state of the roads, a French traveler could not "conceive why the stage does not often meet with disaster." (Library of Congress)

Old Tavern Inn in Middleborough, Massachusetts. The weary traveler and the local citizen mingled at roadside taverns that were frequently nothing more than large houses with serviceable kitchens, reasonably comfortable public rooms, and a few bedrooms that could serve as lodging for several guests at the same time. (Library of Congress)

The *Clermont*. Technology changed lives then as it does now, and the steamboat depicted here—a 1909 replica of Robert Fulton's *Clermont*—was a prime example. Just a few years after the *Clermont* made her historic voyage up the Hudson River, steamboats were plying the inland waters of the new republic, revolutionizing travel and commerce practically overnight. (Library of Congress)

The United States of the Early Republic, 1790–1820. Thinly peopled but blessed with abundant resources and boundless potential, the country had no logical outline yet, but Americans of the period would begin the process of establishing one.

Populations of Major Cities of 1790. The new nation's large communities were sizable towns that eventually would grow into large cities, but at the start, these towns were primarily coastal settlements, and the sparsely populated interior was still a wilderness.

Populations of Major Cities of 1820. Cities experienced phenomenal growth during the period of 1790–1820, increasing in population and springing up in the interior. Even with such remarkable growth, however, America remained a rural country.

Labels on map:

Sheep and Fodder
Dairy — Beef and Fodder
Sheep and Wheat
Wheat Beef Fodder
Wheat
Corn
Pork — Beef — Corn
Tobacco
Hemp Horses
Tobacco — Corn Pork
Corn
Pork
Atlantic

Ocean

Beef Corn Cotton
Corn
Cotton Pork Beef Rice
C o t t o n
Beef — Pork
Sugar Cane

Agriculture 1820

Gulf of Mexico

David S Heidler

Agriculture. Most Americans were farmers during the early Republic, a circumstance that would not change for a century. Most striking was the great diversity that marked the American agricultural community, a variety that with the proper transportation infrastructure would make the country more self-reliant than even Thomas Jefferson had dreamed.

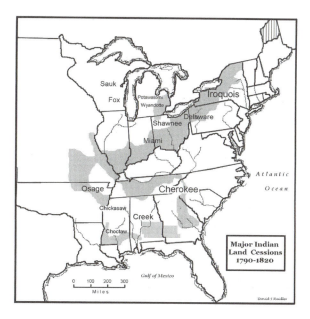

The Land and Population. From the establishment of the first English colonies in the early seventeenth century to the callous policies of U.S. Indian removal in the 1830s, Native American populations were in conflict with spreading white settlement. Taken together, these two maps show the direct relationship between expanding white populations and government efforts to open increasing expanses of Indian land.

Slavery and Freedom. The stark division between freedom and slavery became dangerously geographical by the end of this period. Political polarization was already occurring, and the sectional discord it portended appeared in the bitter crisis over Missouri in 1819–1820. The question of extending slavery into the western territories would finally break the Union in 1860–1861, roughly along the lines shown here, and plunge the country into civil war.

5

LEISURE

Leisure activities during the early Republic were similar to those of the colonial period, especially in that they usually took second place to work. The amount of work required to provide clothes, shelter, and sufficient food for a family meant that only the very young and the very rich could indulge in true relaxation. Older children and most adults sought to add pleasure to busy lives by contriving ways to make their labors entertaining and social.

There was also pressure from a culture that disapproved of pointless play. In the years immediately following the American Revolution, purists argued that amusement for amusement's sake was inappropriate for citizens in a virtuous republic. Americans, they insisted, should avoid the idle dissoluteness of European aristocrats. Ingrained notions of what constituted civic virtue dictated that even leisure should improve one's character, as well as society in general. In addition, the Puritan heritage of New England, the religious revival of the 1730s and 1740s known as the Great Awakening, and the Second Great Awakening of the early nineteenth century prompted many Americans to regard amusements as decadent self-indulgence. They believed that time on Earth should be devoted to its betterment and service to God. The attitude had adherents in all parts of the country, but New England's Puritan tradition of industry, frugality, and piety made it more prevalent in that region.

In cities, not only did limited space restrict leisure pursuits, but business owners and managers of workshops also discouraged activities that distracted laborers from their work. Consequently, pastimes that increasingly resembled later spectator sports arose more or less surreptitiously in cities. Back rooms in bars or saloons were the sites of cockfights, dogfights, and bare-knuckle prizefights. Rural Americans watched the same kind of sports, of course, and wagered on them as exuberantly as their urban counterparts, but Americans in cities and towns exhibited an especially avid enthusiasm for these forerunners of spectator sports.

Like all aspects of American culture, leisure activities were affected by differences in religion, region, social class, gender, age, and race. Even in the most serious and industrious of areas, however, people found the need to relax, socialize, and, on occasion, simply have fun.

HOLIDAYS

Americans did not engage in many leisure activities because they simply did not have the time. The majority of Americans worked six days a week, and most reserved Sunday for worship and sedate activities. While many European countries, particularly those with predominantly Catholic populations, celebrated an abundance of religious holidays that featured a variety of amusements, the United States observed few holidays throughout the nation. Reflecting their Protestantism, many Americans considered holiday festivities sinful and did not observe Christmas with revelry. New Englanders, with their Puritan heritage and the corresponding determination to avoid anything that resembled Catholicism, observed Christmas most somberly. Southerners, on the other hand, at least stopped work for a few days around Christmas, even allowing slaves a week of rest. Special food marked the occasion, but if gifts were exchanged at all, they were modest. Planters typically gave gifts of clothes and extra food to their slaves during the Christmas season.

Areas of the country settled by Germans saw the most enthusiastic celebrations of Christmas. Work came to a stop for a few days, and on Christmas Eve families put up Christmas trees in their homes while drinking beer and singing songs. Areas in close proximity to large German American settlements gradually adopted similar customs, but not until later years did the manifestation of Christmas featuring a decorated tree and presents become characteristic.

Across the country, there were a few regional holidays. Many areas of New England marked the end of autumn with a harvest commemoration that resembled Thanksgiving of the later Victorian era. Most communities set aside days for men to gather for militia training, usually to coincide in rural areas with sessions of the county court. People from miles around traveled to the county seat, either to conduct business with the court or to participate in the militia drill. In the rural Northeast, the nearness of towns and good roads made the journey to these events relatively easy, but in the South and on the frontier, it could take days. Nonetheless people regarded these occasions important and found them enjoyable diversions. Lacking transportation did not stop poor citizens. They thought nothing of trekking long distances to relish even the briefest time with friends and relatives. They crowded those precious times with sporting contests and picnics and allowed their excited children to play past twilight.

Unofficial holidays observed in towns with parades and speeches were the precursors of modern patriotic celebrations. After George Washington's death in 1799, his birthday became such an event. Laborers might be given a few hours to watch the festivities, but they seldom had the entire day off from work. Otherwise, the only holiday officially celebrated by the entire nation was the Fourth of July. On that day, workplaces in American towns and cities closed. People picnicked, played games, listened to speeches, and at nightfall marveled at fireworks.

THE SOUTH

The South possibly enjoyed a greater variety of amusements and leisure activities than any other section of the country. There were fewer religious proscriptions on such pursuits in the South, and because rural inhabitants could not rely on organized amusements like theater, lectures, and concerts—events at the mercy of calendars and clocks—Southerners actually enjoyed more liberty in how they filled their leisure time.

The southern aristocracy likely felt the fewest moral or religious constraints on its leisure activities, particularly the males of this class. Although the elite southern male spent much of his time supervising the operations of a large business concern—such as a plantation or a commercial firm in coastal cities—he pursued leisure activities as well. In addition, societal expectations required wealthy country gentlemen to imitate the lifestyle of European aristocrats. Because it was incumbent on them to maintain appearances, they enthusiastically emulated the pursuits of European nobility. A southern gentleman was expected to own fine horses, extend lavish hospitality to visitors, enjoy excellent music and good literature, know the steps to fashionable dances, and charm ladies of all ages.

Hunting was probably the most popular sport among southern men, whatever their economic class. Country gentlemen **Hunting** rode to their hounds for hours in pursuit of deer, wild boar, foxes, and other animals. Wealthy plantation owners had special horses for the chase, packs of well-bred dogs for the hunt, and specially tailored riding clothes, often made in Europe to imitate more accurately the British aristocracy's hunting garb. Hunts could be gala social occasions, especially the fox hunt, which culminated with dozens of smartly dressed men on first-rate horses, sometimes in the company of ladies clinging to sidesaddles, all pounding after hounds chasing a small, panicked fox. Southerners "loved the yelp of the pack and the excitement of the galloping group of horsemen, and the hard ride."[1]

When not on horseback, southern men scouted forests or stalked marshes for any number of bird species that were considered fair game. Hunters might return home at night with hundreds of birds or other small animals in their sacks. The hunter's reputation in his neighborhood depended on the sheer volume of the animals he killed, and like much of what southerners did in their leisure time, hunting occasionally included wagers, the winner whoever killed the most animals. Among less affluent southerners, hunting birds or game animals such as deer combined leisure with necessity, because their quarry often fed their families.

Contests   Plantation elites enjoyed other amusements such as cock-fighting and horse racing. A major cockfight between two locally famous birds or a race between plantation owners' thoroughbreds brought spectators from miles around to enjoy pre-event libations and to place wagers.

All classes and races enjoyed cockfighting, a sport that attracted audiences anywhere in the nation. A wealthy planter or a yeoman farmer might own the cock, or rooster, but everyone (though mostly males) from the community came to watch the two birds fight, sometimes to the death. While the owner of the victorious bird won a purse, everyone else, through numerous wagers, also had a stake in the outcome.

Most wagers involved animals of one sort or another, and no sport captured the imagination of gamblers more than horse racing. Horse races in the South, which had been regular occurrences since the seventeenth century, could be organized affairs between well-bred horses of the plantation elite or more spontaneous races between farmers simply proud of the speed of their riding horses. In the more organized events, each of the owners would put up money for the purse, or local promoters might supply the purse to bring spectators into town for the event. In any case, as in cockfighting, the purse was only a small percentage of the money eventually involved, for side wagers were usually significant. Every man from miles around would thus be involved in the outcome of the match. Most bettors attended the race, making the event a social gathering for people of all classes and from all backgrounds. Yet organized horse racing stood apart from other sports in the South because virtually all the contending horses belonged to the wealthy elite. Owning such animals and displaying a willingness to wager large sums on them was one way for a man to tell the world that he was an aristocrat. In fact, high-stakes gambling on all sports was a hallmark of those belonging to the plantation elite.

Major towns like Charleston, South Carolina, had at least one major public racetrack, and smaller communities usually maintained a racetrack as well, especially in plantation areas. Race week in Charleston was an important annual social event, and because tracks were owned and maintained by the community's respectable gentry, women could also attend the event. Plantation owners built their own racetracks to show off their racehorses, and buying an expensive racehorse to enter in local races was a convenient way for a newcomer to gain entrée to the privileged circles in the neighborhood. Wealthy planters eager to have competitive racehorses might spend thousands of dollars and scour the country to acquire them. Many hours of training and preparation went into grooming a championship racehorse, for such animals, particularly when they won, added to their owner's prestige.

Horse racing was most prevalent in the South during the early Republic. The religious fervor of the Second Great Awakening caused many northern communities and even some northern states to outlaw the sport because it prompted gambling. In fact, for most southerners, wagering was what made the sport so appealing. Chronically cash poor, they risked such things as livestock, farm goods, wagons, implements, and sometimes even their slaves on the outcome of a race. Those who trained horses and the jockeys who rode them were often slaves who belonged to the horse's owner or whose services he acquired by lease. Jockeys who were especially talented in handling horses often became trainers after age and weight made them unsuitable for competitive riding. Slaves with such talents were extremely valuable, and they often received rewards when their horses won races. Some were so successful, in fact, that they eventually bought their freedom and earned comfortable incomes riding or training racehorses. In any case, their value to their owners gave them a status enjoyed by few slaves during the period. Some jockeys became famous throughout the country while remaining slaves and were treated with a certain amount of deference, even by prominent whites. Perhaps the most famous of the period, Simon, was such a talented rider that on more than one occasion he "alarmed the trainer of the other horse" when he appeared on the racetrack.[2]

As in the later history of horse racing, the most famous contests of the period were match races involving only two horses. Often match races were quarter races, called such because the track was only a quarter mile in distance, a course that tested speed rather than endurance. As breeding practices were refined to produce thoroughbreds, races over longer distances became common, a mile being the standard.

Southerners always enjoyed a good fight, but by the beginning of the period, the brawls that had been a common occurrence on the frontier were being consigned to lower social classes and were becoming less frequent and even illegal in many places. Still, the practice continued of organizing bouts between especially proficient fighters, usually poor whites or slaves whose owners wanted to capitalize on their fighting skills. Although these fights were sometimes referred to as boxing matches, they little resembled modern boxing. The men started in a standing position, but they quickly ended up on the ground, literally descending to a clawing, nasty display of brute strength and feral cunning. If a fight remained too tame for the crowd, it would begin to shout, "Bite, kick, and gouge" as encouragement for the fighters to draw blood.[3] Antagonists rarely emerged without some degree of mutilation, and spectators laid bets not only on the outcome of the match but on the severity of injuries as well.

Spectators of these contests and the fighters who gained their reputations by surviving them might have defined what they were doing as entertainment. Yet more than merely letting off a little steam or enjoying the thrill of wagering on proficient fighters, southern men, particularly in the backcountry, felt compelled to protect their reputations and the honor of their families, almost at any cost. Because a man's status within the community was determined by how his neighbors perceived him, any aspersion on his reputation, whether it questioned his prowess specifically or his integrity in general, required an immediate challenge, or honor was lost. Some scholars have attributed southerners' exaggerated preoccupation with honor to their living with the institution of slavery, especially because slavery tended to equalize the status of white males even as it made them acutely aware of the degraded condition of slaves. To be perceived as inferior to another white male was to emulate the lot of a slave, even if only symbolically. To defend one's honor was to establish as well as sustain one's equality.

As the frontier became more settled, an elite class developed there that aped the habits of its eastern counterpart, not only in dress and daily life but also in how matters of honor were settled. During the colonial period, refined men in the more established parts of the South had abandoned boxing or wrestling matches as ways to resolve disputes, instead resorting to the French custom of dueling with pistols. One would hardly describe the event as a pastime for the principals, but it was for the community. Its interest in such proceedings, particularly in the rituals leading up to a duel, was always keen.

Duels were not spectator events because protocol restricted attendance to the principals, their representatives, a referee, and often a physician. Yet the community at large was usually well aware of an impending contest weeks before it took place. Often insults exchanged in a local newspaper provoked a challenge, making all readers privy to the unfolding drama. After an official challenge had been issued and accepted, gossip—always a favorite leisure activity—quickly carried the news throughout the locale and, if the disputants were famous, beyond. After the duel, gossip broadcast its results, often with grand embellishments that underscored either the altruistic heroism or abject villainy exhibited at the event.

Taverns Every American man enjoyed visiting his local tavern. Most southerners, though, lived in rural areas where the nearest tavern was hours away, an inconvenience that made southern men's visits less frequent than those of northerners. Southerners usually stopped at taverns or inns during their travels to pass the evening with the assembled locals in public rooms before retiring for the night.

Travelers brought news of the outside world and made taverns the best place to gather for both idle gossip about the neighborhood and solid information about major events of the day. When not swapping rumors or news, the men drank ale or spirits, smoked (usually pipes), and played games, most of which involved gambling. Card games such as whist, one of the most popular games, and dice games were almost always played for money. Others diversions like checkers, called "draughts" at the time, could be played simply to pass the time or for serious competitors, to gain local renown.

A scarcity of taverns in the rural South obliged people there to conduct much of their socializing in private homes, **Entertaining** a circumstance that gave birth to the renowned traditions of southern hospitality. Southern plantation owners recorded in journals and diaries how a night seldom passed without a guest in the house. Friends and family, traveling to towns or simply touring the area, often spent nights at private homes while making their way along their route. More than selfless generosity encouraged the cheerful welcome extended to these wayfarers. Aware that their own travels would be occasions for reciprocal hospitality, hosts took care to present their guests with elegant meals and cozy quarters.

The loneliness of rural isolation encouraged frequent parties, barbecues, and dances among the plantation elite as well as middle-class farmers. Smaller dinner parties might begin with a lavish meal of numerous courses followed by a musical recital that featured both talented and marginally skilled musicians on pianoforte, violin, or flute. Ladies might sing. Larger gatherings involved dancing that typically continued well after midnight. Because many attendees came from miles away, they had a persuasive reason to stay and carry on the revelry for days. During the day, men busied themselves with games or sports, such as hunting, fishing, lawn bowling, and horseshoes. The women read, often aloud to each other, sewed, or simply chatted. In the afternoon, everybody reconvened for a barbecue or fish fry followed by more dancing and drinking.

Everyone enjoyed these social gatherings whether the music was lively or sedate and the dancing vivacious or staid. Most people lived in the country, and barbecues and barn dances were more than ways to escape the drudgery of their daily routines. They served as chances to bind together communities and forge friendships with neighbors. They also provided the setting for a timeless dance of another sort, whether in the candlelit ballroom of a plantation house or on the straw-covered planking of a newly raised barn. Flirtation was a high art, and courtships quickly blossomed and just as quickly withered at these gatherings as older boys took their first bashful steps toward blushing girls. Whether powdered and perfumed or clad in simple homespun, the girls were made pretty by the attention of clumsy suitors and watchful fathers.

The ordeals of traveling in the rural South provide a dreary chronicle, whether one was lucky enough to journey by river or, as **Travel** was more likely, doomed to the tribulations posed by consistently bad roads. Little wonder that people generally traveled only if they had to, generally because of business. Yet during the early Republic, some intrepid southerners began traveling for amusement. There were few tourist destinations, but their rarity made those that did exist more attractive. Virginia boasted two of the most popular early resorts, one at Hot Springs and the other at Bowyer's Sulphur Springs, which would eventually be renamed and achieve fame as White Sulphur Springs. Both were mountain communities built around warm mineral springs whose purported healing powers initially attracted the sick. By the early nineteenth century, however, tourists were traveling to the springs as well, where they could escape the summer heat of the lowlands. They lodged in crude, rustic cabins to enjoy the cool mountain air and take the waters of the springs.

In the early years, the journey to these resorts was too difficult for those living farther south. Rich plantation owners in the South Carolina Low Country and along the Georgia coast therefore sought out other ways to escape the summer heat and avoid the diseases it promoted. Some took sea voyages, primarily to the North, but occasionally to Europe. The wealthiest planters also kept homes in Savannah or Charleston, where their families and house slaves could reside during the summer months. Cooler sea breezes made life tolerable, and tropical diseases were usually less rampant. After relocating to their town homes, planters and their families enjoyed a social season so full of balls, dinners, races, and parties that no one was ever at a loss for something to do. Whether set in a large private home or an elite social club, the party's center of the festivities was always a large ballroom. In other rooms, tables laden with splendid food and colorful punches encouraged mingling by those resting from the dancing. Men who wished to smoke retired with brandy to a book-lined study, aptly referred to as the house's library.

The Louisiana Purchase in 1803 officially made New Orleans an American city, but socially it remained a cosmopolitan mélange of European customs as well as languages. It also remained an unendurable cauldron of soggy heat and brewing disease during the summer. New Orleans's Creoles, the people of Spanish or French descent, knew well the discomforts and perils of living there, and they did their best to flee the city during the hottest months. In the winter, though, wealthy Creoles made New Orleans a place so dazzling in its social pursuits that there was no place like it anywhere else in the country. Mostly Catholics, they enthusiastically celebrated every religious holiday on the church's calendar, and hardly a balmy winter night passed that did not include a luxurious ball or an elegant soiree. The season culminated on the eve of Ash Wednesday, the beginning of Lent, a day known as "Fat Tuesday" or Mardi Gras, a celebration so raucous that it made the city as notorious as it was fascinating.

Theater   All southerners enjoyed the theater regardless of gender or class. Classics, especially the plays of Shakespeare, ribald comedies, and slapstick farces found eager audiences in larger cities like Charleston and New Orleans as well as smaller towns. In rural villages, people flocked from the countryside to see anything onstage, awed by the make-believe magic and impressed by the exotica of traveling troupes of actors. Those brave souls might find themselves performing *Hamlet* in an opulent theater to appreciative and respectful audiences in Savannah one week, and to no less receptive but sometimes wildly participatory spectators in a small village's rough-hewn playhouse the next.

THE WEST

The West more resembled the South than the North in its leisure activities, yet the West did exhibit some unique characteristics. Pastimes there were usually more raucous and included both genders as well as broader cross sections of class. The biggest problem for frontier people was their lack of spare time for leisure, because unlike the eastern middle and upper classes, westerners' days were filled with work. They differed from New Englanders, however, in that they regarded work as essential for survival rather than a duty to God. Like southerners, people on the frontier typically lived in rural isolation, craved social contact, and consequently congregated whenever possible to have fun. Visitors to the American frontier commented about how westerners would drop whatever they were doing to watch a fight or a race, or to pursue any other amusement, habits that drew scornful observations about the lack of work ethic among these rough-hewn backwoods people. Although it was true that most westerners were willing to miss an entire day of labor to watch horses gallop over a makeshift track, disapproving visitors did not understand the rigors of frontier life. Isolation was among the pioneer's heaviest burdens. When he had chance to jostle and laugh with other people, he leaped at it.

Whether in small or large groups, western amusements always involved moonshine and gambling. Like southerners, westerners loved a good horse race, though their frontier horses were usually lumbering beasts of burden more accustomed to pulling a dray than running a course. Westerners too enjoyed blood sports such as cockfighting and hunting, but hunting was a practical undertaking to provide meat for the table as well as diversion.

Western gatherings were frequently fashioned to accomplish an important task like raising a barn or clearing a field. **Useful** People always found ways to make such events social as **Socializing** well as work occasions. While the men built the barn, the women visited around the kitchen fire, making food for the party that followed.

Logrolling was another social gathering that revolved around work. Whether it was a new arrival or a neighbor who needed to clear a new field, people would come from miles around to help cut down trees and prepare the huge logs for use as building materials or fuel. Frontier families made harvest festivals some of the most joyous events of the year. After chores such as husking corn, the group would eat a huge meal that the women had prepared and then have a dance. Dancing was prevalent on the frontier, a pastime especially enjoyed by men and women because it was far less formal than dances held in the East. Frontier dances were often held after work, sometimes in the local tavern, boisterous affairs in which couples reeled and capered to loud, energetic music provided by local musicians. Again, the isolation of frontier life made these occasions both memorable as recreation and important as opportunities for older boys and girls to meet and begin courtships. Young couples made the most of such times. They sang, clapped their hands to lively melodies, danced well into the night, and occasionally slipped away for a stroll and a stolen kiss. Older folks watched these proceedings, perhaps sharing a dance or two, but mostly passing the time smoking their pipes, women included, telling familiar stories, and resting from the day's hard toil.

Storytelling Whether in taverns or country stores (which on the frontier were frequently one and the same), or out camping during a hunt or on a front porch at twilight, people filled idle hours with storytelling. The adventurous life of the pioneer was exciting enough, but exploits regularly grew with each telling to produce much of the country's folklore, a series of mythic vignettes collectively referred to as uniquely American tall tales. Frontier folks never tired of hearing tall tales, especially when narrated by one of the period's great storytellers. Legendary feats of strength, fabulously fast horses, invincible fighters, and unerringly accurate marksmen populated the legends, sometimes including comical bungles by early pioneers. Like barn dances, the stories also carried more import than mere amusement. They provided barely literate rural people an oral tradition with which to pass down their heritage to succeeding generations.

Hunting on the Frontier When men on the frontier were not clearing trees, plowing fields, harvesting crops, or mending fences, they were wandering the abundant woodlands hunting game. The profusion of animals on the frontier meant that a skilled marksman was never without meat, but it also meant that an important pastime for many American men was just beyond their front doors. Sometimes they went alone; other times they traveled in groups, driving their prey before them for more efficient killing in volume. Arranging themselves in a large circle, they forced everything within it toward the center. One Kentucky newspaper reported in 1796 that one group of hunters "produced seven thousand nine hundred and forty-one Squirrels killed by them in one day."[4] Contemporary accounts of some group hunts during the period numbered the animals bagged in the hundreds, including bears and deer as well as smaller prey like squirrels and turkeys.

Like Americans elsewhere, western frontiersmen loved to gamble and would wager on almost anything. Betting on the number of animals killed in a hunt was a way of making the outing more interesting. To keep their shooting skills sharp, **Frontier Contests** they staged shooting contests that earned the best marksmen prizes while offering an opportunity for everyone to gamble on the outcome. Such shooting matches were made into social occasions to which entire families came from miles away to watch competitors vie for a barrel of local whiskey or a cow. Marksmen took their turns at the targets, and male spectators placed bets on who would win and side bets on how well others would strike the target.

Shooting-match wagers were carefully organized in comparison to other betting occasions. Most sporting events that westerners wagered on were generally less formal than similar instances in the East. For example, horse racing was popular, but competitors generally rode their own horses, and tracks were not well maintained, if they existed at all. With more than a half-dozen horses running full tilt toward a makeshift finish line, frontier races were a thrilling combination of impromptu and perilous tactics. Riders intentionally interfered with opponents' mounts by thrusting hands in their faces. They cut off an adjacent rider to clip his horse's forelegs with their flying rear hooves. Western horse racing made more violent an already hazardous sport.

Showing off a fast horse and masterful riding ability was a way to demonstrate physical prowess on the frontier. There were others as well. Wrestling was the most popular contest on the western frontier and in the southern backcountry, but men also engaged in footraces and throwing competitions that had them hurling anything from tomahawks for accuracy to large logs for distance. They swung carefully honed axes in log-splitting challenges to test physical stamina and precision chopping. Whatever the activity, numerous wagers were placed in anticipation of the matches, and money or materials changed hands after their conclusion.

Whether organized or not, frontier fights early on became the stuff of legend. A spontaneous fight in a tavern—drinking was always a sure catalyst for these affairs—fetched every man in sprinting distance to see its outcome. Particularly good fighters challenged others in organized contests for prizes as well as renown in a community, but such bouts were organized only in the loosest sense of the word, with no holds barred. Adversaries did anything to win, except use a weapon, in a style of fighting quaintly called Rough-and-Tumble. It was more like gnaw-and-claw, though, what with the gouging of eyes and the biting of ears, noses, and even testicles, gruesome tactics that encouraged the fainthearted to concede victory. Serious fighters grew their fingernails long and filed them to points to better gouge eyes. Frontier life was filled with dangers that carried the menace of accidental injury, but fighters inflicted and risked pre-

meditated mutilation, physical marks of contests that were strange tro-
phies because they were measured by what was missing—fingers, ears,
eyes—rather than what was won. A traveler noted that once he entered
Kentucky, he "saw more than one man, who wanted an eye," noting that
he "was now in the region of 'gouging.' "[5]

THE NORTH

The North was rural in character, much like the rest of the country, but
its farmers, especially in New England, were more likely to live in villages
and trudge daily to their fields. Northerners consequently saw one
another more regularly than did people in the rural South and West. In
addition, some places in the North were tending to urbanization, and city
dwellers naturally lived in much greater proximity to their neighbors and
saw them daily. Northerners had the chance to engage in more social
forms of leisure than people in other parts of the country, but their leisure
activities by circumstance were limited to the kind that could be pursued
in more confined areas.

**Industrialism
and Leisure**

Many employers believed that leisure bred vice and lazi-
ness. The attitude was a legacy of Puritan New England
that viewed idleness as providing an opportunity for evil
thoughts and sinfulness. During the beginnings of Ameri-
can industrialization, the old Puritan idea took on a new practical importance in the marketplace, for employers fretted about employees whose
pursuit of leisure included strong drink that diminished their productivity.

Even Americans who did not work in factories found that urban life
made the workplace inescapably separate from ordinary interactions with
friends and family. Because men in cities worked away from their homes,
the time they spent with their families became their primary leisure activity. Families went to parks together, read quietly or aloud by the fire in the
evenings, or sang songs around the piano to relax from the workday and
renew their household ties.

**The Second
Great Awakening
and Leisure**

As discussed in chapter 6, the Second Great Awakening was important in every region of the country,
but New England probably felt is impact on leisure
activity the most. Ministers everywhere condemned
spectator amusements such as horse racing, cockfighting, and card playing for the gambling they encouraged, denouncing
dancing and drinking for good measure. Yet New England and areas of
New York and the West settled by New England migrants believed the
condemnations most avidly and embraced their prohibitions most
eagerly. Powerful ministers and awakened congregations secured local
laws to ban amusements such as horse racing and gambling, and compel
a strict observance of Sundays. Many feared that an activity that encouraged gambling was "the ruinous pursuit of the idle and the vicious."[6]

Not all the preaching in the world could diminish for some
the pull of the tavern or public house (pub, for short). Its lure   **Northern**
remained as strong in the North as in other parts of the coun-   **Taverns**
try, and many men still spent much of their spare time there.
Drink was not the only attraction. After a long day's work, the cama-
raderie of talking with friends and playing games was appealing.

Taverns and pubs differed in the North, particularly the quaint rural
pubs of farming villages, as contrasted with the great variety of pubs and
inns in larger cities like New York. In cities, pubs catered to a particular
clientele rather than to the various tastes of an entire town or to the random traveler who happened in. For example, some pubs were described
as "coffee houses" to distinguish them from working-class establishments. They served upper-class customers with better food and drink and
generally featured more refined games and entertainments. They were
also inns that offered lodging to more select travelers, typically men in the
city on business. If women accompanied their husbands, the inn provided
private bedrooms and dining rooms that could accommodate ladies. Otherwise, wealthy businessmen of the city could mingle with important
travelers in the common room to discuss everything from the politics of
the day to the prices of imports and exports. They lubricated their discus-
sions with a variety of beverages. Beer, ale, cider, port, Madeira, sherry,
and other fine wines complemented an assortment of mixed drinks such
as "flip" or "syllabub," a mixture of cider, sugar, nutmeg, milk, and cream.
Refinement aside, such concoctions could be the ruin of many a wealthy
patron whose dulled wits at the gambling tables shrunk his pocketbook.

Upper-class inns were primarily set apart by their food. They were
cleaner and presented better appointments than working-class pubs, of
course, but it was the high quality of their board and the variety of beef,
ham, oysters, and the like that determined whether wealthy customers
would return. One delicacy served at finer taverns in the Northeast was
turtle soup, a dish usually unavailable in private homes. Because the tur-
tles that were imported from the Deep South and the West Indies weighed
several hundred pounds, they were too large for private kitchens and in
the days before refrigeration made too much soup for a single family to
consume. Fashionable inns touted the availability of sea turtle soup in
their dining rooms as an irresistible treat, and a kitchen's reputation for
fine food could make an establishment a stylish place for private parties.
Elite clubs attracted such social gatherings with special upstairs rooms
designed for dancing and dining.

Pubs for middle-class males also supplied a practical service for the
community by providing meeting rooms for clubs and a large room for
parties or receptions. The trappings in such establishments were not as
fine as those in the more expensive inns, but the food was hearty and the
accommodations adequate for travelers who could not afford nicer taverns. Just as the affluent citizens did in their inns, clerks and small busi-

ness owners gathered in their taverns at the end of the workday to discuss politics or business affairs.

Those who worked on the city's docks, in factories, or for artisans also had their pubs. More crudely furnished, they served plain food and simple beverages like beer, ale, and rum. The surroundings did not mean that the pastimes pursued there were any different, though. At these establishments, men still came together to gamble, tell stories, and complain about their lot in life. A man too busy to visit a pub could get a bottle at one of the city's many small grocery stores, which sold all types of beverages. For some, these "grog shops" were a regular stop on the way to or from work, a fact that made them prime targets for the emerging temperance movement. One British observer noted that while rarely did one see Americans in a falling-down-drunk state, "many are throughout the day under the influence of liquor."[7]

Colonial times and the years of the early Republic were the heyday for the tavern and inn. By the 1820s, their time as places for wealthy businessmen and travelers to congregate was waning. Instead, hotels and restaurants were becoming popular as local gathering places for the economic elite. For other classes, the growth of the temperance movement was to make the sociable tavern into the iniquitous saloon, and the patronizing of it a cause for reproach rather than a source of relaxation.

Hotels and Restaurants   Cities like New York took the lead in establishing luxury hotels on the European model. These businesses served not only travelers but also the city's upper and middle classes as social gathering places. The first floor included a bar for gentlemen, a dining room, and a parlor where women could have tea. For posh social clubs to hold annual or semiannual balls, the second floor typically included a large hall that could accommodate an orchestra for dancing with smaller side rooms for serving refreshments. The third floor's smaller rooms were for club meetings or smaller receptions, and guest rooms were on the fourth floor and above, up to the sixth floor, which was the highest built before the advent of steel girder construction.

The popularity of hotel dining rooms encouraged some entrepreneurs to open establishments devoted to serving full meals in a relaxing atmosphere. Like hotels modeled on European establishments, these restaurants were more socially suitable for ladies than taverns and pubs. As cities such as New York developed a more refined nightlife featuring concerts and theater productions, it became both necessary and lucrative to provide establishments catering to women who attended these functions. Some restaurants even began serving elaborate late-night meals during the usually lengthy theater intermission, special repasts that were the forerunners of today's post-theater supper. On most evenings, though, restaurants were packed primarily with men, relaxing over a good meal and fine brandy.

Wives no doubt craved the same level of social activity as their husbands, but etiquette considered it inappropriate for respectable women to patronize pubs. The exceptions were community social occasions like wedding celebrations. Only **Women's Leisure** on theater or concert nights did their husbands invite them to a restaurant. Otherwise women socialized at home with other women. Those who did not work outside the home usually found opportunities to socialize casually with neighbors every day as well as during more organized activities. Middle- and upper-class women called on one another regularly. During such visits the hostess or her servants would serve tea or other light refreshments, and the ladies would discuss mutual friends, their charitable or church activities, or make plans for other social gatherings. Such visits were often unorganized and unannounced, while other women's social activities could be painstakingly planned. Formal tea parties included friends, wives of their husband's business associates, or new women in the neighborhood. Women who accepted such an invitation were expected to reciprocate at some time in the future.

Women in the urban North also organized sewing circles to allow participants to congregate in one house to do their family's sewing while visiting. Such social events were sometimes charitable exercises in which ladies sewed garments for the poor. In the rural North, South, and West, women met in quilting bees to stitch blankets for themselves and the community. While centered on a useful activity, these events were cheerful chances for busy women to chat with neighbors.

As northern cities grew in population and area, the opportunity for shared pastimes like hunting, fishing, and other outdoor pursuits declined. As a result, northern urbanites turned **Spectator Sports** to spectator sports and activities to fill their brief leisure time. Though increasingly frowned on by churches, gambling was often a central part of spectator activities. Northern cities held indoor cockfights and dogfights as well as human wrestling matches. Prizefighting did not become widely popular until the 1830s and 1840s, but such contests occurred, especially after formalized procedures for matches were imported from Great Britain.

Northerners enjoyed horse races, but the influence of the Second Great Awakening led to their being outlawed in some communities. Before that, horse racing had had a long tradition in the North. It was especially popular in New York from colonial times, and Long Island was the site for some of the country's most famous races, drawing people from great distances to watch renowned horses compete. The events were uniquely democratic, anticipating the egalitarian impulses of the Jacksonian Age, as people from all classes took ferries operating from Manhattan or New Jersey to Long Island, carrying picnics to spend the day watching races and enjoying the company of friends and family. The upper classes owned the thoroughbreds, but people from all strata of society enjoyed the races and were dismayed when laws banned the sport in many parts of the North.

Theater   In large northern cities, particularly New York and Philadel-phia, the theater was a popular diversion. America's first profes-sional actors were primarily from Great Britain and had performed in these theaters during the American Revolution. Avid theater-goers welcomed these actors back enthusiastically during the period of the early Republic. Like all Americans, northerners loved the variety of enter-tainment available in the theater. Offering musical reviews, instrumental recitals, and classical or fashionable plays, northern cities provided an assortment of amusements that most southerners and westerners could only dream about. In fact, larger cities in the North boasted an abundance of theaters, each of which offered several different kinds of entertainment nightly. Because of their popularity, theaters of the early Republic were quite large and offered a broad range of ticket prices from the most expen-sive private boxes to balcony seats that even working-class patrons could afford. European visitors found the quality of American theater amazingly good, partly, as one observer noted, because of "the enormous emigration, caused by the French Revolution," that supplied "theaters with excellent orchestras" and "a great mass of patrons,"[8] and were shocked to see in the audiences "men that, if in London could hardly buy a pint of porter."[9]

The clergy argued that attending the theater did nothing to improve the average person, some even insisting that "to endulge a taste for playgoing means nothing more nor less than the loss of that most valuable treasure the immortal soul."[10] Yet the quality of performances, as well as their con-tent, particularly productions of the works of Shakespeare and other important playwrights, revealed a growing sophistication among Ameri-can theatergoers in the latter part of the period.

Participatory Sports   Despite the growing number of spectator activities, city dwellers still tried to find ways to engage in physical activ-ity during their leisure time. The proximity of rivers and lakes made it possible for many of the upper and middle classes to take up boating, both sailing and rowing, as recreation. Again, the proclivity for gambling meant that both participants in, and spectators at, such events inevitably began to wager on their outcomes. The upper class dominated most of these boating activities, and certainly all the yacht clubs, but like many spectator activities, the races were watched and followed by people from all classes.

Aristocratic Leisure   Just as in the South, the upper classes of the North had the most leisure time and made the most of it. The affluent worked hard, but their wealth gave them time to enjoy read-ing, concerts and plays, and travel. Though general tourism did not become popular until transportation improvements made travel comfortable, the wealthy enjoyed pleasant carriages with shock-absorbing springs that softened the rattles of bumpy roads. Thus equipped, they made trips to places like Saratoga Springs to escape summer heat or to Newport, Rhode Island, to enjoy the sea breezes.

Those who wanted to make trips over greater distances found it increasingly easy to do so in the North. After 1790, several enterprising northerners opened stage lines for travelers. While most of their customers were men traveling on business, middle-class patrons increasingly began using stagecoaches to visit relatives in distant towns. When women also began buying tickets, owners made efforts to increase creature comforts. Yet a persistent problem that prevented travel from becoming a mainstream activity in the early Republic was the necessity for sleeping arrangements along the way. The country was dotted with taverns and pubs that provided lodgings for overnight travelers, but they were rarely clean enough to be considered suitable for ladies. A night spent in a wayside inn would often leave travelers itching from bedbugs and fleas that shared the filthy bedding. A British traveler put to bed in the communal dormitory of one roadside inn complained that after falling asleep, "I was soon awoke in torture from a general attack made on me by hosts of vermin.... I started from the bed, dressed myself, spread a coverlet on the floor, and lay down there to court a little more repose, but I was prevented by a constant noise in the house during the whole night."[11]

Improving roads in the latter part of the period meant that travel in the North for rest and relaxation not only increased in volume but varied in destinations as well. In addition to Saratoga Springs, other places began providing services as resorts, particularly scenic areas such as Niagara Falls and the New Jersey shore. The heyday of these resorts was still years in the future, but changing middle- and upper-class perceptions about leisure travel as a proper way to spend time gave them their start.

The wealthy could not only afford better accommodations when they traveled; they could also entertain at their homes in a much grander fashion than the other classes. People graced with invitations traveled miles to attend these affairs, some of which were destined for legendary status with their extravagant multicourse meals served by uniformed retainers. Well-dressed ladies and gentlemen sat at the dining table for hours while they were served the finest food available not only in the nation but in the world.

Northern cities made it easier for the gathering of social, literary, or musical clubs, and they were accordingly more prevalent in that region than in other parts of the country. Upper- and middle-class men and women alike belonged to clubs purportedly founded to advance a common interest or promote a shared activity, but whose actual purpose was to provide a social outlet.

SELF-IMPROVEMENT

The idea that leisure time should be used for self-improvement, particularly of mind and character, gained wide currency during the early

Republic. To become more virtuous citizens, the upper and middle classes spent much of their leisure time reading serious literature, developing musical skills or listening to others display theirs, and attending lectures to broaden their understanding of the world around them.

Literature   Books were quite expensive, but they were not particularly rare inasmuch as Americans loved to read. While most of the literature during the period came from Europe, many Americans had come to the conclusion that avoiding the corrupting influence of aristocratic Europe required developing a national literature. As part of the initiative to instill the values of a virtuous republic, many of the period's writers extolled the attributes of the Founders, often depicting them through gross exaggerations and sometime with sheer inventions. The most notorious example of this type of laudatory writing was the extremely flattering and largely fictional biography of George Washington written by Mason Weems. It was the source of myths such as young Washington's insistence that he could not tell a lie when admitting to cutting down a cherry tree.

Other historians who examined the relatively brief American past, however, did a better job of explaining why the Republic had been founded and of defining its essential philosophy. Notable historians of the American Revolution were Mercy Otis Warren (also one of the most important woman writers of the early Republic), David Ramsay, and biographer John Marshall (who was chief justice of the Supreme Court). Such authors were the best-selling celebrities of their day, and they were widely read not only because they inspired pride in the American past but also because they entertained audiences with a lively literary style.

In addition to history, Americans improved themselves intellectually by reading scientific treatises. Many were published in Philadelphia, the city with the largest scientific community during the early Republic. Works focusing on what that age called political philosophy (ours refers to it as political science) sought to make relevant in American terms the political theory of the Enlightenment.

American fiction had to wait a few more years to truly come into its own, but Americans loved to read foreign fiction, especially from Britain, from whence they imported it in large volumes. There were those who condemned the widespread reading of fiction as unproductive of republican virtue, but fiction that taught a moral lesson was considered acceptable.

Americans also enjoyed reading newspapers and magazines. Virtually every town of any size produced at least a weekly newspaper, and men interested in politics usually subscribed to other newspapers from large cities. Places like New York had many newspapers that appealed to various interests and different political affiliations. As discussed later, politics increasingly were a spectator sport in the United States during the early Republic, and newspapers were a convenient way to keep up with both sides of the battle. They also became increasingly scurrilous in their attacks, thus adding to their entertainment value. For example, one paper during the presidential campaign of 1800 charged that if Thomas Jefferson were "elected to the Presidency, the seal of death is that moment set on our holy religion, our churches will be prostrated, and some famous prostitute, under the title of Goddess of Reason, will preside in the Sanctuaries."[12] Such passages were sure to titillate even the most apolitical citizen.

Magazines, especially those for ladies, were also quite popular. Ladies' periodicals might have been dismissed as frivolous had they not always included practical tips about housekeeping and child rearing. Other magazines catered to people interested in the latest literature, art, and scientific pursuits. In keeping with the desire of many intellectual Americans to emphasize American contributions in those areas, many publications, in the words of the editor of the *Columbian Magazine,* hoped "to shew, that, the source of all improvement and science, a liberal encouragement was offered, at this early period of her independency."[13]

Music

Music was a part of most Americans' daily life. There were work songs, children's songs, and church songs that most people knew by heart. The period also saw a growing belief that knowledge of music and skill at playing a musical instrument were important parts of a proper middle- and upper-class education. Children took music lessons, and adults in urban areas spent time practicing the works of European composers such as Joseph Haydn and George Friedrich Handel. Even the most modest communities regularly staged concerts that featured local musicians and vocalists. In large cities, wealthy patrons of the arts established musical associations—the New York Philharmonic Society was an early example—to foster the development and performance of what became known as "classical music."

Hymns or other religious melodies were by far the most important music in most people's lives. Similarly, many fondly recalled and frequently sang or played the music of their fathers and mothers, the origins of a musical heritage later called "folk music." Families sang these songs around their fireplaces, and workers warbled them to pass the time of day, an age-old way of making the toil of daily chores lighter with a song. Taverns were always a popular place to hear old folk tunes or new, popular songs where soloists or groups performed. In fact, some of the most popular tunes were drinking songs deliberately fashioned to appeal to the partially inebriated, in both their ease of melody and their vivacity of verse.

Lectures

The prominence of the lecture circuit or lyceum movement did not occur until after 1820, but the custom of traveling experts expounding on everything from astronomy to zoology began during the period. Because Americans believed that education and self-improvement were imperative ingredients for economic success, public lectures attracted a surprising number of working men whose direct interest in some topics could only be surmised as marginal. Yet they trusted that increasing their knowledge in a general way could start them up the ladder of success. Beyond such a utilitarian goal was the doctrine that the expanding right to vote required that everyone be an informed citizen. It was a powerful incentive for individual self-improvement in all areas of knowledge.

Public Gardens and Parks   By the beginning of the nineteenth century, public gardens and parks became an innovative addition in many American cities. Sometimes for a small fee or free of charge, city dwellers could enjoy a taste of nature. Because French and British designers built some of these first public gardens, they often imitated those of Paris and London. The forerunner of the amusement park also appeared during these years. These parks were designed to provide a broad array of amusements, and competition caused proprietors to expand attractions by adding music, fireworks, outdoor plays, and refreshments, diversions that were especially popular in the summertime. Patrons whiled away hot evenings strolling through flowers, listening to music, and sipping lemonade. A popular treat at many of the gardens was frozen cream (or ice cream, as we know it), a novelty for Americans in the early nineteenth century.

Politics   Political education was supposed to produce a more informed, educated citizenry, and many men brimming with such edification felt a keener interest in public affairs; some even exhibited a growing desire to participate in politics. Most adult white males could vote in elections from the beginning of the Republic, but the elite nature of national politics had caused many to lose interest. In many ways, local politics could be just as discouraging. Voters frequently had little say about who would stand for office because the patricians in a community typically merged into political cliques that chose candidates from their own ranks. Elections consequently were often boring, preordained affairs. Not only was it considered undignified for candidates to campaign, but they were expected to act like reluctant aspirants who stood for election only to fulfill their duty and oblige the will of the people.

Still, during the early part of the period, independent urban artisans and craftsmen took an interest in elections and showed their support for candidates with parades organized by trade. Celebrating a victory could produce grand spectacles as men turned out in the clothes of their occupation, some carrying the tools of their trade, others carrying banners, to march down the streets of American cities, their destination frequently a tavern.

The tradition of political parades persisted and reached its peak during the 1830s and 1840s. Indicative of a growing democratic spirit among the electorate, these later parades not only celebrated the election of a favorite candidate or a party victory but also served as rallies during campaigns to whip up support. In fact, by the end of the period, the expanding franchise that included a growing number of urban working men noticeably invigorated politics. Candidates found it necessary to court these new voters, and the best place to do that was where they congregated after work—the saloon. Consequently, ensuing decades saw the urban saloon become the gathering place for organizing urban politics, and it was the odd fellow who was not affiliated in some way with a political club that gathered in these drinking establishments.

The nation's rural areas, which characterized most of the country, saw politics changing there as well after the War of 1812 as more smaller landowners became involved in public affairs. Again, as the franchise expanded to include previously unaffiliated voters, they too had to be wooed. Rural folk needed little excuse to gather for eating, drinking, and generally having fun, and the tradition of the barbecue as political rally gained rapid and eager acceptance. Candidates pooled resources to pay for food and drink, and voters brought their families to hear speeches while feasting themselves full. Thus did politics become a leisure activity during the early Republic, resembling their manifestation today as a spectator sport, one the average voter found increasingly entertaining.

The European tradition of having periodic market fairs to sell goods and meet friends and family never took hold in America. In the South and on the frontier, distance discouraged the custom, and New England towns were close **Agricultural Fairs** enough to farms to allow regular visits. Instead, the goals of self-improvement and scientific inquiry led agricultural societies to organize local fairs to promote the dissemination of useful knowledge. Beginning in the early nineteenth century, organizers in New England, the mid-Atlantic states, and the South began holding livestock shows to encourage more scientific methods of animal breeding and husbandry. These predecessors of today's county fairs at first gave prizes to farmers displaying the best animals, but they quickly evolved into more broadly conceived events. They became venues for exhibiting agricultural products and handicrafts and for educating farmers about new agricultural techniques. These early fairs also fostered national pride with displays vaunting American manufacturing. Moreover, such festivities, with their practical underpinnings, provided communities with recreational events that allowed people to mingle, hear an educational lecture, and listen to a local band without feeling guilty over being away from plows and churns.

CHILDREN

As noted in chapter 2, the new emphasis on the importance of childhood meant that people placed a greater importance on play and toys than in earlier times. A main reason for the change in children's clothes, for example, was to make play easier. From the time they could walk, small children of every class and race spent most of their time playing, and middle- and upper-class children had toys. Boy and girl toddlers generally played together, but when most children reached the age of three or four, their play was usually segregated by gender, though there were exceptions. Typically, though, the types of play activities, games, and toys became gender specific. We have noted how many believed that adult recreation should be useful, and likewise many thought that children's play should center on self-improvement by preparing them for adulthood. Considerable thought was given about how best to accomplish this goal. Pamphlets outlined what was appropriate and what was inappropriate for children's play activities. One urged that "amusements of our youth shall consist of such exercises as will be most subservient to their future employments in life."[14]

When not in school, boys in rural areas spent much of their time in outdoor pursuits. Older boys learned the leisure activities of their fathers, especially how to ride horses, shoot guns, and catch fish. Outdoor games were designed to produce strong bodies able to plow fields, build barns, and shoe horses. Boys played with balls and sticks and had organized outdoor games like "shiny" or "bandy," the early equivalents of field hockey. In these games, boys were organized into teams and used sticks to knock something through a goal. Often they had to make do with whatever round object they could find or fashion, because real balls were rare. The opposing team tried to prevent the score and to steal the ball. In colder climates, boys played an early form of curling. On frozen ponds, teams of four players pushed around as many as eight large, heavy stones at the same time. The object was to move your own stones while obstructing those of the other team. In addition to such organized sports, boys made up games or played make-believe as children have in all times. They pretended to be soldiers fighting the British during the Revolution or the War of 1812; they pretended to be pioneering scouts seeking a new trail to the frontier; they pretended to be great hunters. The games they played and activities they participated in were little different from those of their fathers and would remain largely unchanged when taken up by their sons.

Little girls were not only more regulated in their outdoor activities; they were encouraged to do much of their playing indoors, a formula designed to prepare them for their roles as homemakers. Yet girls did have outdoor games, and on occasion they were even able to persuade boys to play with them. Boys and girls, for instance, were allowed to play battledore and shuttlecock, an ancestor to badminton. A game called "the needle's eye" was much like the modern game of Red Rover: children arranged in two parallel rows stood holding hands as a child from one row ran toward the other with the object of breaking the chain, all to the cadence of chanted verses. All these activities were literally considered child's play, for adults rarely participated in anything akin to modern team sports. Rarely did female children, for that matter. Since girls were considered more delicate than boys and in little need of physical strength, they spent most of their time indoors with their dolls or playing parlor games. During inclement weather, boys might join girls' parlor games, but they would never play with dolls.

Many children's parlor games of the early Republic were similar to those of today. For instance, blindman's wand was similar to the modern game of blindman's buff. In the earlier game, a blindfolded child tried to find playmates by touching them with a stick (hence the wand) and asking them questions to determine their identities. The unlucky child who was first found and then found out became the next "blind man."

The growing emphasis on the importance of play meant the appearance of more elaborate toys. Children had always had toys, but they were generally homemade and hence quite simple. For poor children, this remained the case, but for others of even modest means, increasing numbers of manufactured toys or playthings crafted by artisans were brought into American homes. Girls played with realistic dolls that ranged from those of superb craftsmanship for the affluent to simple cloth figures that nonetheless became prized possessions of girls in humbler homes.

The birth of the American factory system all but eliminated leisure time for poor children. They always had to work harder than their middle- and upper-class counterparts, and during these years their use as factory laborers meant even less time than before for play. Such children worked 10 to 12 hours a day, six days a week, leaving them with little energy to play even if they found the time. Yet except for the impoverished and those unfortunates who were born into slavery, children's lives showed a marked improvement during the early Republic. Their importance as future citizens made adults look at childhood in a different way than had previous generations. Play became an important part of a child's development, helping to mold the boy into the reliable husband and upright father, the girl into the virtuous wife and tender mother, and both into citizens able to sustain the Republic and advance its ideal of liberty.

CONCLUSION

By the end of the period, the religious revival known as the Second Great Awakening had changed many people's ideas about diversions and amusements even as the birth of the American factory system altered the tangible aspects of leisure. Calls for more useful amusements sprang from both spiritual concerns about the orderliness of society and utilitarian fears that laborers dissipated by saloons and gambling dens would be ineffective in the factories. The amusements that church and mill condemned did not go away, of course, but they became less acceptable in polite society and increasingly became the exclusive pursuits of the lower classes. Games and sporting events that had flourished in the colonial and early national period declined in importance, even as people spent time watching spectator sports. Children played games, while adults spent their leisure hours trying to improve their minds and refine their characters. Good books, serious theater, fine music, and public lectures allowed American adults to relax without feeling guilty about wasting time. Occasionally they even had fun. Yet it is most certain that the typical American man often pretended to embrace the need for reform rather than completely endorsing it in his heart. Even as he accompanied his wife to the weekly lecture downtown, he longed for the pleasures of the acrid saloon and the thrill of wagering on a fast horse. A less abstract impulse for improvement and time usefully spent persisted on the frontier, where snippets of leisure time were most often consumed by useful pursuits that strained to integrate socializing afterward. When those isolated, rough-hewn people did have free time, though, their leisure activities were rustic, boisterous, and sometimes violent. They played as hard as they worked, and they worked very hard indeed.

NOTES

1. Francis Butler Simkins and Charles Pierce Roland, *A History of the South*, 4th ed. (New York: Alfred A. Knopf, 1972), 147.

2. Edward Hotaling, *The Great Black Jockeys: The Lives and Times of the Men Who Dominated America's First National Sport* (Rocklin, Calif.: Forum, 1999), 44.

3. Dick, *The Dixie Frontier*, 140.

4. Foster Rhea Dulles, *A History of Recreation: America Learns to Play* (New York: Appleton-Century-Crofts, 1965), 71.

5. Ibid., 74.

6. Henry Chafetz, *Play the Devil: A History of Gambling in the United States, 1492–1955* (New York: Clarkson N. Potter, 1960), 49.

7. Michael Batterberry and Ariane Batterberry, *On the Town in New York from 1776 to the Present* (New York: Charles Scribner's Sons, 1973), 43.

8. Barnard Hewitt, *Theatre U.S.A., 1665–1957* (New York: McGraw-Hill, 1959), 44–45.

9. Bruce McConachie, "American Theatre in Context, from the Beginnings to 1870," in *The Cambridge History of American Theatre*, vol. 1, ed. Don B. Wilmeth and Christopher Bigsby (Cambridge: Cambridge University Press, 1998), 132.

10. Dulles, *The History of Recreation*, 89.

11. Philip D. Jordan, *The National Road* (Indianapolis: Bobbs-Merrill, 1948), 63.

12. Jim Cullen, *The Art of Democracy: A Concise History of Popular Culture in the United States* (New York: Monthly Review Press, 1996), 46.

13. Cynthia A. Kierner, *Revolutionary America, 1750–1815: Sources and Interpretation* (Upper Saddle River, N.J.: Prentice Hall, 2003), 330.

14. Quoted in Jesse Frederick Steiner, *Americans at Play* (New York: Arno Press, 1970), 4.

6

FAITH AND CHARITY

A remarkable continuity marks the American experience with religion, despite the fact that Americans prided themselves on the diversity of faiths in their country. From the earliest years of the colonial period through the early Republic, a central theme of American religious faith was the belief not only that divine providence guided the destiny of peoples and places but that the American setting was the site for a new chosen people. As one clergyman put it: "In the discovery and settlement of this country God had some great end in view."[1] In addition, Americans believed that their civic system was God's gift of liberty and opportunity not only for Americans but also eventually for the entire world. In all events and dangers, God would protect the nation and its people, preserving them for some future service in a broader plan of good works. It was a perception handed down from the first Puritan congregations of New England. By the early nineteenth century, it had become thoroughly interwoven in the complex American religious fabric. The American Revolution—an undertaking that succeeded against the longest odds—and the eventual formation of the new government under the Constitution were regarded as self-evident proofs of greater accomplishments to come.

The importance of religion in the function of American society was therefore immense. The Puritan mind was possibly more influential than the dazzling intellectual innovations of the Enlightenment. Although some intellectuals gravitated to Deism, the idea that God was more an objective observer of his perfect mechanical machine than a prime mover in the affairs of men, the great bulk of the population believed God was not only supreme but also actively involved in charting human affairs. A good example of this belief can be seen in the diary of the dying Quaker Samuel Cole Davis, who confided to himself and future generations to "remember it was the Lord that sent this affliction on thee."[2] Such a notion made for an energetic religious faith that occasionally achieved levels of phenomenal vigor, such as during times of fervent religious revivals. It also bolstered a patriotism that extended far beyond a devotion to one's country simply because it was one's home: Americans believed that God's divine will was directing the destiny of the Republic, and in its early years, patriotic loyalty to that republic was a form of what sociologists and historians would eventually characterize as "civil religion." Moreover, religion convinced many "that it is possible to produce such a change in the moral character of man as shall raise him to a resemblance of angels."[3]

The religious diversity that flourished in the American setting has always been a perplexing riddle for scholars. What made the infant United States a place where so many different and occasionally antagonistic faiths could coexist? The circumstance certainly ran counter to history. The rise of Roman Catholicism from the ruins of the ancient world set the pattern for religious conformity that was considered the ideal, both by the Catholic community and later by the various sects of the Protestants. The concept of religious conformity, in fact, was virtually unbroken in the history of the Western World from the fifth-century fall of Rome through the establishment of colonies in North America. One church all-encompassing and dominant was the quest, and attempts to establish such a church labeled all outside it as dissenters at best, heretics at worst. Much mischief and some malevolence resulted under the banner of religious conformity, from the imposition of annoying social disabilities to appalling physical persecution. Yet the United States refused to establish such a dominant church, and by deliberately contriving ways to separate any church from government sponsorship, the new nation sought to prevent such domination from occurring by accident. As one American Presbyterian wrote, "there is not a single instance in history in which civil liberty was lost, and religious liberty preserved entire."[4] Political and religious liberty were inseparable. For instance, during the early Republic, President James Madison refused to sign a bill chartering an Episcopal Church in Alexandria, District of Columbia, arguing that "the bill exceeds the rightful authority to which governments are limited by the essential distinction between civil and religious functions."[5] In another case, evangelical groups decried the breaking of the Christian Sabbath, especially by the U.S. Post Office, which under an 1810 statute was directed to deliver mail seven days a week. Nonetheless, their intense lobbying proved to no avail. Congress upheld Sunday mail delivery as a central bulwark of the separation of church and state.

In short, no particular religious group was allowed to decree governmental policy, and the result was an incredible religious diversity. The First Amendment to the Constitution not only prohibited the establishment of a state church; it also set the circumstance in which the new nation could become a haven for virtually every species of faith (and nonfaith) that the human mind could contrive. Most Americans subscribed to some sort of faith, or as one observer noted, "those that have it [religion], shows it, and those that have it not wish to be considered religious for the credit it gives in the society."[6] The civil religion of the American experience—that amalgamation of spiritual faith and civic obligation—encouraged tolerance through a sense of community that crossed denominational lines. And the conspicuous absence of the government promoting a particular faith made all the others feel less threatened. The United States was unique in its approach to a problem that had troubled cultures since the time of the Romans.

We should not, however, leap to the conclusion that religious differences and disputes did not exist in the early Republic. Even the predominance of Protestants did not mean that most Americans were bound as one in a common religious belief. The early Republic continued the tradition of religious debate and doctrinal argument that had begun during the earliest colonial times. Congregations continued to split hairs and divide into new groups, new sects formed, and some groups embraced emotional revivalism while others rejected it with sniffing disapproval. Rationalism, that great intellectual ornament of the eighteenth century, seemed sensible to some, troubling to others, and atheistic to the anxious. In fact, about the only thing that all these disparate and various groups, sects, and denominations could agree about was the prudence of religious freedom. And even given that point of agreement as an ideal, there were boundaries to it in reality. The First Amendment could not stop Protestants from being suspicious of, and sometimes persecuting, Catholics. States were not constrained by the Constitution from promoting or excluding religion. Virginia was unique in its adoption of statutory religious freedom, for many other states collected taxes to support religion or imposed special restrictions on others. However, because of the Constitution's legal guarantees, Protestants proselytized from each other's denominations without violent reprisal, and new sects could usually be regarded with wariness and misgivings without their being snuffed out by vicious attacks.[7] Religious rivalry was neither nationally dire nor dangerously violent in a sustained, systematic sense. Even in 1819, during the storm over Unitarianism in New England, one of the bitterest arguments in American denominational history, a visitor from England declared, "All is harmony." He concluded that "here are no disputes about religion; or, if they be, they make no noise."[8] While this testimonial was something of an exaggeration, it was a tribute to the American tradition of religious freedom that it contained more truth than overstatement.

DIVERSITY AS AN ARTICLE OF FAITH

The concept of denominations—separate religious entities that offer different belief systems within a broad framework of agreement—was essentially a creation of the nineteenth century and in many ways was a reflection of religious pluralism in the early Republic. It is not the purpose here to recount the theological history of the nation and its various faiths, but before examining the effects of religion on daily life during the period, we should take a few moments to acquaint ourselves with the major and minor varieties of belief that made up the incredible range of religion in those early years of the nation. The following capsule descriptions are arranged alphabetically.

African Methodist Episcopal Church   Those unfortunate Africans traded into slavery in British North America and their descendants during the colonial period experienced a varying and an intricate mixture of compulsory acculturation and voluntary integration into Protestant Christian traditions. The sweeping evangelism of the late 1790s and early 1800s increased the number of black Christians just as it did white ones, and in the South, where slavery not only persisted but was fixed in place by the rise of the plantation system, slave owners tried to use religion as a way to promote obedience to masters as a condition for salvation. Slaves, however, just as frequently connected their plight to that of the ancient Hebrews in Egyptian captivity, and their hymns ("spirituals," in their parlance) remain a testament to the longing for freedom in this world and, barring that, salvation in the next.

In the North, freedom in this world did not always mean equality, even at the church altar. In 1787 black members of Saint George's Episcopal Church in Philadelphia left the parish to protest prejudicial treatment and thereafter met in a rented stockroom to hear sermons by their leader, former slave Richard Allen. This initial group formed the nucleus of additional black congregations that formed throughout the city and in 1816 joined to establish the African Methodist Episcopal Church. Allen became the denomination's first bishop upon being ordained by the fading Francis Asbury in one of his last official acts, a tie to the Methodists that saw the AME church emulating Methodists in doctrine, church polity, the General Conference system, and eventually wide-ranging missionary work.

In 1796 a similar break by black parishioners occurred in New York when their displeasure over being marginalized in the John Street Methodist Episcopal Church prompted them to establish a separate congregation. With the blessings of Francis Asbury, they built their own church and named it Zion in 1800. The new denomination soon spread to Connecticut, New Jersey, and Pennsylvania, although it did not formally withdraw from the Methodist Church until 1820. Almost 30 years after that, the denomination honored the original New York congregation by adopting the name American Methodist Episcopal Zion Church.

Baptists   Many Protestants in the United States were Baptists, a denomination that began in early-seventeenth-century England that embraced five cardinal principles. Baptists believed in separation of church and state, thorough congregational independence, faith based exclusively on the Scriptures, conversion and membership in the church as a result of a personal religious experience, and baptism by complete immersion. Although Roger Williams is sometimes described as the founder of American Baptists and his church in Providence, Rhode Island, established in 1638, as the original Baptist congregation in America, some scholars argue that Williams and his followers did not practice complete immersion. Nonetheless, during the colonial era, Rhode Island was the hub for the dissemination of Baptist theology and in 1764 became the site of the first Baptist college in America. Elsewhere in New England, Baptists were subjected to harsh harassment until the end of the seventeenth century, and their numbers were mostly confined to the mid-Atlantic colonies, where English and Welsh immigrants brought the faith with them in increasing numbers, especially to New York, Pennsylvania, Maryland, and Virginia.

As with other denominations, the Great Awakening, discussed later in this chapter, had a profound impact on the Baptists, leading to a faction committed to religious revivals. Following untrained and unpaid farmers who took on the mantle of preachers, this faction grew swiftly in Virginia and North Carolina, especially among the poor, and by the late eighteenth century, southern Baptists had become plentiful and powerful. Because they devoutly believed in the separation of church and state, they strenuously urged the new American government to embrace the idea, a mainstay in sustaining religious liberty in the early Republic. Meanwhile their reliance on farmer-preachers meant the Baptists would rival even the Methodists during the Second Great Awakening in establishing new churches on the American frontier.

Because like Baptists, members of the Church of the Brethren believed in total immersion for baptism, they were known as "Dunkers," often modified as Dunkards. **Church of the Brethren** Their baptismal observance required that they be plunged three times for each entity of the Holy Trinity. Originally appearing in the German states in the late 1600s, Dunkards came to America in the early eighteenth century to settle in Pennsylvania, Maryland, and Virginia. Eventually they spread westward, establishing simple farming communities that adhered to an unadorned faith in the Bible, the Trinity, and baptism as the basic requirements for deliverance. Dunkards refused to swear to oaths, rejected tobacco and alcohol, and passionately opposed slavery. They just as avidly embraced pacifism.

The rites of the Dunkard faith were a daily event centering on emulating Christ's washing of feet, ceremonies of fellowship, the breaking of bread, and finally the observance of the Eucharist. Congregations enjoyed autonomy to elect their own ministers.

Catholics had been among the first English colonists with the establishment of Maryland in 1634 as a refuge for those **Catholics** fleeing persecution in England. Yet they were never numerous in the colonial establishment and even in Maryland suffered maltreatment under punitive laws throughout the colonial period, a reflection of the anti-Catholic animus dating from the English Reformation. Yet there were Catholic signers of the Declaration of Independence, Catholic soldiers in the officer corps and ranks of the Continental Army, and Catholic delegates to the Constitutional Convention. They remained a minority, however, and were slow to secure civil rights in various states.

Colonial Catholics had relied on the Jesuit order for spiritual guidance, but in the decade after the Revolution, the suppression of the order and the break with Britain saw a greater reliance on American prelates. Marylander and cousin of a Declaration of Independence signer, former Jesuit John Carroll became the first bishop of Baltimore. At that time, Catholics numbered about 35,000 in the mid-Atlantic states and scattered French settlements on the frontier. Meanwhile the Catholic Church's presence in the United States grew solely because of disruptive European events, especially the French Revolution, which sent many French priests into exile in the United States. The presence of these French churchmen created a problem in itself when Americans divided over the Anglo-French war in the early 1800s. Yet the long history of Catholic educational and charitable work that had begun in 1737 with Ursuline nuns in French New Orleans continued unabated. Georgetown Academy served all faiths, and St. Mary's, the first Catholic seminary in the United States, opened in Baltimore. Maryland's Elizabeth Ann Bayley Seton, destined to become the first American-born saint, founded the Sisters of Charity of St. Joseph and in 1809 a school for girls in Emmitsburg.[9] The Sisters of Charity opened America's first Catholic orphanage in Philadelphia, and in South Carolina plans to publish a Catholic weekly bore fruit in 1822 when Bishop John England brought out the first issue of the *United States Catholic Miscellany*.

Even after the absorption of French Louisiana in 1803, Catholic numbers remained slight throughout these years, and Catholics were abided because they were unobtrusive. When political and agricultural problems in Ireland during the 1820s brought a flood of Catholic refugees to American shores, their growing presence meant growing resentment from Protestants in competition for jobs and social status. The result was a new round of informal persecutions, some resulting in violent incidents, fueled by occasionally scurrilous charges of corruption in the church and scandalous misconduct in the convents.

Congregationalists

Congregationalists were theologically descended directly from the Puritans of England and consequently enjoyed pride of place as one of the oldest, most numerous, and most significant religious groups in the colonies. For later generations, they would come to define the persevering and innovative American spirit. The first of their number, Separatist Puritans, had in 1620 established a colony at Plymouth against all odds after agreeing to the celebrated Mayflower Compact, the first statement in the New World of the ideals of democratic government. In religious terms, they were also seminal in establishing Congregationalism as the desirable standard for church organization in several New England colonies. Although detractors in England mounted attacks on Congregationalism, the denomination continued to develop its own identity throughout the colonial period, especially as Puritan immigrants swelled the population. Harvard and Yale Colleges were established to supply educated ministers during these years, and broad-minded Congregationalists adopted the Halfway Covenant to moderate the necessity of having a religious experience to qualify for church membership, a measure that angered traditionalists and caused some to gravitate to Presbyterianism. While the Great Awakening in the 1730s and early 1740s swelled Congregationalist numbers, it also led to serious doctrinal arguments that ultimately fractured Congregationalism into conflicting camps, a prominent one eventually becoming Unitarians. Politically, however, Congregationalism supported the American Revolution, and its clergymen readied their flocks for the sweeping cultural and governmental changes that the break with Britain portended.

The Congregationalists undertook noteworthy missionary and educational initiatives during the early Republic. America's first missionaries to foreign lands hailed from the organization the Congregationalists created in 1810, work that continued in the 1820s and 1830s in remote frontier areas of the United States itself and beyond its borders. Congregationalists also sustained important colleges they had established at Williams, Amherst, Oberlin, and Carleton.

Yet in the years of the early Republic, Congregationalism remained a regional presence in New England that failed to accompany the large migrations of New Englanders westward, mainly because of the Congregationalist insistence on an educated clergy. The Plan of Union of 1801 proposed to merge their scattered adherents on the frontier with more numerous and better established Presbyterian congregations, and the results were predictable. Most such worshippers did not merely join Presbyterians in church attendance; they became Presbyterians in fact, and Congregationalism remained both regional in character and small in size.[10]

Deism was more a philosophy than a theology. Deists believed in a supreme being but rejected revelation and denied mystical **Deists** canons of Christianity, such as the occurrence of miracles that violated natural laws. Coinciding with the rationalism of the Enlightenment, Deism came to America in the late eighteenth century when some notable American intellectuals and influential figures embraced the philosophy during the revolutionary era. Higher education was affected by Deism—some would have said "infected" by it—and traditional denominations reacted to it with growing dismay, especially in New England, where it gave impetus to the Second Great Awakening. Yet Founders such as Benjamin Franklin and George Washington were attracted to Deism's tenets of rationalism and toleration. Thomas Jefferson openly espoused Deism, leading to the eventual charge by his political enemies that he was an atheist (which he was not), as did Thomas Paine, who undoubtedly was an atheist, thus muddying the waters regarding the philosophy's potential consequences in attracting a large number of believers. The romanticism of the early Republic, however, would greatly erode the attractions of Deism as a philosophy-faith, while some basic facets of it were incorporated into the rationalism of Unitarianism and Universalism.

Disciples of Christ   The Great Revival on the American frontier had a direct impact on the formation of this denomination, especially because its principal leaders were the dynamic Thomas Campbell and his son Alexander. Originally Presbyterian ministers, the Campbells established in 1811 a congregation in Pennsylvania based on Thomas Campbell's Christian Association, which he had founded two years earlier. Frequently referred to as Campbellites, the denomination officially called itself Disciples of Christ and advocated not just the revival of the Christian faith but also the restoration of Christian principles based exclusively on a fundamental interpretation of the Bible, especially the New Testament. The denomination was attractive to frontier settlers and spread rapidly westward. By the 1830s, various other revival movements were also embracing the Disciples of Christ, the Kentuckian Barton Stone and his flock prominent among them.

Episcopalians   During the colonial era, the Church of England (known informally as the Anglican Church) was the established state religion, but the Revolution's break with England and the subsequent acceptance of the principle of separation of church and state required the restructuring of their church by American Anglicans. They adopted the formal title of Protestant Episcopal Church and informally became known as Episcopalians. In a rapid sequence of reorganization, Episcopalians developed a national organization and obtained consecration of American bishops. By then, the entire church had been brought under central governance.

During the early Republic, the Episcopal Church concentrated on healing the damage to it caused by the Revolution. Many of the faithful who saw allegiance to the British crown as a bulwark of their church had been alienated. By 1811, the vigorous spirit of revival that had swept through other denominations a decade earlier also began to take hold in more staid Episcopalian circles as so-called Low Church advocates embraced the evangelical imperative and gained control from High Church traditionalists. Important achievements and growing numbers reflected the denomination's rejuvenation. An Episcopal seminary was established in 1817, and general missionary work began three years later. Starting in 1810 and for the next 20 years, Sunday schools became a fixture in almost all parishes. Doctrinal disputes again emerged in the 1830s when the Oxford Tractarian Movement in England—an endeavor to revive Catholic principles in the church—appealed to the defeated High Church faction and encouraged them to mount a determined effort to regain their control of policy. The quarrel that ensued continued for decades.

The Protestant Reformation began in the German states in the early sixteenth century when Martin Luther systematically began challenging Roman Catholic doctrines. Lutherans were thus the first protesters to Catholic policies and practices. They came to America early **German Denominations in Pennsylvania** with seventeenth-century Dutch, German, and Scandinavian colonists, and in 1742, the first Lutheran synod was established. Ethnic and linguistic diversity characterized the faith, and the growing immigration of Lutherans after the American Revolution further diversified congregations during the early Republic on the basis of language alone.

The Reformed Church was also a part of the Reformation that swept the German states. The denomination first appeared in Pennsylvania and in 1793 assumed the official name of German Reformed Church.

Moravians were the American manifestation of a denomination founded in Saxony in 1727. Settling in Savannah in 1734, Moravians soon relocated to Pennsylvania and were quickly joined by other Moravian immigrants from Europe. Additional settlements were established in North Carolina near what is now Winston-Salem. Moravians were devoted to the notion of religious consistency and consequently closed their communities to outsiders until the middle of the nineteenth century. They were nonetheless enthusiastic missionaries to Indians and others seen as needing spiritual revelation, carrying their faith in the Bible as the exclusive guide to behavior. Moravians believed in infant baptism but accepted members upon a declaration of faith.

Mennonites derived from a splintering of Reformation denominations that had separated from more traditional elements over the issue of infant baptism. Their spiritual founder was the Dutch cleric Menno Simons, hence the name Mennonite. Rejecting baptism except upon voluntary declarations of faith, Mennonites were Anabaptists (or rebaptizers) whose primary spiritual guidance was based on the tenets from the Sermon on the Mount. They submitted to civil laws but would not breach their inherent belief in pacifism, their resistance to swearing oaths, or their aversion to participating in civic affairs. The most conservative elements of the faith eschewed modern conveniences and fashionable forms of dress. Their first American presence was in 1683 at Germantown, Pennsylvania, where they established a farming community. Swiss and Dutch immigrants swelled their numbers in the following years and included subsects of the faith, such as those following the Swiss Mennonite Jakob Amman, who were thus known as the Amish.

The Amish followed the teachings of their founder that stated control of the church required strict penalties for deviations from traditional doctrine and customs. The Amish consequently practiced social restraint by shunning the excommunicated. Shunning forbade all routine contacts with the wrongdoer, even sexual intimacy with a spouse who was under reprimand by the community. In keeping with their Mennonite heritage, the Amish embraced pacifism, kept neat farms isolated from outsiders, adhered to plain dress, and renounced modernism. Their concentrated numbers in Pennsylvania apparently originated the term "Pennsylvania Dutch," a misnomer because it was an American distortion of "Deutsch," meaning German.

The Church of United Brethren in Christ was an amalgam of Mennonite and earlier evangelical Protestant denominations. In 1800 a conference officially established the church in Frederick, Maryland, and 15 years later a General Conference amplified and refined its doctrines. Members embraced a form of Methodist Arminianism and performed baptisms only upon voluntary conversions.

Judaism   Jewish religious community life was established in North America when two dozen Sephardic Jews fled Brazil for the Dutch colonial city of New Amsterdam in 1654. When New Amsterdam became New York City in 1659 with the transfer of the colony to British colonial administration, the small Jewish community there enjoyed minor privileges that enhanced their religious identity and practices, such as the establishment of a separate Jewish cemetery. During the colonial period, Jewish numbers grew with the arrival of eastern European immigrants seeking to escape religious persecution and political maltreatment. These immigrants, known as Ashkenazim for their German and east European ancestry, settled in coastal towns such as New York, Philadelphia, Charleston, and Savannah, where they formed the bulk of the Jewish communities. The minority was the older, more established Sephardic Jews, sometimes called Portuguese Jews because of their Iberian roots. In addition to differing in social rank, these two congregations also differed over rituals of worship, a circumstance that continued beyond the colonial period into the early Republic. The result was a significant departure from some aspects of Jewish doctrine, such as the strict observance of the Sabbath, especially because the nature of exilic Judaism tended to congregational autonomy. In fact, under Jewish law, 10 adult males could form a congregation and appoint a rabbi whose only qualification might be a detailed knowledge of Jewish texts.

Jewish life in the early Republic resembled that of the colonial years. Working at traditional trades such as shop keeping, merchant trade and shipping, wig making, and gemstone cutting, they prospered as a small but industrious minority. Their numbers remained quite small—fewer than 3,000 Jews lived in the United States at the close of the American Revolution—and not until the 1820s did that situation begin to change. After the Napoleonic Wars, immigration from eastern Europe greatly increased the number of Ashkenazim in both coastal regions and the interior, so that by the 1840s, Jews were a noticeable presence as far west as the Mississippi River.

American Judaism did not remain a static theology during the early Republic. Time-honored and conventional practices such as obedience and loyalty to the Jewish community became less important in the politically free and economically dynamic American setting. Autonomous congregations became more responsive to the social wishes of their members and less likely to adhere strictly to traditional Jewish religious laws and customs. That is not to say that Jews were secularized by the American experience of the early Republic, but they did respond in predictably secular ways to the energetic social, political, and economic forces that described life in the United States during the first part of the nineteenth century.

Originating in England in the 1730s as an Anglican religious club at Oxford that "methodically" studied the scrip- **Methodists** tures, Methodists were in sufficient number in America to be noticed about 30 years later. Methodists accepted the doctrine of Dutch Calvinist Jacobus Arminius, which celebrated human free will as compatible with God's omnipotence. In essence by accepting Arminianism, Methodists rejected the strict Calvinist notion of predestination, the belief that God has already determined the fate of every soul on earth.

Beginning in 1769 and for the next few years, the celebrated Methodist preacher John Wesley dispatched a total of eight missionaries from England to spread the word, but their small numbers belied the influence they wielded. For one thing, the charismatic Francis Asbury, who would become the primary leader of Methodism in the United States until he died in 1816, was among them. Secondly, a homegrown group of ministers arose in Maryland and Virginia. Lacking ordination, they did not administer the sacraments, but some ordained Anglicans with evangelical inclinations admitted Methodist converts to their folds or administered the sacraments to them separately.

Of Wesley's British missionaries, Asbury alone remained during the Revolution, and after victory over Britain, Wesley's influence waned because he had supported the king. In the face of such American opposition, Wesley set aside petty issues of church governance to grant American congregations ecclesiastical autonomy, if not complete independence. Because no American Methodist preachers had been ordained and could not administer the sacraments, Wesley ordained two English preachers and sent them to America with plans to establish a superintendence of American Methodists that would have included the popular Asbury. Subtly attuned to the new American political climate, though, Asbury was disinclined to accept any role in church governance without the blessing of his preachers. The remarkable result of his reluctance was a conference in Baltimore during the Christmas season in 1784 in which the Methodist

Episcopal Church was formally established, complete with ordained preachers and protocols for service. The assemblage even adopted a hymnal. A publishing house, the Methodist Book Concern, was established in 1789 to produce religious pamphlets, books, and official tracts of the church.

During their work before the Revolution, Wesley's missionaries, including Asbury, had used the circuit system that had proved so effective in England, and its continuance during the 1790s was greatly responsible for the increase in Methodist numbers. By following a migrating population with the Methodist message of unencumbered grace and individual accountability, preachers won a phenomenal number of converts on the frontier during the Great Revival. By 1820, Methodist membership in America was more than 200,000, a rate of increase that continued for the next 30 years to nearly a million souls.

Presbyterians   American Presbyterians represented a mix of Scots Irish immigrants and New England Puritans. The first Presbyterian congregation was at Snow Hill on Maryland's Eastern Shore in 1684, and by the eighteenth century, the Philadelphia Presbytery had assumed leadership of the denomination, which was growing because of continuing Scots Irish immigration. Disaffected Congregationalists also swelled Presbyterian numbers, as they were attracted to inherent traditionalism, and like the Congregationalists, Presbyterians almost universally supported the American Revolution, further adding to their luster. In 1788 a central assembly took on the task of governing the faithful, and its organizing potential meant that Presbyterians would be poised to take advantage of the great religious surge of the revival movement at the beginning of the 1800s. The Plan of Union of 1801 formalized cooperation on the frontier between Presbyterians and Congregationalists, and many Congregationalists became Presbyterians, but as the years passed, the church was increasingly racked by dissension brought on in part by such converts resisting Presbyterian traditionalism.

Although they were to become a significant influence in shaping the culture of an expanding America, Presbyterians would not be as omnipresent on the frontier during the Great Revival as Baptists and Methodists. In part, their comparatively high educational standards meant that their ministers were in shorter supply. At first, ministers hailed mainly from New England (Aaron Burr's grandfather Jonathan Edwards and his father were examples), but the College of New Jersey (later Princeton) eventually supplied the bulk of the denomination's leaders, and Presbyterians would be tireless in establishing colleges to match the westward march of American migration.

Quakers   Officially called the Society of Friends, they were colloquially known as Quakers because they were said to have spasms as they underwent religious experiences. The Society of Friends originated in England during the mid-seventeenth century in response to the preaching of George Fox, whose message focused on the notion of an "inner light" in every person and the doctrine of Christ residing in all people. The Anglican establishment in England regarded Quakers as heretical, and they suffered severe persecution. They came to American shores early in the colonial period, but Puritan New England reflected Anglican suspicion about them and tried to persecute them out of existence with fines and floggings. When those measures failed, the Quakers were banished, but the persistence of the faith saw it taking hold nonetheless, and they were actually welcomed in some places such as Rhode Island and New Jersey. William Penn founded his colony of Pennsylvania as a refuge for persecuted Friends from all over Europe, and by the time of the early Republic, they were quite numerous and ethnically diverse. When Quakers ceased active proselytizing in the eighteenth century, systematic persecutions ended, but other denominations continued to regard them with suspicion, especially for their rigid pacifism, which prohibited them from serving in the military, and for their clannish discipline that enforced marriage exclusively within the faith. They were early advocates of humane and fair treatment for Indians and early proponents of antislavery. By 1787, not a single Quaker owned slaves. During the early Republic, Quakers participated in the great westward migrations that motivated the rest of the population, though they mainly moved into the Northwest Territory because of its ban on slavery.

Because they believed that God exists in everyone, Quakers stressed human decency and always strove to eliminate evil with sincerity, simplicity, honesty, and pacifism. Quaker shopkeepers and their customers did not haggle over prices, and they were noted for their use of "plain speech" that substituted "thee" and "thou" for what they regarded as the formal pronoun "you." They observed equality between the sexes in worship and accepted anyone into their faith who indicated willingness to acknowledge its tenets and fulfill its obligations. Quakers worshipped in unstructured and unprogrammed "meetings" that assembled the faithful at least once and sometimes twice a week in plainly constructed and unadorned meetinghouses. They sat quietly unless members were moved to speak, offering themselves as witnesses by sharing religious thoughts and experiences for the group to discuss freely.

A splinter group from the Society of Friends was the United Society of Believers in Christ's Second Coming, which had formed in the mid-eighteenth century in England. They were known at first as Shaking Quakers and later simply as Shakers. The first Shaker community in the United States was established in New York at Watervliet in 1776. Because Shakers were celibate even in marriage, they did not naturally increase their number, and the sect grew only by attracting converts. During the early Republic, it eventually numbered almost 20 communities of about 6,000 members. Shakers owned property in common and were noted for their exquisite but simple craftsmanship, which produced a distinctive style of furniture. Shaker hymns were equally simple, but they were also lyrical celebrations of uncomplicated pleasures, such as "Simple Gifts," which the twentieth-century American composer Aaron Copland wove into several of his most famous compositions.

Another Protestant sect similar to the Quakers formed in Germany under the leadership of religious reformer George Rapp. In 1803 persecution by Lutherans forced the sect to move to Pennsylvania, where they founded the town of Harmony. They were called Harmonists and have usually been identified as the Harmony Society. Like Shakers, they practiced strict simplicity, owned all property in common, and strove for celibate marriages. In 1815 most Harmonists moved to Indiana and founded the town of New Harmony, but their new location proved a harsh and uninviting spot for many members, who either left the faith or trudged back to Pennsylvania after selling their property to Robert Owen, who had plans to establish his own utopian community there.

Unitarians   Unitarianism grew out of theological challenges during the Reformation that questioned Roman Catholic doctrines, especially that of the Holy Trinity, the belief that God exists as one being in three entities: the Father, the Son, and the Holy Spirit. Unitarians, however, regarded the Trinity as negating the fundamental Judeo-Christian belief in monotheism and insisted instead that God existed in only one entity. In old Europe, even other Protestants regarded Unitarians as highly heretical because they essentially denied the divinity of Christ. For a time, they were able to exist only in Poland and Transylvania, but eventually Unitarian émigrés carried their beliefs westward, sometimes suffering martyrdom as they did so. Not until 1813 did they gain any kind of recognition as a viable faith in Britain.

The origin of American Unitarianism defies a simple explanation. In essence, the Puritan congregations of old New England underwent a profound transformation in the first two decades of the nineteenth century. A moderate body of Liberal Christians became Unitarian Congregationalists, as contrasted with traditionalists who remained Trinitarians. The split basically resulted from the dissent of certain Congregationalist clergymen in New England who rejected Calvinist doctrines that had formed the core of the Great Awakening. Those doctrines included absolute predestination and original sin (the concept that man is naturally depraved). Instead, Unitarians insisted that God was compassionate rather than angry and that man had a free will to choose righteousness over iniquity. A formal break occurred in 1796 when Boston's King's Chapel seceded from the Protestant Episcopal Church and officially embraced Unitarianism, and during the years that followed, additional New England congregations became essentially Unitarian in belief and practice, if not formally in name. Finally in 1819, the influential Congregational minister William Ellery Channing delivered a sermon entitled "Unitarian Christianity" that gave formal voice to the fundamental philosophy of Unitarianism, and that date is usually taken as the birth of organized Unitarianism. Rather than adhering to a specific doctrine or dogma, Unitarians believed in rational thought and individual ethics as the basis for their conviction and also believed that revelation was not an event but a continuing process that made religious learning a lifelong process.

Another religious belief that ran a parallel course to Unitarianism was Universalism, also a movement born of opposition to the notions of inherent human wickedness and predestination. In 1790 three disparate groups representing these thoughts met in Philadelphia and formed the Universalist church. The congregation remained small, however, and was mainly extant in New York and eventually some portions of the Midwest.

REVIVALISM

One of the most profound episodes in the early Republic centered on the religious revival called the Second Great Awakening. Its impact on daily routines for a considerable number of Americans was as immeasurable as it was intense. In some respects, it was also a brief interlude of heightened religiosity in an increasingly secular social, political, and economic environment. The expanding religious sentiment that began swelling in the 1790s and resulted in a sustained burst of revivalism at the turn of the nineteenth century, however, is a vital part of the story of those Americans.

Even during the colonial period, the broad geographic expanse and irregular establishment of American colonies brought about a growing variety in religious faiths. A level of tolerance was necessary merely to keep the civil peace even in the face of the established Church of England, but such forbearance might actually have been a reflection of religious indifference. By the beginning of the eighteenth century, time and distance had lessened the Old World's religious hold on distant flocks, no matter what their faith. An effort to renew flagging religious fervor was in part responsible for a revival movement in the 1730s and 1740s that is popularly called the Great Awakening. Revivals not only sought to reanimate the faithful but also endeavored to win new converts. Glimmerings of this development were seen in New Jersey's Dutch Reformed Church as early as the 1720s, but the movement took flight in New England in the 1730s when Jonathan Edwards delivered a series of fervent, vivid sermons that convinced listeners that they were indeed "sinners in the hands of an angry God."[11] Spurred by the equally moving addresses of George Whitefield, who took his message on the road, the Great Awakening continued into the 1740s, gaining converts and finally kindling dissent, the latter among those who objected to the absolute statement of Calvinist doctrines such as predestination and original sin. Nonetheless, the Great Awakening soon broke regional boundaries to spread southward and breathe life into Presbyterians, Baptists, and, by the American Revolution, Methodists as well.

Origins

The Great Awakening did more than enlarge church congregations of the various Protestant denominations. It also served to counter the rationalism of Enlightenment philosophy, which was essentially unreceptive to notions of revealed religion. Nonetheless, the appeal of rationalism, evidenced by the lure of Deism among American intellectuals, did work to dampen religious fervor in the latter part of the eighteenth century. The constitutional prohibitions on a state church also seem to have diminished the influence of the organized churches. Finally, the westward migration of the American population following the Revolution put into play the same geographical factors of distance that had earlier loosened the ties between colonial populations and Old World churches. Organized religion in the eastern United States saw its influence waning among pioneers.

The Second Great Awakening   Church leaders responded to this development by renewing the revivalism that had proved so successful in the Great Awakening. Beginning in New England, the Second Great Awakening got under way in the 1790s as devotees of Jonathan Edwards sought to overcome the appeal of Deism, what some called the " 'French infidelity' that was threatening to sweep away every vestige of Christianity."[12] Occurring within customary church ceremonies, the eastern revival effectively invigorated church attendance and encouraged missionaries to travel abroad as well as to scattered pioneer communities on the American frontier. Nobody, however, was prepared for what happened in sparsely populated frontier regions. The Second Great Awakening in the western American wilderness was to become the Great Revival.

The western manifestation of revivalism was intensely emotional, broadly interdenominational, and exceptionally infectious. By 1799, Presbyterian, Baptist, and Methodist ministers were riding circuits throughout the frontier to inspire the faithful and convert the unchurched. The western wilderness did not appear a promising vineyard for the Lord's work, and its tough, profane, hard-drinking denizens might reasonably have been judged as beyond salvation. Yet initial sermons—passionate orations delivered in crude log buildings serving as unembellished churches—began drawing folks from all over, especially after word spread about the extraordinary physical reactions among attendees. Some observers then and now have attributed the attraction of these services to the irresistible desire of lonely pioneers to seek out social occasions, whatever their purpose. Leaving aside speculations about their motivation, the number of people attending the sermons grew so steadily that they finally resorted to congregating at large camp meetings, an old idea that found new life as remarkable things began to happen. Organized as multidenominational events in Kentucky by ministers such as Presbyterians James McGready and Barton W. Stone, camp meetings rapidly spread as a method of religious revivalism. They took place in woods and clearings, usually near streams that provided water, and attracted settlers from both near and far, some traveling for days to the event and remaining for days to hear preachers exhort the faithful, extol the blessed, condemn the profligate, and save the willing. Services occurred virtually nonstop, several preachers bellowing at the same time just out of earshot of each other. Darkness did not stop them, and only the flicker of bonfires and pine resin torches broke the otherwise impenetrable night of the deep woods. Some of the men drank liquor, of course, and the doings of some young men and women in distant shadows were decidedly more physical than spiritual. Yet even cynics who came to scoff at these events were often swept up in the contagion of them. The swaying crowds, the fatigue caused by long travel and little sleep, the eerie shadows thrown by the fires and guttering torches made for an evocative scene. Pioneers were not used to crowds, and they were certainly not accustomed to late nights. Sooner or later, for reasons that are not at all clear, something would snap, and the tension of the meeting would erupt into frightening, bizarre displays of emotionalism. Burly men sobbed uncontrollably, women barked like dogs, children rolled violently on the ground; people broke into frenzied dances, spasmodically jerked their arms and legs, and spoke in unintelligible tongues. Some even injured themselves in free "falling exercises" or banged their bloodied heads against trees.

In 1801, Barton Stone was the moving force behind the most stunning camp meeting revival of the period. It took place in the second week of August in Bourbon County, Kentucky, at a place called Cane Ridge, some seven miles from the community of Paris. The event attracted a phenomenal number of people. By some estimates, as many as 20,000 souls came to Cane Ridge, and there were possibly more who drifted in and out over the course of the meeting, making it briefly one the most populated places in the United States. "From Friday until the following Thursday, night and day without intermission," there were people "engaged in some religious act of worship."[13] Generating a sound like Niagara Falls, the crowd shouted, barked, and jerked for six days while listening to continuous sermons, sometimes as many as seven occurring at once. On occasion, hundreds of people were simultaneously struck by the falling exercise, dropping to the ground as though felled by artillery, "like men slain in a mighty battle."[14] They rose up, though, and, after it was over, continued to feel the intense glow of the experience, enlarging Methodist, Baptist, and Presbyterian congregations or forming new sects such as the Christian Church or the Disciples of Christ. Some joined the Shakers.

The growth of evangelical denominations such as the Baptists and Methodists, actually to outstrip older groups like the Congregationalists and Episcopalians, was instrumental in the growing democratization of society and politics at the close of the early Republic and the start of the Jacksonian period. The years after 1820 saw emotional revivals spread eastward, and upstate New York experienced such an extended period of religious commotion that it was dubbed the "Burned-Over District" and became the seedbed for new faiths such as the Latter Day Saints, popularly known as Mormons, and Adventists, who believed in the looming end of the world to coincide with the return of Christ. By then, the revival was firmly embedded in the practices and rituals of American evangelism, a fact forged by the astonishing and unexpected events that had swept across the frontier in the first years of the century.

WORSHIP

Urban churches during the colonial period essentially copied the architectural designs prevailing in England, and those structures naturally remained in place after the Revolution. New construction in the years that followed, however, consciously sought to break with British influences and establish a unique American style. The period's general architecture is often called Federalist, to match the dominant political culture of the day, and though it bore distinctive American characteristics, it was actually derivative of Georgian architecture then dominant in England. Church architecture thus mirrored this trend, and not until the later decades of the nineteenth century did it become a distinctive American style with the appearance of neo-Gothic designs.

In new settlements on the frontier and in established but remote rural areas, church construction tended to be quite simple and often produced nothing more than a log meetinghouse with crude benches and a plain raised platform for the preacher. Sometimes, the "church" was simply a clearing where wagons could be drawn so that their occupants could listen to a sermon delivered from a tree stump.

Sermons and Services   In established eastern churches, the patterns of worship were staid and traditional. Christian church services took place on Sundays, and the congregation was expected to dress formally for the event. Even the lower classes reserved special clothes, nicer than ordinary attire, to wear while attending worship services. In the early years of the period, indigent or unsupervised children might be rounded up in certain cities to attend Sunday schools, a facet of church life that went through distinct phases, as discussed later in this chapter.

The eastern Protestant denominations had always been intellectual centers and continued to be during the early Republic. In 1800, Congregationalists and Presbyterians still held considerable sway with about half the congregations in the entire country and with a long tradition of establishing colleges to educate their clergy. College-educated ministers sermonized weekly on both spiritual and temporal matters and did not hesitate to illuminate current events with the light of religious thought. In Congregational and Presbyterian churches, that thought centered on the belief that Adam in the garden had damned all men and women with his original sin, the Passion of Christ had atoned for mankind's sins, and only the elect who had been "born again" would see Heaven, regardless of their good works or adherence to the sacraments.

On the frontier, traditional and established denominations encountered a different environment of worldly concerns. **Frontier** Toughened pioneers rejected church hierarchies just as **Methodism** ardently as they scorned political ones. Formal modes of worship in fancy clothes were unlikely, and the intellectualism of refined eastern pulpits was regarded as both irrelevant and pretentious. Instead, most pioneers relied on the circuit rider, frequently a Methodist minister instantly recognizable by his clothing: a broad-brimmed hat, prominent collar, and dusty, long coat. He rode a circuit that covered a hundred miles to visit remote cabins and preach the Bible through John Wesley's explanations. His scattered flock accepted him precisely because he had not been to college. Instead, he was an alumnus of the school of hard knocks, steeped in useful, relevant knowledge about life rather than esoteric theories from books, and as familiar with every tree and brook on his journey as he was with the people who eagerly awaited his arrival. In spite of its simple trappings and the unpredictability imposed by a wilderness setting, circuit riding was neither disorganized nor haphazard. The preacher rode his circuit for four years, during which he held services every single day, two on Saturdays and Sundays, and was expected to be on time for them with clocklike reliability. His sermons were not the sober, contemplative discourses of eastern churches but were stirring declamations in ordinary language that vividly portrayed the horrors of damnation and the splendors of deliverance.[15]

More informal than even the Methodists, the Baptist frontier preacher was frequently a local resident whose qualification for **Frontier** the pulpit was simply "the call" from the Lord. That condition **Baptists** made him competent in the eyes of his church to spread the Gospel after the Council of Brethren had duly assessed him and had conferred ordination through prayer. These farmer-preachers continued to till, sow, and harvest their fields because they received no salary from the church. They could move with congregations or, wanting one, seek it out in unchurched regions. They posed no financial burden on the church, and their guidance from regional associations was minimal.

Baptists primarily differed with Methodists about total immersion in baptism, but the frontier also saw lively theological debates over issues such as predestination, free will, and original sin. Methodist circuit riders occasionally conducted services for Baptist congregations, but Baptists remained vigilant against the chance that such intermittent contact with believers in "infant sprinkling" did not contaminate their congregations.[16]

The goal of salvation was central to the cycle of birth, life, and death in the Judeo-Christian culture of the early Repub- **Living** lic. Adhering to the early Roman Catholic belief that only the **and Dying** baptized were in the community of Christendom and that even innocent souls dying unbaptized could not enter Heaven, infant baptism was the custom of Roman Catholics and most Protestant churches.[17] For Protestants, however, it was more a ceremony establishing the covenant between the individual and God than a ritual relating to sin and salvation. In the Protestant church, Baptists were unique in rejecting infant baptism, holding to the belief that it derived from no biblical authority. Further, Baptists insisted that only adults could be guilty of sin and only adults could understand the significance of the baptismal experience. Baptists also refused to baptize by affusion (sprinkling water) but insisted on total immersion to emulate the experience of Jesus at the hands of John the Baptist.

Explaining death and instilling confidence that it impinges only on the body, not the soul, is a key function of all theologies. Funeral practices are intimately tied to religious beliefs about the meaning of life and the reality of an afterlife and as rituals serve a vital psychological purpose for the bereaved. Dressing and preparing the corpse, offering the opportunity to family and friends to view the remains, holding a wake, participating in processions, crafting eulogies, joining in prayer, and tolling church bells were ways to celebrate life as much as mourn death. As we have seen, for Americans in the early Republic, death from accident and especially from disease was a pervasive likelihood, and the commemoration of life with assurance of salvation was a central part of their daily lives.

CHARITY

The birth of new denominations and the strengthening of others was not the only feature of the Second Great Awakening, for within this increased variation of faith there was also a reaffirmed commonality of basic theology that eroded differences in the Protestant community. Unlike the original Great Awakening, which had focused on fixing belief in predestination and human corruption, the Second Great Awakening preached a message of universal deliverance and the essential goodness of people as demonstrated in their good works. The buoyant idea encouraged missionary work, educational endeavors, and reform movements that campaigned for temperance and against vices such as gambling.

Although working outside the home was socially unacceptable for married mothers, charity work offered women an outlet because such activity was seen to complement their role as nurturers. Just as women tended to be more prone to conversion experiences during the Second Great Awakening and tended to outnumber men at camp meetings and church services, so they took the lead in organizing church projects to aid the poor, such as collecting and distributing food and clothing. They were also responsible in the early nineteenth century for establishing the first Sunday schools, institutions designed to teach poor children how to read and write through religious instruction. In charity work, women performed as "republican mothers" for those women who were too poor or ignorant to take on that role themselves.

The American Board of Commissioners for Foreign Missions was founded by the Congregationalists in 1810 and attracted the backing of Presbyterians as well. Nondenominational groups included the American Education Society, founded in 1815, and the American Sunday School Union, founded in 1817, that formed the basis for a network of generous charitable institutions that crossed religious lines by including a variety of religious leaders. Beginning in 1816, the American Bible Society undertook the task of providing translations of the Bible to all peoples of the world, frequently at no cost and always unadorned by commentary.

The pervasive problem of inebriation was an early target of reform. As a result of custom and to take the edge off daily **Temperance** routines that were both demanding and tedious, American men and women drank spirits as a matter of course. Festive events such as weddings and somber ones like funerals saw excessive drinking and sometimes devolved into fracases. The aftereffects of strong drink kept workers at home on Fridays and Mondays, and drunken fathers were apt to mistreat their children and abuse their wives. In what would amount to a long campaign against hard liquor, temperance societies sprang up in New York in 1808, Massachusetts in 1813, and Connecticut in 1813, leading to the formation in 1826 of the American Society for the Promotion of Temperance in Boston, which a decade later had a million members on its rolls. Frequently led by women, these moral reform movements helped to elevate their status as social and moral arbiters.

First established in the United States in the 1790s, Sunday schools emulated British efforts to expose impoverished child **Sunday** workers to a basic education, using the only day free of labor **Schools** those children enjoyed. In America, such schools began appearing in larger eastern cities and emergent factory towns, especially in New England, where children received Bible-based instruction in the three Rs of reading, writing, and 'rithmetic. At its outset, the enterprise was unique in that it broke with a tradition of spiritual instruction for children that emphasized religion over attaining even rudimentary skills, a practice that dated from colonial times. Instead, early Sunday schools focused on literacy as much as spiritual teaching, convinced that good citizenship depended on turning children into educated adults. Before the appearance of these Sunday schools, unsupervised children tended to gather on Sundays to engage in raucous play that frequently led to mischief. Sensing a developing social problem, education-minded reformers established Sunday schools both to take these rowdy children off the streets and to impart to them at least some proficiency in reading and writing. In this form, the Sunday school enjoyed a mixed success at best, and had it not been transformed by the advent of revivalism, the institution might not have survived its early structure and purpose. In addition, the beginning

of public schools that functioned as regular weekday educational institutions reduced and ultimately eliminated the need for Sunday schools in
that role.

Under the influence of the Second Great Awakening and the sustained
evangelical zeal it inspired, the concept of Sunday schools gradually
changed in the first years of the nineteenth century to make them primarily a tool of religious instruction. Correspondingly, the rapid expansion of
these schools led the evangelical movement to formalize them as an integral part of Protestant religious custom, adapting the content of lessons as
well as pedagogy to the renewed importance of spiritual development. In
this fashion, the Sunday school became an extension of church activity
rather than a philanthropic gesture to promote primary education. And in
that regard, the Sunday school became a melding of charitable impulse
and evangelical purpose, a design both to uplift the children of the church
and to sustain them as Christian citizens of a virtuous republic.

Colleges
Continuing the colonial tradition, higher education was intimately tied to religion during the period, and the Second Great
Awakening encouraged in ensuing years the establishment of
denominationally sponsored liberal arts colleges throughout the South
and West. Their primary function was to educate young men for the min-
istry, and their curricula replicated the traditional course of study to that
purpose. Latin, Greek, mathematics, and moral philosophy not only
formed the curricular core; those studies frequently formed the whole of
the educational experience at these new, rough outposts of learning.

In the East, however, many of the universities that had been founded
during the colonial period as training grounds for clergy from various
denominations moved away from church sponsorship and instead
became schools where wealthy young men could acquire some finish.
These developments shocked and dismayed the clergy, who worried that
young college men no longer "made any pretensions to piety," and that in
these universities "the name of God is blasphemed, the Bible denounced,
the Sabbath profaned, the public worship of God is neglected."[18] Still,
American belief that knowledge and virtue were tied together kept colleges and universities at the top of many people's list for charitable giving.

CONCLUSION: THE PERFECTIBLE WORLD

The early Republic was a time of flourishing reform movements and the
roots of more to come. Efforts to advance women's rights, the invention of
so-called miracle cures and treatments, the introduction of communal living, and the practice of polygamy or celibacy were all foreshadowed or
actually appeared during these turbulent years. Societies against drinking
alcohol, smoking or chewing tobacco, uttering profanity, and delivering
Sunday mail either were in formation or were established. The long strug-

gle against slavery began uncertainly and quietly among certain religious denominations that the mainstream regarded as "odd," but it began.

Most reformers were gifted optimists who thoroughly believed in a perfectible world, and the legions of Americans who enlisted in their movements were idealistic and compassionate. Even those Americans who were not particularly religious, such as Thomas Jefferson, believed that "no definite limits could be assigned to the improveability of the human race."[19] The influence of the evangelical movement inspired by the Second Great Awakening was central to the renewal of a vision nurtured by colonial Puritans. Those forebears wanted a world emancipated from the malice of petty men, the mayhem of war, the blight of whiskey, the shackles of poverty. Americans of the early Republic strove just as valiantly to liberate their world as well, with women frequently in the vanguard of the effort and thus working to change, however gradually, their place in public enterprises.

Faith and charity were the twin bulwarks that could confirm and endorse established values amid a world rapidly transforming itself from the simpler ways of agricultural communities and artisan workshops into a market economy and the industrial age. Factories and their workers were still too scattered and novel to merit much notice, but that condition was swiftly changing as well. The coming years would test faith and strain charity, but both proved resilient and durable, thanks in part to the early Republic's burst of religious conviction in the western wilderness and the eastern cathedral. Americans' innate belief that the world could be made better, that God had chosen them for the task, and that they therefore had a duty to fulfill their destiny proved as enduring as the Puritan vision of the fabled City on the Hill, an article of unshakable faith renewed in these early years that would prepare Americans and their heirs to weather many tumults ahead.

NOTES

1. John R. Bodo, *The Protestant Clergy and Public Issues, 1812–1848* (Princeton: Princeton University Press, 1954), 7.

2. Steven E. Kagle, *Early Nineteenth-Century American Diary Literature* (Boston: Twayne Publishers, 1986), 11.

3. Russel Blaine Nye, *The Cultural Life of the New Nation, 1776–1830* (New York: Harper Torchbooks, 1960), 30.

4. Ibid., 196.

5. James D. Richardson, *A Compilation of the Messages and Papers of the Presidents, 1789–1897*, vol. 1 (Washington, D.C.: Government Printing Office, 1896–1899), 489.

6. John Mayfield, *The New Nation, 1800–1845*, rev. ed. (New York: Hill and Wang, 1986), 13.

7. The fate of the Latter Day Saints, or Mormons, in various eastern communities during the 1820s and 1830s is the exception that proves this rule.

8. William Cobbett is quoted in William R. Hutchison, *Religious Pluralism in America: The Contentious History of a Founding Ideal* (New Haven: Yale University Press, 2003), 14.

9. Saint Elizabeth Ann Seton was canonized in 1975.

10. The Congregationalists would eventually reject the Plan of Union and in 1832 form the American Congregational Union.

11. This was the title of one of Edwards's most famous sermons. Its tone, indicated by the title, was nothing short of frightening. "O sinner!" Edwards declaimed. "Consider the fearful danger you are in: it is a great furnace of wrath, a wide and bottomless pit, full of the fire of wrath, that you are held over in the hand of that God, whose wrath is provoked and incensed as much against you, as against many of the damned in hell." The entire sermon can be found in Jonathan Edwards, *Works of President Edwards*, vol. 4 (New York: Leavitt, Trow, 1844), 313–21.

12. Nye, *Cultural Life*, 213.

13. Ibid., 218.

14. The description is Peter Cartwright's in Cartwright and W. Strickland, *Autobiography of Peter Cartwright: The Backwoods Preacher* (New York: Carlton and Porter, 1856), 38. Also see Richard McNemar, *The Kentucky Revival, or, A Short History of the Late Extraordinary Out-Pouring of the Spirit of God, in the Western States of America, Agreeably to Scripture Promises, and Prophecies concerning the Latter Day: With a Brief Account of the Entrance and Progress of What the World Call Shakerism, among the Subjects of the Late Revival in Ohio and Kentucky. Presented to the True Zion-Traveller, as a Memorial of the Wilderness Journey* (Albany, N.Y.: E. E. Hosford, 1808), 25.

15. James MacGregor Burns, *The Vineyard of Liberty* (New York: Knopf, 1982), 494–501, provides a colorful description of frontier religion.

16. The phrase appears in an anecdote about Methodist minister Peter Cartwright recounted in Sydney E. Alhstrom, *A Religious History of the American People* (New Haven: Yale University Press, 1972), 444.

17. The evolution of Catholic doctrine on baptism is complex. Before A.D. 500, the belief that the absolution of postbaptismal sins could be accomplished only once encouraged the delay of baptism as long as possible. After the 500s, however, the development of penitential procedures through confession made postbaptismal sins less alarming, and the earliest possible (infant) baptism became an imperative.

18. Nye, *Cultural Life*, 205.

19. Ibid., 30.

7

BEYOND THE MAINSTREAM

Many people during the early Republic lived differently from ordinary Americans. In most cases, as when cultural differences dictated a different lifestyle, they did so by choice. Indians, immigrants from other countries, and pioneers who chose to leave established settlements for the wilderness are examples of those who deliberately took paths that diverged from the conventional. In other instances, however, people fell out of the mainstream involuntarily. African American slaves especially exhibit that unfortunate circumstance. Criminals obviously chose the way of misfit, but society leveled compulsory punishments that ranged from incarceration to death. In short, a significant number of Americans lived differently from their fellow countrymen, attesting to the fact that long before it was fashionable to admonish it to be, America was a place of diversity.

INDIANS

Most Indians east of the Mississippi River during the early Republic lived in permanent towns and villages where daily routines stemmed from a primarily sedentary, agricultural existence. Considerable intermarriage between Indian women and white traders did not change the fact that most Indians still lived apart from European American communities. Yet frequent contact with white society, especially through trade, changed Indian culture in the years following the early colonial period. White trade goods such as cloth, metal pots, hatchets, hoe blades, and guns lessened the effort necessary to produce food and sustain shelter, but they also created a creeping dependency. Each generation suffered a gradual erosion of basic knowledge about how to make the items essential to sustain their culture. White society eventually possessed the means through dependence to force ever larger land cessions from Indian tribes. Daily life became easier in some ways, but the heritage of Indian existence as marked in their birthright of land steadily diminished. To many Indians, the land was their "life and breath."[1]

Farming and Hunting   Despite their use of labor-saving devices and manufactured goods, most Indian cultures persistently clung to their customs. While they produced most of their food by farming, their agricultural techniques remained the same as before contact with Europeans. For instance, women did most Indian farming, with the exception of clearing fields. In Iroquois, Creek, and Cherokee cultures, women owned their fields and passed them down to their daughters, reflecting the matrilineal structure of most Indian cultures. (Lodgings also belonged to women.) In the spring, the women of a town spent most of their time preparing the fields and planting the season's crops with seeds saved from the previous year's harvest. Although some crops were exclusive to different regions, corn was the mainstay of virtually all Indian nutrition. Various beans, squash, and pumpkins supplemented their diets. Women spent much of the growing season tending their plants while minding children, keeping house, making clothes, and preparing food. In the fall, they worked together to bring in the harvest and preserve food for the winter. Corn was parched to be eaten later or to be pounded into meal for bread or mush. Beans were dried.

Men spent much of their time in activities that largely centered on providing food as well. Indians acquired most meat by hunting, and animal hides and furs served as the primary goods to barter with whites for manufactured items. To supply their towns with meat as well as an adequate number of hides to trade with whites, Indian men often had to range great distances from home. The most important long-distance hunts occurred in the fall and winter for southern Indians and in the late summer or early fall for northern tribes. By the period of the early Republic, untrammeled hunting had depleted many traditional Indian hunting grounds of game, particularly of deer, whose skins were a prized trading article with whites. Federal Creek agent Benjamin Hawkins reported in 1799 that some hunters "have returned from hunting without any skins and I have heard from one town who have not killed fifty."[2] Declining resources and far-ranging hunting parties made for conflict with other Indian tribes who were vying for the same food supplies, and sometimes the result could mean war. Moreover, dwindling resources meant that by the early nineteenth century, Indians were finding it increasingly difficult to support their families. Southern Indians, particularly the Creeks and Seminoles, sought to ease the problem of decreasing game by adopting white cattle-herding practices with European breeds. The temperate climate and large expanses of open land favored such husbandry, and these Indians became particularly adept at raising cattle. Tending herds became one of the primary responsibilities of a town's men and boys.

In addition to hunting and husbandry, men might help wives and daughters prepare fields for planting, especially if clearing **Games** were necessary. Otherwise, they built the town's buildings, carried out heavy repairs, sat in governing councils, and served as warriors in times of conflict. Among the Creeks, a particularly numerous linguistic group, warriors often outnumbered the standing army of the United States. To hone war-making skills, Indian boys and men spent much time playing violent ball games. In existence long before Europeans arrived in America, these extremely rigorous games served as important rituals as well as practical exercises. In the North among the Iroquois, the game was the predecessor of modern lacrosse. It was played primarily during the harvest season. A team of approximately 15 to 20 members, each wielding a staff with a small basket at the end, tried to deposit a deerskin ball in a goal guarded by the opponent. The contest featured a good deal of physical contact, including the use of the sticks as cudgels.

In the South, Creeks and Cherokees played a similar game. A match between two towns included large wagers that could make or break a town's economy for the coming year. Perhaps more important than material considerations, a town's honor and prestige often rested on the outcome of a match. The night before the game was filled with religious ceremonies and dancing that resembled rites preceding a war. In the Creek and Cherokee ball game—"stickball," as it was called by whites—two posts made of stripped trees sat about 10 feet apart at each end of a three- to four-acre field. Teams tried to knock a small deerskin ball through these goals. Players carried two sticks similar to those used by Iroquois but shorter, with small leather baskets on the ends to catch the ball. As in the Iroquois game, the sticks were also used as clubs. The ball carrier ran it down the field to toss through the goalposts while opposing players could use any tactic to stop him and his teammates. Injuries abounded during a typical contest, which ended only when a team scored 12 goals. For evenly matched teams, a game could take all day. Most Indian groups staged these ritual ball games between towns of the same tribe or confederation, though there were instances of Creek towns challenging Cherokee towns. Within a particular confederation, such as the Creeks', contests determined status for individual warriors and their towns.

The importance of its clans and its place within the governing structure of the confederation primarily established a **Matrilineal** town's status. Within the town, the clan determined a per- **Clans** son's place in everything from social status to marital opportunities. Matrilineal societies sustained clans through their females. Property such as houses or fields descended to daughters from the mother, and though rank for males and females was a function of her standing, the actual practices attendant to matrilineal descent could be quite complicated. For example, a male's inherited titles or positions came from his mother's side of the family. That meant that his standing came from his maternal uncles rather than from his father. Correspondingly, important positions held by his father came to him through his father's mother and were passed on to his father's sisters' sons. Once a boy came of age and began his training for hunting and as a warrior, maternal uncles conducted much of his education. Girls, whether in a matrilineal or patriarchal structure, learned at the hands of their mothers.

Towns When not tending crops, most girls and their mothers spent their time in the town. Indian towns east of the Mississippi River were situated near flowing bodies of water on defensible ground. Many had been in the same location for decades or even centuries by the time of the early Republic. Beyond this generality, all similarities from region to region ended. The architecture and layout of Indian towns varied not only for different locales but for different tribes as well. In the North, the six nations of the Iroquois (the Oneida, Cayuga, Seneca, Onondaga, Mohawk, and Tuscarora) typically constructed fortified towns surrounded by log palisades. Iroquois men built platforms behind the palisades for defenders to stand on while shooting attackers. By the early Republic, Iroquois numbers within the United States were greatly diminished, a result of many Iroquois siding with the British during the Revolutionary War. Those who had not fled to Canada still clung to traditional ways, however, including the plans of their towns and the style of buildings in them. Some Iroquois who had married whites or lived near them began to build houses much like those of their white neighbors, but those of the old towns continued to construct the traditional building called the longhouse. These structures, sometimes as much as 100 feet long, consisted of a long central hall from which numerous rooms extended that served as living quarters for individual families. Each town also had storage buildings for food and other essentials and a large meeting hall for important gatherings and celebrations.

In the South, extended families of the Creeks, Cherokees, Seminoles, Chickasaws, and Choctaws—groups that whites had dubbed the Five Civilized Tribes—lived in individual wattle and daub houses. These structures were framed with small trees and limbs and covered with mud or clay mixed with straw (daub). By the early Republic, many southern Indians had begun building log cabins and framed houses with mud or stone chimneys. The changing architecture did not, however, alter their traditional ceremonies and festivities, including the placing of a ceremonial structure in the center of town.

Similar to all cultures, Native American society revolved around rituals and ceremonies. Because the town's survival depended on a good yield of crops, the most important festival coincided with the earliest harvest. For Creeks, this was the Green Corn Ceremony, aptly named because it occurred when the earliest corn was ready for collecting. In honor of this significant event, the town was thoroughly cleaned, and a new fire was started in its ceremonial center. The town then enjoyed a week of celebrations and games. In anticipation of a celebratory banquet, people not only fasted but also purified their bodies by taking a powerful emetic known as the Black Drink. Thus cleansed, the people of the town shared a grand feast.

Like people of all cultures, Indians conducted particular rituals attendant to the death of any of their members. Some groups, like the Creeks, buried their dead, though generally in a sitting rather than prone position, and usually put items with the body that the person had owned in life. Perhaps the Choctaws had some of the most elaborate death rituals. The deceased was placed on a platform in the open for a number of days until the flesh was "putrid, so as easily to part from the bones." A group of specially trained Choctaws then stripped the flesh from the bones, which were then "deposited in the bone-house."[3] When the bone-house was full, relatives of the dead took its contents out of the village and in a solemn ceremony covered the bones over with dirt, creating an earthen mound.

During the early Republic, Indians east of the Mississippi witnessed profound and troubling changes that would have a direct impact on their daily lives. The end of the American Revolution removed British-imposed restrictions on western **Troubled People** migrations of whites, and settlers poured into the regions that would become the new states of Kentucky, Tennessee, and Ohio. As these pioneers encroached on Indian lands, trespassed on Indian cornfields, and killed game in Indian hunting grounds, Indians retaliated. The years between the American Revolution and the War of 1812 saw wars on the frontier between settlers and Indians that gradually changed everything for the land's original inhabitants. Some Native Americans in both the North and South deemed that Indian unity might stem the seemingly endless and irresistible tide of white settlement, and they sought to strengthen existing confederations or organize new and more broadly conceived ones. Creeks in the South and the great Shawnee warrior Tecumseh in the North were the most determined, but ultimately both were defeated. Tecumseh fell in the War of 1812, and the Creeks suffered a crushing loss to Major General Andrew Jackson, who forced them to sign the Treaty of Fort Jackson, a coercive arrangement that ceded 23 million acres of their land to the United States. The wholesale defeat of Indians during the War of 1812, in fact, opened the floodgates to white settlement in the West while providing the government with the way to separate Native Americans from their lands. The result was the removal policy that relocated most eastern Indians to areas west of the Mississippi during the 1830s.

AFRICAN AMERICAN SLAVES

Spreading migrations that expanded tobacco and cotton increased the demand for slavery while changing its demographics. Under provisions agreed to at the constitutional convention of 1787, the foreign slave trade was outlawed in 1808. Thereafter an increasing need for slaves was met partly through natural increase, but also through an illegal trade. Between 1808 and 1820, probably more than 15,000 slaves were smuggled into the South. Meanwhile a domestic slave trade transferred slaves from plantations in declining agricultural areas of the East to sell them to the newly settled, burgeoning plantations of the Old Southwest. Under the demand of these labor-hungry regions, the price of slaves rose steadily during the period, particularly for young and healthy men. In 1800 a young black man's average price was about $500; 20 years later, that price had doubled. Almost everyone regarded the slave trader with contempt, but his activity was abided nonetheless. It was a disagreeable necessity, went the reasoning among those in the East who had more slaves than their limited or depleted lands needed. Although most states had laws prohibiting the sale of young children from slave mothers, they were seldom enforced, and there were never any laws against separating husbands and wives. While many planters faced with bankruptcy ultimately put aside their normal revulsion against the family heartbreaks that slave trading caused, many others would not tolerate it and were careful to direct in their wills that their slave families be kept together.

American prohibitions against the international slave trade took effect in 1808, but before that, between 1790 and 1808, the international slave trade flourished, and the lives of some of those eventually bound for slavery in the United States included its horrors.

The Slave Trade   Most Africans brought to the United States came from the agricultural areas of West Africa, meaning that they had spent most of their lives planting, cultivating, and harvesting crops. How they fell into slavery varied, but by the years of our period, many either were prisoners of African tribal wars or had been captured by fellow Africans specifically to be sold into slavery. These captives' journey to the coast for sale to white traders was only the first stage of a prolonged, ghastly ordeal. Their hands bound and their feet hobbled, they were formed into lines and tied together to walk for days to the coast, receiving little food and water as they did so. After they reached the ocean, a slave-trading ship captain selected them, branded them with his mark, and loaded them aboard his ship with less care for their health and comfort than would have been shown to livestock. Thus began the infamous Middle Passage of the transatlantic slave trade. Chained together, slaves lay prone in rows in the cargo hold, "frequently stowed so close, as to admit no other posture than lying on their sides."[4] Only occasionally allowed above decks, they spent the bulk of the voyage wallowing in urine, feces, and vomit, their food and water apportioned so inadequately that only the hardiest survived. It is, in fact, only surprising that more did not die. Some were driven to suicide by the horrors of the voyage. An appalling 15 to 20 percent perished in the Middle Passage. Most of these desolate people were imported to Latin America rather than the United

States. Only about 5 percent of the slaves exported from Africa came to the United States.

Slaves born in America were the products of over a century of acculturation and adaptation between Americans of African, European, and Native American descent. As a result, the cultural context of their daily lives bore influences from all **American Slavery** these traditions. By far, however, the overriding feature of their existence was the fact that they were slaves by force of law. It bears remembering that while their lives, like those of most Americans, revolved around work, they worked completely for the benefit of someone else: neither their labor itself nor the products it created would improve their lot or benefit them directly.

Most slaves worked on small farms or middling plantations. They lived near the main house in slave quarters, log or clapboard cabins that could be marginally comfortable or barely livable, depending on the plantation. The "quarter" was usually arranged along a dirt lane, sometimes collo- quially called "the street." On large plantations, an overseer, the planter's factotum, supervised daily activities with the help of assistants or "driv- ers," specially chosen slaves who supervised the gangs in their specific tasks each day. Slaves working on a small farm were less specific in their labor and performed many different tasks on a daily basis. Work com- menced at first light, stopped for a long midday lunch of corn bread and occasionally salt pork to avoid labor in the hottest part of the day, and then continued until dusk. In addition to the proficiency necessary to plant, cultivate, and harvest crops, slaves could acquire special skills to become talented brick masons, blacksmiths, carpenters, or seamstresses and enhance the self-sufficiency of the farm or plantation. During growing season, most slaves worked hoeing grass and weeds away from crops. Women were often employed at spinning thread or yarn and weaving cloth, especially during rainy periods when they could not work in the fields. In any case, slaves who did not labor in the fields worked long days as well. House servants rose long before their masters to light kitchen fires, cook breakfast for the household, iron clothes, help master and mis- tress dress for the day, or begin another round of endless housecleaning. Most plantations did not have hundreds of slaves, and one or two people performed most of these duties.

Slave families consisted of about the same number of children on aver- age as white families, but slave women probably gave birth to more chil- dren in their lifetimes than the average white woman did. Roughly one in three slave children died before the age of two, an appalling infant mor- tality rate even for a time when all children were vulnerable to disease. Slaves, however, suffered under especially taxing conditions that featured poor prenatal care and nutrition and the work schedules that kept moth- ers in the fields and away from breast-feeding responsibilities. Even erratic feedings could do harm as slave infants suffered from their mother's poor diet, and small children who were too young to work often served at best as marginally neglectful babysitters.

Leisure and Lore
When slaves finished their daily work, they returned to simple lodgings for an evening meal and a few hours with friends and family. With time to prepare rations provided by their owner and vegetables grown in their gardens, slaves could enjoy a more restful and agreeable meal than during the day. The planter supplied the basics for their diet, most often an allotment of salted or cured pork, dried corn or cornmeal, molasses, and salt. Slaves planted gardens with foods that would have been familiar to tables in Africa. Peanuts, yams (called sweet potatoes), and rice grew well in the South and were important sources of nutrition for whites as well as slaves. In fact, the expertise of Africans in growing rice had made it a lucrative cash crop for plantations during the colonial period. Slave men supplemented their families' diets by fishing in nearby rivers, streams, and lakes. Southern states had laws prohibiting slaves from owning guns, but owners would sometimes lend shotguns to slaves for hunting.

After the evening meal, slaves visited neighbors in the quarters, watched their children play, listened to stories, and sang and danced. Storytelling was important for slaves, not only as a diversion but also as an oral tradition that preserved their history. In a ritual as old as the fables of Aesop, adults used folktales to teach children important lessons about ethical behavior, some of these stories originating in Africa from the seventeenth century and passing from generation to generation. Considered among the wisest people in the quarters, storytellers wove parables that often followed the exploits of anthropomorphized animals learning life's lessons the hard way.

They told their tales in English, but like everything about slave culture, there were vestiges of African influences. This was especially true on larger plantations, where slaves had less contact with whites. Yet African languages existed only as relics because even those who recalled the old ways of talking found themselves awash in a sea of alien tongues. The wide array of West African languages simply frustrated the emergence of a common, native vernacular. Instead, learning English and integrating it with pidgin variations of their own vocabularies and syntax was the only way for them to communicate within the slave community as well as with the white one.

Their music also had strong African roots and was an extremely important part of their lives, in both the quarters and the fields. In Africa, people at work passed the time singing verses in the form of chanted declarations and responses. Slaves sang the same type of songs at their work with different words rendered in English but cadenced in the rhythms of Africa. The lyrics of these songs, however, had a distinct American flavor and often told of "the usage they have received from their Masters and Mistresses in a very satirical stile and manner."[5] African influences also framed dancing done by the slaves during evenings and holidays. Musical instruments such as the banjo and various drums featured in their compositions also had African origins.

Slave funerals were another example of how succeeding generations sustained African customs even after the passing years had **Faith** clouded their origin. Although it was not a convention in Africa to hold funerals at night—slaves did so partly from necessity because they were often deprived of the necessary time during the workday—they emulated West African practice by dancing and singing in celebration of the deceased's return to a true home. Interment in the slave cemetery included placing belongings on the grave to make the journey home easier.

By the early Republic, most slaves practiced a Christianity marked by vestigial African influences. For years, slaves on large plantations gathered on Sunday to conduct their own services and to hear sermons by their own preachers. Following revelations about possible slave insurrections, however, the custom of allowing such unsupervised worship fell into disfavor because of white fears that slave gatherings encouraged conspiracies and risked rebellions. Increasingly, planters insisted that white ministers preside over slaves' services or that their slaves attend white churches. During these services in white churches, the ministers often took the time to instruct slaves to "obey your masters and mistresses" so that "your back won't be whipped."[6] Farmers and planters who owned only a small number of slaves especially adopted the practice of taking their slaves to their churches. Whether openly or secretly, however, most slaves continued to hear sermons by black preachers, who often even awed white observers with the "wonderful sympathy between the speaker and the audience."[7] Wherever they worshipped, afterward most slaves had the balance of Sunday off from work. The exceptions were house servants, whose work of preparing meals knew no holiday.

In the late fall after the harvest came hog-killing time. Slaughtering was almost as important a time as reaping **Other Tasks** for the well-being of the farm or plantation. Most of the meat that the master's family and slaves had during the winter would be prepared during hog killing. The largest hogs were chosen for slaughter and killed either with a bullet to the brain or by having their throats slit. They were strung up by their hindquarters and cut open to remove their internal organs, which would be boiled to make them edible for various dishes. After skinning the carcass, slaves cut up the hog to smoke and salt cure, necessary techniques for preserving the meat during the coming year. Plantation slaves were the primary laborers for this lengthy and unpleasant chore, and because nothing went to waste, they received the parts of the hog that whites did not want, such as the intestines. These were cleaned, boiled, and fried to produce what became known as chitterlings or chitlins.

In addition to hog killing, numerous other tasks needed completing before the planting season. Fences had to be mended, roofs patched, hay baled for livestock fodder during the winter and spring, and tools and plows repaired. These jobs were purposely postponed during the busy growing season for when there would be time during the off months. Thus the only real break from the grind of daily labor came at Christmas. Most slaves received about a week off at Christmas, days filled with extra food and perhaps a bit of spirits to celebrate the season. During this week at the end of the year, they enjoyed music, dancing, and visiting, even with slaves from other plantations. Yet the simplicity of their life was structured around want and deprivation, and nothing illustrated that fact more than the marginal clothing they received as part of their "gifts" at Christmas. Men were usually given trousers and work shirts, and women either simple dresses or the cloth to make them. Children wore only simple shifts or shirts until they reached working age, and their mothers were given cloth to make these simple garments.

Punishments   Slave misconduct was usually punished by whipping, a bad enough experience, but atrocious cruelties also occurred, such as branding or other forms of mutilation. Even planters who considered themselves humane often resorted to these practices, which were almost always meted out by the overseer. Aside from the indignity and deprivation inherent in the system, deliberate mistreatment of slaves was rare, however. Even the most uncompassionate owner realized that starving slaves or depriving them of clothing and shelter risked causing sickness and was economically imprudent. Yet any system that gives individuals absolute power over others will have the potential to promote instances of extreme cruelty. One South Carolina slave owner and his wife beat one of their slaves until his back resembled raw meat and then "applied a pickle of *pepper and salt* to his wounds." "The miserable wretch died a few hours after in the most excruciating tortures."[8]

Most slaves endured their lot, showing defiance in passive ways, such as working at a slow pace or feigning illness, but a very small minority ran away, some in a bid for freedom, some in sad attempts to return to former owners after being sold. In the wake of the 1790s slave insurrection in Santo Domingo and the barely thwarted 1800 Gabriel Prosser revolt in Richmond, Virginia, whites installed harsh slave codes to stem defiance, snare fugitives, and prevent insurrection. Yet the rules were only marginally effective. Their enforcement in rural areas would have required the constant vigilance of whites. As it happened, regulations that theoretically prohibited slaves from unsupervised or unauthorized travel were honored more in the breach, as slaves moved around quite a bit, especially when owners used them as couriers for long errands or hired them out to work for neighbors. Some planters even permitted their slaves to learn to read and write, a direct violation of laws that were designed to prevent the circulation of seditious ideas. The vast majority of slaves, however, remained illiterate and hopeless, completely and ironically dependent on the system that consistently exploited and repressed them. In contrast to other Americans, even the lowly convict, the slave's lot was utterly forlorn and bleak. One hard day was much like the hard days that preceded and followed it. While some had better masters than others in terms of treatment, food, and punishments, their lives were not their own, and their children were condemned to the same wretched state, and as far as they knew, their children's children as well, generation unto generation, forever.

FREE BLACKS

Whether they lived in the North or the South, free African Americans during the early Republic had a status at best marked by ambiguity. As runaway slaves, freed slaves, or descendants of freed slaves, African Americans in the North were typically placed in economically and socially inferior positions. In the South, free African Americans were generally descendants of former slaves who had won freedom either through extraordinary service to their masters or because of an owner's moral qualms about the institution of slavery. In some cases, free African Americans in both the North and the South were descendants of indentured servants from the colonial period who had actually never been slaves. At best, the free black was regarded as a second-class citizen, and more frequently he was viewed not as a citizen at all. The section of the country determined how well he lived.

The tide of antislavery feeling that gripped many southern slave owners following the American Revolution increased **The South** the number of free blacks in the South as altruistic owners manumitted their human property. By the early years of the nineteenth century, free blacks made up almost 10 percent of the black population in the South. Yet the surge in manumissions quickly subsided when whites began to fear the influence of free blacks on slaves. Legislatures actually began to make it more difficult for owners to free their slaves. Yet freed slaves and other free blacks were uncomfortable reminders both to their brothers still in bondage and to whites that African Americans could succeed in a region that made most of them slaves.

It was a strangely replicated world. Free blacks lived apart from whites while nevertheless making their livings in much the same way that whites did. White society, however, made it clear that "be their industry ever so great and their conduct ever so correct, whatever property they may acquire or whatever respect we may feel for their character, we could never consent, and they could never hope to see...their descendants visit our houses, form part of our circle of acquaintances, marry into our families, or participate in public honours or employment."[9] The attitude persisted and took greater hold in the 1820s and 1830s, the period ironically lauded as that of Jacksonian Democracy, when white men enjoyed an expansion of political rights while disenfranchising free black men in states like North Carolina and Tennessee where they earlier had the vote.

Some whites would have preferred that no free blacks live in the slave South, but in some instances, their presence was economically indispensable. They performed tasks that even the poorest whites considered beneath them, and they provided an extra source of workers that was more cost-effective than slave labor for seasonal jobs. Small landowners could hire free blacks to harvest crops without having to pay their living expenses for the rest of the year. Oystermen, fishermen, and crabbers could hire free blacks to help during their busiest season and afterward send them on their way. In cities, black men recently freed from slavery labored as dockworkers, teamsters, and day laborers while their wives worked as domestic servants for middle-class tradesmen. Descendants of slaves or servants from the colonial period were often artisans or craftsmen, their skills passed down through generations of skilled laborers. In rural areas, particularly in the upper South, many free blacks were small farmers who were descended from slaves or servants who had acquired land during the colonial period. They went about their daily lives in much the same way as other small farmers.

Whether they were urban workers, craftsmen, or small rural farmers, the daily lives of free blacks in the South might have appeared little different from those of their white neighbors, at least at first glance. Yet differences made subtle by casual observation were quite profound. Free blacks in rural settings had a very limited circle of friends. In areas where schools for white children were scarce, educating black children was nearly impossible. Only parents who were literate could teach their children to read and write, and such rudiments were the only education their children would receive.

In cities their situation was somewhat better. There, free blacks living in closer proximity to other free blacks and urban slaves had people with whom they could socialize and attend church. Urban free blacks were more successful in establishing churches for their communities as well as schools for their children. Against white opposition that feared any assembly of blacks, whether they were free or slaves, independent black churches were established in southern towns at the beginning of the early Republic. In addition to the African Methodist Episcopal Church, numerous other black denominational churches sprang up throughout the South.

Many early abolitionists, especially Quakers, established schools for free black children and sometimes set up night schools for free black adults to teach them the rudiments of reading and writing. By the early nineteenth century, free blacks operated most of these urban schools, many times in association with black churches. White fears meant that many of these schools were short-lived. Responding to their limited opportunities for economic upward mobility and the increasing inability to educate their children, many free blacks migrated to northern cities during the first half of the nineteenth century. There were also more compelling reasons to do so. The increasing value of slaves saw unscrupulous whites abducting free blacks and taking them out of state to sell into slavery. The rise of this deplorable practice gave added urgency to northern migrations.

The only free blacks who remained were those who either practiced a craft or plied a trade that made them familiar in a community and hence difficult to kidnap or those who were simply too poor to relocate. The former continued to live in close-knit black communities of the urban South, while the latter simply scraped by, usually as urban day laborers. Free black farmers were another story. The rural isolation and the danger of falling victim to abduction gradually persuaded most free black farmers to leave the South.

Important exceptions to this pattern were free blacks in Louisiana. Slavery had existed in Louisiana for most of its history, but under French and Spanish rule, attitudes toward race were considerably different from those that would prevail after the United States took possession of the territory in 1803. French and Spanish colonists had frequently come to the region without families and had settled down with black women. These arrangements resulted in a sizable population of mixed-race children whose social and legal status was distinctly different from that of their counterparts in the United States. There, liaisons with slave women were seldom admitted, and their offspring almost never recognized. In French and Spanish Louisiana, however, it was not unusual for white fathers to recognize such children and free them and their mothers. When the United States took possession of Louisiana, there were a large number of free black households descended from these unions.

Most of Louisiana's free blacks of mixed heritage lived in New Orleans, where they formed a separate class of largely middle-class tradesmen and artisans. During French and Spanish rule, some free black families had amassed considerable wealth and property, sometimes ironically including slaves. At the beginning of American administration of Louisiana, about a quarter of the population of New Orleans were the so-called *gens de couleur*. Their numbers significantly increased over the next decade as a result of large free black migrations from the Caribbean.

French and Spaniards in Louisiana had never treated free blacks as social equals, but they had not imposed serious legal restrictions on them either. American officials and settlers found shocking the fact that free blacks in Louisiana were also a part of the territory's armed militia. Despite such reflexive fears, enlightened territorial officials like Governor William C.C. Claiborne realized the value of having additional men to repel foreign invasions or to put down slave rebellions. The free black militia thus remained in existence throughout the early Republic, and with happy results for the United States in its greatest hour of need, when the famous "free men of color" rallied to Andrew Jackson's standard to defend New Orleans from the British at the end of the War of 1812.

Yet Louisiana's territorial legislature could not repress fears that a successful, prosperous free black community provided a dangerous example to the slave population. The free blacks of New Orleans could educate their children and attend religious services with far fewer restrictions than free blacks of any other southern state, but the legislature enacted laws explicitly defining the status of free blacks as inferior to that of white citizens. Less formal but no less insulting was the expectation that free blacks show extreme deference to whites.

Although the custom was most prevalent in Louisiana, some free blacks throughout the South owned slaves. Most lived in towns and cities, where their slaves toiled in workshops or merchant enterprises. Successful black business owners occasionally made enough money to buy land and in some instances, especially in Louisiana, owned plantations that used slave labor no less industriously than neighboring operations owned and operated by whites.

The North   Slavery had existed throughout the North during the colonial period, but it never became as integral to the northern economy as it did to the southern one. Because slaves were far less numerous in the North, social pressure to maintain the system was not as intense, and attitudes that emerged from the American Revolution had more leverage in bringing about slavery's abolition. In fact, reconciling the principles of the Revolution with actual practice saw northern legislatures that had not done so already enacting gradual emancipation laws during the 1780s and 1790s.

The relatively sudden occurrence of northern emancipation created two groups of free blacks. There were those people who had been born free, descendants either of freed slaves or of indentured servants from the colonial period, and there were former slaves recently freed by northern statutes. People born into freedom tended to be more comfortable economically than the recently manumitted, and though they typically resided in segregated communities, those communities were usually stable. Recently freed slaves, on the other hand, had to scramble for work and settle for makeshift lodgings in a world that reflexively relegated them to the lowest economic and social level. Many recently freed slaves were illiterate and could find only the most menial jobs. A sense of black community emerged, though, even in the face of these glaring differences of place and circumstance. The total number of blacks in most northern communities was small, and empathy for the poor among them encouraged the development of solidarity that knew no caste and counted no income.[10]

In the absence of white fears about a combination of free blacks and slaves organizing rebellions, northern cities and towns displayed greater tolerance toward the establishment of black churches and schools. In fact, the segregated nature of northern communities encouraged the founding of black churches that became important social as well as religious centers for African Americans. In addition, some regions at first did not have segregated education. At the beginning of the early Republic, their relatively unobtrusive numbers meant that free black children often attended school with white children, especially in New England. Yet as northern manumission increased the number of free blacks, white prejudice also grew. White parents objected to the presence of black children in schoolhouses, and white children predictably responded to the negative attitudes exhibited by their parents by mistreating their black schoolmates. Black parents addressed the growing problem by seeking the creation of segregated schools, a practice that had become standard in most northern communities by the end of the period. Black schools were almost always inferior to white schools in both instruction and facilities, and free black children often left school no better prepared for the demands of a competitive world than when they had entered. By the 1830s, leaders in northern black communities were calling for an end to school segregation, but more than a century would pass before the situation changed.

Poor schools were little better than no schools at all, but discriminatory hiring practices placed even well-educated free blacks in the lowest-paying jobs. Their segregated schools were mirrored by their segregated neighborhoods, always in the poorest part of town, whose principal feature was substandard housing. When the man of the house left in the early-morning hours to take on whatever day labor he could find, his wife fed and dressed the children for school and then either left the house as well for a job as a domestic servant or remained at home to take in laundry from the white part of town. Most families barely scraped by on their meager earnings, and in the few cases where free blacks found lucrative work as skilled craftsman, the white community rarely treated them as equals. Even the supremely talented mathematician and astronomer Benjamin Banneker was never accorded the celebrity or acclaim he deserved. By the time he died in 1806, Banneker had shown himself to be one of the country's most accomplished scientists. Like many free blacks of his generation, he was a descendent of an English indentured servant and a freed slave in Maryland, but his accomplishments were anything but typical. A farmer by profession, he was only self-taught in mathematics and mechanical design but nevertheless devised and built an exceptionally reliable clock. He also became proficient in astronomy, primarily by using his extraordinary powers of observation, and began publishing an almanac in the 1790s that featured the movements of planets and the position of stars from his own calculations as well as wide-ranging literary excerpts for the amusement and enlightenment of readers. His mathematical skills made him a valuable member of the surveying commission that laid out the District of Columbia. Banneker was by no means an activist, but neither was he falsely modest. In a celebrated exchange, he challenged

Thomas Jefferson's supposition that blacks were mentally inferior. Yet when sending a white friend calculations for astronomical events, he nevertheless felt the need to preface his predictions by asking his reader "to view with an eye of pity .... the first attempt of the kind that ever was made in America by a person of my complexion."[11]

Free African Americans during the early Republic might have started the period with a sense of hope born of expectations that the revolutionary rhetoric of freedom and opportunity would extend to them. Especially in the North, where some even fought in the Revolution for the same ideals that white citizens had embraced, the promise seemed realizable. Yet the promise was only partly fulfilled, and the dream was often tragically denied. The Revolution did result in freedom for many slaves in both the North and the South, but this change in legal status did little to improve either their economic or social circumstances. In the lower South, the situation for free blacks so deteriorated during the early Republic that many migrated to the North. There they found their liberty less tenuous, but they still enjoyed few opportunities for advancement and remained firmly lodged at the bottom of the social and economic ladder.

PIONEERS

Life on the frontier was naturally more difficult than in the more settled parts of the country. The journey itself could be the most arduous part of the experience, as explained by one pioneer when he wrote in his journal that the party "then sailed for Kaintucky. Arove at Limestone the 18th, after 10 days of the fertigueinest time I ever saw."[12] Pioneers found densely forested lands in need of clearing to make them into farms. The frontier had no lumber mills and brickyards, so homes had to be built from materials at hand and by the people who would live in them. All of these demanding chores had to be accomplished before settlers could begin planting crops and establishing stable routines.

Forests to Farms The most common method of clearing fields involved a protracted process of girdling trees by cutting a ring through the outer layer of bark to produce a wound that gradually killed the tree and made removing its stump easier after it was cut down. Very old trees left enormous logs that had to be moved away before a field could be plowed and planted. Abandoned Indian cornfields were obviously more attractive farmsteads because they allowed one to avoid this tiresome job. Draft animals such as mules, oxen, or horses helped to pull felled trees out of the way. If other settlers lived nearby, the chore became a social occasion called logrolling. Neighbors brought their draft animals to make the work go quicker while women prepared a feast for the party to follow.

The varying condition of frontier land dictated the type of farming practiced there. It might take years to clear enough land to yield a surplus of crops for sale rather than subsistence. Most frontier farmers had small vegetable patches and exerted most of their effort raising corn. Corn could be used for fodder, mainly for pigs, and ground into meal for the family's bread. When farmers finally cleared enough land to produce a surplus of corn, it could be distilled into whiskey for easy transport to local or distant markets.

Generally, women worked with their husbands to plant and harvest the crops. Children who could walk often pitched in as well. Though frontier farms rarely divided labor between the sexes, certain jobs were the special province of females. Women tended vegetable gardens, fed the animals, cooked, cleaned, and raised the children, chores familiar to farmwives in every section of the country. Men cleared additional fields, repaired tools, for blacksmiths were scarce on the frontier, and hunted. Most men enjoyed hunting, but what was often a sport in eastern rural areas was a necessity on the frontier. Game frequently provided the family's only meat, and a good hunter could not only set his family's table but also have enough additional game meat to trade for other necessities.

Frontier families went to bed earlier than eastern ones. Backbreaking labor encouraged the habit, of course, but the expense of candles and lamp oil did so as well. Twilight sent many families to bed. Before dawn, the wife and older daughters rose to stir the banked fire to life and warm the usually single room of their home. They prepared breakfast, and the long day's labors began anew.

As more land was cleared and put under cultivation, the western frontier increasingly resembled the rural East. **Elbow Room** Houses and barns were newer and made from cruder materials; streets of scattered villages were muddy and fewer in number, and they were lined with fewer businesses and contained fewer professionals like doctors and lawyers as their residents. Yet these people aspired to the stability of civilization and the comforts of established, thriving settlements. This desire for stability and even civilization led at least one observer to describe many of these pioneers as a group "possessing remarkable traits of character and manners which are a compound of civilization and barbarism."[13] Other pioneers, however, particularly men, moved to the frontier to escape eastern society. Some of them brought their families, and when another wave of wanderlust overtook them, they simply uprooted and moved them again. When the economy thrived and farm prices rose, they could pocket nice profits for farms with cleared fields and structures, certainly more valuable than uncleared woodland.

Some even found the presence of family too constricting and preferred to move out to the frontier or beyond alone. If they settled in one place at all, they cleared only enough land for subsistence. They usually preferred more mobility, hunting for their food and trading with Indians for furs and animal skins.

Mountain Men
Immediately preceding the War of 1812, entrepreneurs realized that riches were to be made by cutting into the British monopoly on the Canadian fur trade. The most famous of these men was John Jacob Astor, whose American Fur Company was a short-lived attempt to eliminate the British domination of the fur trade in the Pacific Northwest. Manuel Lisa's Missouri Fur Company cultivated trade with the Indians of the upper Missouri River, depending on a rough breed of frontiersmen to bring in the furs and skins from the Rocky Mountains and the upper plains. These characters were the fabled mountain men whose activities became the stuff of legend on the American frontier.

The mountain man actually spent most of his life well beyond the frontier. He lived in a shadowy, often unmapped region of plains and mountains far from white settlements. Much of the year he was either alone or paired with a temporary partner trading with Indians of the far West, people removed from eastern awareness. The mountain man mainly trapped animals for fur companies, the type of animal depending on the company. Companies that specialized in the upper Missouri trade generally dealt in buffalo robes or skins. Traders hunted buffalo, which were still abundant on the upper plains, and traded for their skins with Indian tribes in the region. Mountain men in the Rocky Mountains typically trapped beaver for pelts, which were valuable in the East and in Europe for making men's hats.

Though a mountain man made his living from trapping, he had to be proficient with a gun as well. Defending himself from animals, particularly the aggressive grizzly bear, and the occasionally hostile Indian was an everyday possibility. Indians of the plains and the Rockies traded with these trappers but also naturally saw their presence as a threat and their activities as impinging on vital resources. Sometimes Indians tried to force these intrepid trappers out of a region, and mountain men could be either stubborn or compliant as the case required.

Life for mountain men revolved around the seasons. They usually spent winter in makeshift cabins or among the Indians to be near hunting and trapping regions at the start of spring and then traveled to a company fur-trading post. These summer journeys were lengthy in time and distance, but worthwhile because they allowed for the purchase of supplies and whiskey, with perhaps a bit of money left over. In the fall, mountain men took advantage of the hunting season before the harsh winter again forced them into a sort of human hibernation, hoping that they had bagged enough game to sustain them through the long white months. Some were not so lucky and starved to death during particularly severe winters when no game moved through their isolated camps.

It was meant to be a lonesome life, for mountain men thrived on solitude and wide open spaces. Yet its days were numbered from the start. During the 1820s, the practice of holding rendezvous in the mountains began so that trappers and company men could exchange goods. The rendezvous was no doubt a welcome break from utter isolation, but that it even became possible was a sign that the wilderness was not as distant and as empty as before. By the end of the early Republic, the romance of the solitary mountain man was all but finished. Some still clung to the lifestyle, but competing with the trapping systems employed by organized companies proved impossible. Most mountain men by the 1820s traveled in large groups, sometimes numbering 50 trappers, and divided their labors for efficiency. Some looked for food, others hunted or trapped, and others maintained the camp and did the cooking. Not only were they more productive in their labors, but these groups could better defend themselves against Indians and rival companies. In addition, the number of traps necessary to procure large numbers of beaver pelts required a sizable investment, and lone trappers could not compete with these company operations. Only those outfitted by the big companies could make a living from trapping and hunting by the 1820s, and by the 1830s and 1840s, this prototypical frontiersman, while not extinct, was finding that changes in the market and the unrestrained trapping of beaver had altered his world. Other pursuits allowed him to remain on the frontier, but that too was steadily changing. He led exploring parties through the Rockies and across western deserts or guided wagon trains to the Pacific Northwest and to California, earning him a living, but one tinged with the irony that his new activities placed him among the very people he had labored so hard to escape.

IMMIGRANTS

The number of immigrants who came to the United States between 1790 and 1820 was small compared to the tremendous numbers to come in the mid- to late nineteenth century. Yet they became a significant part of the population nonetheless and had a considerable impact on the country's course and development. Most were hardly indigent, but they shared the same motives for coming to America as later immigrants—to make a better life for themselves and their families.

Most immigrants during the early Republic came from northern and western Europe. Though the greatest waves from Ireland and Germany would not come until the 1840s, immigrants traveled from there during these years, as well as from England, France, and other European countries. They sought out the economic opportunities and political freedoms that the United States offered, but they were also running away from hardships in their native countries. Farmers who had divided their lands beyond the point of further division to provide sons with a way to make a living believed that the abundant land in America was the best chance for them to continue the agricultural traditions of their ancestors.

Many of these people thus came to the United States expecting to maintain as well as improve their way of life. They were to find, though, that while land was plentiful, getting to it and buying it, as well as the tools and livestock needed to work it, was an expensive undertaking. The result was often a dream deferred as a pattern developed that would persist over the next century for immigrants who landed in America's cities and remained there. They took what work was available and struggled to save enough money, their constant hope that one day they could buy a farm.

Germans   The immigration of indentured servants is an important part of the American story in the colonial period, but the practice of selling one's services to pay for one's passage to America continued during the early Republic as well. It was especially prevalent among impoverished Germans, sometimes called "redemptioners" because someone would have to redeem their services to free them from years of servitude. Their status was legally little better than that of a slave during their indenture, and they were sometimes subjected to unspeakable brutality while being deprived of the necessities of life.

The misfortunes of redemptioners began aboard the ship that brought them to America. During the voyage, they were obligated to the captain of the vessel for their passage, and upon arrival in the United States, he sold them to the highest bidder. Frequently deprived of all but the most negligible food and drink, redemptioners often arrived in the United States quite ill from malnutrition and the close confines of the ship. Children suffered the most on such voyages. One reformer wrote that "the cry of the children for bread was, as I am informed, so great that it would be impossible for man to describe it."[14] Some passengers actually starved to death on the voyage. Others did not complete it for other reasons. In 1805 a captain stopped his ship in Great Britain and sold some male passengers against their will to British army recruiting agents, despite the fact that they were leaving wives and families aboard. An observer who came aboard one of these ships when it arrived in the United States described conditions on board as a "revolting scene of want and misery. The eye involuntarily turned for some relief from the horrible picture of human suffering."[15] German Americans already in the United States, many of them descendants of Germans who had come during the colonial period, formed relief societies to mitigate the suffering of these new German immigrants, but many continued to suffer under abusive masters long after arriving in the United States. Their dreams of quickly saving enough money to buy a farm faded as redemptioners were sold to work as house servants or manual laborers, often under terms that took years to fulfill. Even after years of backbreaking toil and after they had obtained their freedom, they had little more than what they had brought to the United States in the first place, which was often only the clothes on their backs. Many more years would pass before they had the money to buy the tools necessary to work for themselves and begin saving for land.

Impoverished immigrants from Ireland also suffered terrible
hardships. Many Irish came to America during the colonial   **Irish**
period, and their letters home to friends and relatives encouraged
an almost continuous immigration to America well into the early years of
the nineteenth century. A much larger number of Irish immigrants came to
the United States in the late 1840s fleeing the great Potato Famine, but they
would be inspired to do so by these earlier pilgrims.

More than half of the Irish immigrants of the eighteenth century were
the so-called Scots Irish from the northern part of Ireland in Ulster.
Although they were called Scots Irish, they did not recognize the distinction and simply referred to themselves as "Irish." The label, however,
derived from the fact that they were descendants of Scot migrants to Ireland. These colonial immigrants were mostly Presbyterian Protestants
who had been unable to support families on the poor soil of northern Ireland and unwilling to abide oppressive British land policies. Some reports
have as much as half the population of Ulster immigrating to the American colonies during the eighteenth century. Some migration from the
Catholic parts of Ireland occurred during the colonial period and would
continue after 1790, but Catholics migrated in far smaller numbers and
generally not in family groups. Most Irish Catholics who came over before
the Potato Famine were single men looking for economic opportunities.

Instead, many Ulster migrants came as families and found few economic opportunities in America's small colonial cities. They consequently
traveled as extended families or clans to the colonial backcountry, where
they soon became the largest European ethnic group on the American
frontier. In fact, by the beginning of the early Republic, people of Irish or
Scots Irish descent made up about 15 percent of the American population.
Most lived in the southern backcountry in the way most pioneers did,
occupying crude log homes, planting corn, and raising pigs. Eastern elites
disparaged their primitive lifestyle, but these hardworking people produced some of the country's most important leaders. American presidents
Andrew Jackson, James K. Polk, James Buchanan, William McKinley, and
Woodrow Wilson were descended from these robust Ulster Irish folk.

The establishment of an independent United States did not stop Irish
immigration. Yet these later arrivals found a changed situation. The
chance to find jobs in growing American cities had increased, and the
greater distances involved in getting to land on the frontier made it less
available. Many of these Irish immigrants had been farmers, but they also
possessed other skills that made them valuable in a country short of experienced laborers. Unlike German redemptioners, most Irish immigrants
before the Potato Famine paid their own way to the United States and frequently brought savings as well as tools with them. They fled political
oppression, particularly after the failed uprising against the British in
1798, and a declining economy that had assailed traditional crafts such as

linen making that had earlier sustained a large part of the population. They were skilled artisans whose customers no longer had the money to buy their handiwork, schoolteachers whose pupils could no longer take the time from work to attend schools, physicians who no longer had solvent patients, and business clerks whose businesses had locked their doors and let them go. They saved their money or sold their businesses and came to the United States.

This relatively well-educated group of immigrants, largely from middle-class origins and fleeing what they regarded as British economic and political oppression, was eager to embrace the American experiment in republicanism. Irish males threw themselves into American politics with a will as newspaper editors, pamphlet writers, and political operatives. They embraced the most radical of republican ideas, were strong supporters of the Jeffersonian view of republican government, and were at least partially responsible for the increasing democratization of American politics at the end of the period.

The Ulster Irish spoke English, though in a very distinct dialect, followed a form of Protestantism already familiar to most Americans, and often plied trades that were much in demand in the United States. Thus their everyday lives were little different from those of other European Americans. Children attended the same schools as other children, wives performed the same domestic chores as other wives, and husbands engaged in the same types of work as other men, both in rural and urban settings.

French French immigrants also came to the United States in large numbers during the 1790s and in the years following the Napoleonic Wars. Immigrants of the 1790s came for a variety of reasons ranging from their admiration for the American experiment to flight from the excesses of the French Revolution. Still another group came as a result of the slave uprising in what would become Haiti.

French immigrants who fled the French Revolution fell into several groups. In the early days of the Revolution, many were monarchists who feared the empowerment of the French lower classes. People with such fears were unlikely to come to the United States with its philosophy of greater liberties for its citizens, and in fact few of these so-called Royalists did head for America, preferring instead the refuge of European monarchies. Royalists who did come to American did not remain long. Splits among French revolutionaries regarding the best course for France spawned dissent and power struggles that caused another wave of departures from France. As the revolution turned violent, many revolutionaries ran to America rather than risk the Reign of Terror. Generally well educated, these refugees took up the professions they had practiced in France, including journalism, medicine, and the law, and consequently they quickly fit into American society. They also introduced a great deal of French culture to the United States, particularly in food, art, and literature, and entered into the numerous political debates that consumed so much of the American middle and upper classes' time.

Other French immigrants to the United States during the 1790s were refugees from the slave revolt on the island of Santo Domingo. As many as 20,000 French merchants, plantation owners, and families fled to the United States when slaves working the sugarcane fields successfully revolted. Many of these refugees spent only a brief time in the United States before taking passage to France or other French colonies. Most of these émigrés ultimately departed for France or Spanish Louisiana, where they could speak French, acquire cheap land, and resume plantation agriculture under a more congenial government. Yet one group's arrival in 1793 was probably responsible for the transmission of yellow fever to Philadelphia, one of the worst epidemics of that disease in United States history.

Another wave of French immigration followed the fall of Napoleon in 1815. When Napoleon was sent into his final exile to the island of St. Helena, many of his followers feared reprisals from the restored Bourbon monarchy. Several hundred of these refugees persuaded Congress to sell them a parcel of 100,000 acres of Alabama land on the Tombigbee River for two dollars an acre. The ostensible purpose was to relocate to Alabama on land recently taken from the Creek Indians, transplanting a grape and olive culture in the process and hence the name of the settlement—the Vine and Olive Colony. The settlers who established the town of Demopolis consisted of upper-middle-class supporters of Napoleon, military officers, and their families. Hardly experienced in commercial agriculture, they fairly quickly failed at it, and most of them moved back to France after receiving promises of pardons. Those who remained in the United States moved to Louisiana or to Mobile because of their large French Creole populations. In their less than a decade of residence at Demopolis, however, they exerted considerable influence on the culture of the region's newly established planter class. Their dress, food, drink, dances, music, and general joie de vivre made Demopolis one of the most festive places in Alabama as well as the country.

Wherever they settled, in fact, French immigrants influenced American culture far out of proportion to their actual numbers. The American middle and upper classes associated the French with sophistication and attempted to emulate them whenever possible. New restaurants appearing in American cities consciously copied French recipes and advertised their dishes as the latest in French cuisine. American hairstyles for both men and women changed dramatically with the influx of French refugees in the 1790s. Only older men continued to wear wigs, while the rest tied their hair behind at their necks in simple queues. When men in Napoleonic France stopped wearing the queue and cut their hair short, such became the fashion in the United States. Men's fashions that had adhered to British styles began to incline toward the French in the 1790s.

By the early nineteenth century, long pants had replaced knee britches, and men wore beaver hats and high-collared coats. Women also followed the French in matters of dress and hairstyles. In the 1790s, fashionable American women adopted the loose, narrow, high-waisted dresses that presaged what became the Empire (after Napoleon's empire) style of the early nineteenth century. The elaborate coiffures of the eighteenth century gave way to simpler styles worn around the face and cascading down women's shoulders.

Jews   Though a few did immigrate during this period, most Jews in the United States during the early Republic were not recent arrivals, and the largest immigration of Jews into the United States was still a number of decades away. Jews had come to the American colonies as early as the seventeenth century, the first group from the Portuguese colony of Brazil to the Dutch colony of New Netherlands in 1654. These Sephardim (Jews from the Iberian Peninsula) were the first of thousands who found in the New World a refuge from the extreme persecution of the old. Other groups of primarily Sephardic Jews came to other colonies as well. The religious toleration practiced by Rhode Island made Newport the primary haven for Jews in the English colonies. The southern colonies of South Carolina and Georgia also proved very tolerant of these persecuted people, and Jews migrated to those colonies in the eighteenth century as well.

During the colonial period, the English colonies placed restrictions on the open, free exercise of the Jewish faith, but such proscriptions were mild compared to those imposed in Europe and in Latin America. Therefore by the time of the early Republic, most American cities—especially New York, Philadelphia, Newport, Charleston, and Savannah—had thriving Jewish communities.

The new nation's constitutional protections meant that Jewish congregations could practice their faith without fear of legal reprisals, but by then, most American Jews were so thoroughly acculturated into their communities that they had not experienced serious impositions in years. In addition to following their faith in peace, they participated in the social and political life of the community the same as their Gentile neighbors, leading one British visitor to comment that he was "surprised that all who profess the Hebrew faith do not emigrate to the United States, as they would there not only be free from civil incapacities…but would even find themselves eligible to the highest offices in the Republic."[16] The descendants of those first Jewish immigrants worked in the professions of medicine and the law, engaged in politics, business activities, and various trades and crafts, and in general were indistinguishable in their daily lives, except for the day they celebrated the Sabbath, from any other European Americans.

Beginning in the early nineteenth century, however, a new wave of immigration established another group of Jews in the United States.

Spurred by discriminatory laws in most of the German states, German Jews, or Ashkenazim, began coming to the United States in small numbers. Most of these immigrants were young, single men who planned to save enough money to send for family members. Some were successful; some were not. For the most part they initially settled in northeastern cities, where they worked as day laborers. The few who were skilled workers might work for established craftsmen and, if they were fortunate, might save enough money to open their own business.

Those never joined by families often blended into the Gentile community, married outside their faith, and lost much if not all of their Jewish heritage. Language and cultural differences deprived them of ready acceptance by the older American Jewish communities, which primarily spoke English and were generally part of the upper economic echelons of American society. Only after larger numbers of Jews in family groups started arriving in the 1830s did American Jewish working-class communities begin to take root in urban areas.

Most immigrants to the United States came from England, where the shortage of good farmland and the restrictive nature **English** of skilled trades drove many working-class people to emigrate. Colonial America had been a destination for such people since the early seventeenth century, and its change to a sovereign republic did not stem the tide. Because they not only spoke English but did so with pronunciations indistinct from the American accent of that day, these immigrants quickly blended into American society.

The most employable English immigrants were those who had worked in the growing number of English factories, particularly in the textile industry. The British government placed restrictions on the immigration of such people and made it illegal to export machinery plans, but many Britons seized the economic opportunity and found a way to America, some with important machinery blueprints, even if only in their memories. Men such as Samuel Slater brought valuable information to America to transform the country's economic life by giving birth to the American factory, the basis for the American version of the Industrial Revolution.

Rather than moving to rural areas and taking up life on farms, most immigrants during the early Republic stayed in **A Nation of** the cities where they first arrived. Seeking familiar lan- **Immigrants** guage, culture, and religion led some groups, especially Germans, to form urban neighborhoods that became small enclaves of particular European nationalities. During the day, mothers in working-class neighborhoods congregated to watch their small children play and talked over problems. In the evenings after work, a sense of community developed as the men and older children returned from labors to visit with neighbors, attend parties, and socialize in neighborhood pubs. On Sunday (Saturday in Jewish communities), these neighbors attended church together and socialized afterward. In short, the pattern of their daily lives differed little from that of other Americans. Although languages may have been alien or accents distinct, and though they resided a few streets away from other groups, acculturation was relatively easy in these years, and the time it took was relatively short. Not until the tremendous tide of immigration in the 1830s and 1840s did Americans begin questioning the value and wisdom of having millions of immigrants arriving in the United States.

Many people came to the United States during the early Republic because they wanted to be part of the great American experiment in liberty and equality. Yet the large numbers of people who initially did not seem to fit in gave rise to worries that ideas incompatible with American institutions were coming with them. In the 1790s, for example, French immigrants brought with them ideas that some Americans believed to be excessively democratic. Congress had as early as 1790 passed naturalization laws that required a two-year residency in the United States before applying for citizenship, but such regulations were not particularly restrictive. By 1795, however, the residency requirement had been increased to five years. Three years later, when many French immigrants were seen as favoring the Democratic-Republicans, the party in opposition to the Federalist majority in Congress and the John Adams administration, Congress acted again. Prompted by an undeclared naval war with France, a new Alien Act extended the residency requirement for citizenship to 14 years. Coupled with the Sedition Act, which made it illegal to criticize the sitting government, this distressing legislation was in part an attempt to stifle political opposition, an effort that miscarried by contributing to the backlash that handed victory to the Democratic-Republicans in the 1800 elections. In such indirect but no less tangible ways, immigrants could profoundly affect mainstream American politics.

CONVICTS

As in all times, some people who chose to live outside society's conventions did so maliciously. The early Republic had its criminals who justified their actions with the same rationalizations that have always informed the illicit deed: necessity drove this one to theft, or unfairness drove that one to felony. Crime has always been part of the human story, but the years of the early Republic were a transitional time in which new explanations for criminal behavior and new techniques for dealing with it made their first appearance. Punishments, for instance, contrasted markedly with those meted out during the colonial period, when criminals were more likely to be whipped or branded. Public humiliations had been routine, with offenders placed in stocks confining hands and feet between two notched wooden boards or in pillories with an additional hole for the head. Habitual crooks were banished, and in extreme cases, some were executed. Jails were used for temporary incarceration before trial or sentence, not for punishment.

During the early Republic, though, convictions for criminal offenses increasingly meant a sentence to spend a specified amount of time in a state prison. In fact, the establishment of the earliest prisons coincided with the elimination of the death penalty in most states for many crimes. By the nineteenth century, most states executed only those found guilty of treason or murder. Although these same states preserved the right to impose death sentences for robbery, arson, assault, and counterfeiting, they usually did so only after multiple convictions. In any case, a person under sentence of death was never sent to a prison. Prisons were not used as places for executions until the 1830s. Instead, the condemned was kept in a local jail until the appointed time for the execution. Those executed in the United States during the early Republic were typically hanged in public ceremonies, a practice that continued into the 1830s. By then, humanitarian objections finally overcame the public's fascination with such exhibitions.

Following British tradition, public executions had been conducted in America since colonial times. Such spectacles were thought to deter potential criminals while meting out just deserts to the convicted. Some victims doubtless took pleasure in seeing their assailants punished, but most of the people who traveled miles to see executions came out of morbid curiosity. The days before an execution were garish and grotesque. Salesmen hawked their wares, and traveling entertainers performed for crowds who gathered to see the hanging. Executions became social occasions for rural communities and cheap entertainment in cities. The actual event was a short affair, lasting only a few minutes. The condemned mounted the gallows, a minister prayed with him for a few minutes, a hood was placed over his head, his legs and hands were bound, and a noose was placed around his neck. A competent executioner could ensure a broken neck, and a quick death followed the drop through the scaffold's trapdoor.

These gruesome events, however, declined sharply during the early Republic because of the Enlightenment belief that every man was perfectible and religious con- **Rehabilitation** victions that all people were redeemable. Such beliefs inspired Massachusetts to establish the first state prison in 1785, and other states soon followed suit. New theories developed in Britain proposed that the controlled environment of a properly arranged prison could alter behavior, thus to "rehabilitate" criminals, weaning them from wickedness and preparing them for productive lives in society. Enlightenment thinkers posited that sentences in "penitentiaries" (the term was another British modernism) could be spent learning the value of hard work while contemplating the consequences of bad behavior. Such theories rested on the belief that criminals actually were good people who had gone bad because they had not been raised correctly.

Undoing childhood misdirection became a serious undertaking, and the daily regimen of prisoners resembled extreme military discipline. They awoke early to a simple breakfast such as corn mush. Prisoners were then placed at various tasks where they learned basic skills in trades, a remedy for idleness and the boredom it encouraged, the theory being that monotony perpetuated criminality. The most popular skills were in carpentry, weaving, and nail making. Prisoners in urban areas could be taken out during the day to work on various public works projects such as street repairs, a practice condemned by free laborers who rightly claimed that convict labor drove wages down at best and put honest workers out of a job at worst.

During work periods, male inmates could not idly chat with fellow prisoners, even those sitting next to them. Guards allowed only work-related conversations. Women prisoners, given jobs considered appropriate for their gender such as sewing or spinning, were allowed to talk. An incentive for good work included a modest wage from which the cost of room and board was deducted, leaving a small amount of money to help parolees make their way after serving their time. Although working in prison was considered a privilege, the work itself could be arduous and uncomfortable. A British observer who witnessed the work in a Connecticut prison's blacksmith shop noted that when the shackled prisoners entered "the smith, some went to the sides of the forges, where collars, dependent by iron chains from the roof, were fastened round their necks."[17] Prisoners who misbehaved or disobeyed rules were not allowed to work and could not earn money, one of the most persuasive punishments that could be used against a prisoner.

Prisoners whose crimes were heinous or who were considered too dangerous for the regular prison population were not allowed to work at the outset of their sentences. Instead, they were placed in individual cells and only saw guards when their single daily meal was brought to them. Such prisoners were only rarely even allowed books. A record of unblemished behavior might earn such prisoners the right to join the main prison population and begin a work regimen. Some prisons actually had several gradations of punishment, including "solitary confinement in a dark cell...as the severest usage; next, solitary confinement in a cell with the admission of light; next, confinement in a cell where the prisoner is allowed to do some sort of work; lastly, labor in a company with others."[18]

At the end of their 10- to 12-hour workday, prisoners returned to dormitories. Early in the penitentiary experiment, they slept, socialized, and ate in large rooms. The evening was the only time when they were not completely regimented in their activities. After the evening meal, they could visit as long as the sound of conversations did not reach to their guards' ears. If prison officials thought the noise too loud, conversations were stopped.

Because the purpose of these early prisons was reform, the conditions in them were probably better than many inmates had ever enjoyed on the outside. They were somewhat spartan, but they were clean and relatively warm in the wintertime. Food was nutritious if not plentiful, and medical care was available to everyone. Alarming problems, however, began marring the noble experiment in rehabilitation. Reducing the number of capital offenses meant that by the end of the eighteenth century, relatively new state prisons were terribly overcrowded. Overworked and undermanned, these institutions frequently became places to keep criminals rather than reform them. Extremely crowded prisons abandoned solitary confinement even for hardened criminals, integrating them with the general prison population, where they became master criminal tutors for hosts of criminal apprentices. The only training many prisoners received during their incarceration was how to become better criminals.

As these problems became so obvious that officials could not ignore them, a new round of reforms was put into place in the early nineteenth century, including a return to single-cell prisons, not just for violent offenders but for all inmates. Prisoners were let out of their cells during the day for work and to eat meals, but they were ordered to remain silent. Officials believed that quiet, contemplation, and hard work would restore criminals to the right path. Work was redesigned not only to teach prisoners good habits but also to produce necessary items like shoes and nails that would offset some of the cost of inmates' upkeep. It is hard to say if these reforms, the precursors to more than two centuries of like-minded efforts in penology, resulted in the rehabilitation of significant numbers of good people who reformers reasoned had gone bad through no fault of their own. No solid statistics relate levels of recidivism for late-eighteenth- and early-nineteenth-century prisoners, but we do know that prisons of the period continued to be very crowded.

CONCLUSION

Even in colonial times, America was a place of broad cultural diversity. Depending on where one lived, diversity was tolerated, if not generally encouraged. The mixture of indigenous people, the large number of immigrants coming to the country during the colonial period from such diverse backgrounds and ethnic groups as German pacifists to Portuguese Jews, and the presence of large numbers of African American slaves made for a rich mélange of cultural experiences. Yet some Americans chose to live apart. The vast expanses of land on the frontier drew farmers to what they believed was a better economic life. Others simply could not tolerate the increasing density of eastern populations and longed for open spaces. Americans who chose a life of crime were shut away in new state prisons designed initially in the optimistic hope that misfits could be made into productive members of society, but ultimately serving as places to separate criminals from law-abiding Americans. For all these reasons, the United States remained what it had always been and will always be: a culturally and spiritually diverse place for those who are dissimilar by choice or circumstance.

NOTES

1. Kathryn E. Holland Braund, *Deerskins and Duffels: Creek Indian Trade with Anglo-America, 1685–1815* (Lincoln: University of Nebraska Press, 1993), 175.

2. Ibid., 178.

3. Noel Rae, ed., *Witnessing America: The Library of Congress Book of Firsthand Accounts of Life in America, 1600–1900* (New York: Stonesong Press, 1996), 531.

4. Ibid., 35.

5. John W. Blassingame, *The Slave Community: Plantation Life in the Antebellum South*, rev. ed. (New York: Oxford University Press, 1979), 115.

6. Ibid., 132.

7. Ibid., 131.

8. Jane Louise Mesick, *The English Traveller in America, 1785–1835* (New York: Columbia University Press, 1922), 135.

9. Ira Berlin, *Slaves without Masters: The Free Negro in the Antebellum South* (New York: Pantheon Books, 1974), 187–88.

10. Even in Boston, where slavery ended very early in the period, African Americans made up less than .5 percent in 1800. See James Oliver Horton, *Free People of Color inside the African American Community* (Washington, D.C.: Smithsonian Institution Press, 1993), 26.

11. Banneker to Andrew Ellicott, 6 May 1790, in Carter G. Woodson, ed., *The Mind of the Negro As Reflected in Letters Written during the Crisis, 1800–1860* (New York: Russell and Russell, 1969), xxiii.

12. Dick, *Dixie Frontier*, 21.

13. Ibid., 24.

14. Andreas Geyer Jr. to Henry A. Muhlenberg, 27 April 1805, in Wayne Moquin, ed., *Makers of America—Builders of a New Nation, 1801–1848* (New York: Encyclopaedia Britannica Educational Corporation, 1971), 6.

15. Mesick, *English Traveller*, 45.

16. Ibid., 266.

17. Albert Bushnell Hart, ed., *American History told by Contemporaries*, vol. 3 (London: Macmillan, 1897–1929), 45.

18. Mesick, *English Traveller*, 116.

8

THE MARTIAL LIFE

A FRONTIER ARMY

The U.S. Army in 1790 was quite small and mostly concerned with duty on the frontier. Excluding officers, the authorized strength of the army was 1,216, although that figure was seldom reached. Soldiers were all enlistees and were mainly posted in the wilderness of the Ohio River valley, where they were supposed to overawe potentially hostile Indians. It was a job that took them far away from friends and family, and it could be both dangerous and frustrating. Scattered garrisons were neither large enough to intimidate angry Indians nor able to prevent settlers from riling those Indians by moving onto their lands and stealing their possessions. The army was also powerless to prevent Indian retaliation that such misdeeds spurred. Instead, soldiers were huddled in isolated posts, eating bad food and sleeping in austere barracks while waiting for the government to send enough men and supplies to maintain the peace.

When the growing violence on the Ohio River frontier finally captured the government's attention, the little army was forced into combat. Under mounting political pressure, the War Department ordered the army's commander, Josiah Harmar, to attack the Indians. The army's consequent introduction to Indian warfare proved enlightening, at least for the men who survived it. Poorly trained militia supplemented the paltry number of regulars, and the resulting force proved shockingly ineffective. In fact, it was chased back to its headquarters at Fort Washington (near Cincinnati) in the fall of 1790. More soldiers, also exhibiting the awkwardness of too little training, were sent to the Ohio River in the summer of 1791 and placed under the command of territorial governor Arthur St. Clair. That November, northwestern Indians walloped them as well. Such defeats were stern tutors, and the government grimly learned its lesson to increase the frontier army to 5,000 and install a rigorous training system that became a major part of these soldiers' daily lives. Led by General Anthony Wayne in 1794, this capable and disciplined force finally dealt Indians in the Ohio country a decisive defeat at the Battle of Fallen Timbers.

Most of the military history of the 1780s and 1790s has focused on these few battles, perhaps to give the impression that military life after the Revolution was marked by incessant Indian war. In reality, the average soldier on the western frontier saw little combat, and daily schedules were more described by the routine of drill and the tedium of garrison duty than the perilous excitement of battle. After the victory at Fallen Timbers, the government again sharply reduced the army's numbers, sacrificing preparedness to frugality but also calming widespread fear that a standing army posed a threat to the civilian government. Nonetheless, the inconsistent nature of frontier affairs for the next decade caused the army to swell in times of crisis and ebb in periods of calm. The soldier's lot was at best hard and unpredictable, and when no threat loomed, he was usually unappreciated and sometimes disdained by a suspicious and skeptical citizenry. Little wonder that during good economic times, both officers and enlisted men left the army in droves. During peacetime, most soldiers and officers remaining in the early Republic's army were there because they had no other prospects of employment.

Officers   During these years, a man became an officer more frequently as a result of his influence than his worth, for having powerful political friends was indispensable in obtaining promotion, even for the experienced and meritorious. This unwritten but persistent policy of giving preferment to men with proper political connections resulted in an officer corps that was both highly politicized and essentially incompetent, or as one officer characterized them, "Beasts & Blockheades."[1] As with most political patronage, the practice endured only as long as its consequences were trivial. Appallingly poor officer performance in the War of 1812 imperiled the country, however, and brought rapid and meaningful changes to the way commissions were granted and promotions earned.

Officers during the period suffered from a surprising lack of job security. Periodic military increases to meet Indian threats at home or international ones abroad were usually followed by reductions. Officers were never certain that their jobs would last for more than a year or two. In fact, many were released during cutbacks with the idea that they could always be recalled when needed, an idea that the government embraced in theory but found wanting in both application and results. Not only was the army's stability of command seriously impaired, but many competent officers found civilian positions that were at least more secure and frequently better remunerated than their military careers. Understandably, they had no desire to reenter the service, whether the country needed them or not.

The average private received a considerable amount of training over the course of his enlistment from officers and noncom- **Training** missioned officers, but officers who did not attend the United States Military Academy—the great majority during the early Republic— received virtually no formal training. Usually, newly commissioned officers were taken under the wing of a more senior officer or noncommissioned officer and informally taught the job. In the absence of such a mentor, the new officer learned his profession through observation. Exceptions were officers assigned to artillery or engineering units. President George Washington established an artillery and engineering training school at West Point, New York, in 1794, an institution that eight years later became the United States Military Academy. After the War of 1812, junior officers increasingly came from West Point, but though better trained than non–West Point graduates, these young men had a lot to learn about life in the army.

Indeed, one of the greatest impediments to developing a strong, professional officer corps was the lack of training provided for young officers. Nowhere was this more evident than during the few occasions when officers led their men into combat. Because battles were rare occasions until the War of 1812, Congress, at least, did not see the dearth of officer training as a valid worry. The executive branch, on the other hand, was another matter, for presidents were well aware that the army had tasks other than fighting battles. Not just Washington, with his military background, but thoroughgoing civilians John Adams and Thomas Jefferson also decried the lack of technical expertise of American engineers and the reliance on foreigners to carry out those functions in the United States Army.

Newly commissioned officers were usually young men whose first task was the thankless and frustrating chore of recruiting **Duties** those they would command. The new officer was usually expected to sign up a company, a unit that usually numbered from 75 to 100 men. He could undertake this assignment in a variety of ways, but the most promising approach was to travel to a city where the pickings would at least be more plentiful. Printed handbills and posters, paid for out of his own pocket, advertised his purpose and with any luck would generate some interest and produce a few takers. Even while continuing to accept recruits for his quota, the new officer commenced rudimentary training for his new charges, a job that could include instilling simple concepts such as distinguishing left from right but also teaching, "by gentle methods, regularity of conduct."[2] Sometimes he had to hunt down those whose second thoughts about joining the army prompted them to desert. Meanwhile everything had to be documented in regular reports to his commanding officer or the War Department. As soon as the officer had filled his ranks, he joined his regiment, where the serious training of the men commenced under the more practiced eyes of toughened, experienced sergeants.

Recruiting chores did not end there. When soldiers did not reenlist, recruiting was necessary to reinforce existing units. It was one of the most undesirable jobs in the army, one usually given to junior officers, who spent a large part of their early careers at it. Yet there were also compensations. Recruiting assignments allowed young officers to leave the frontier for more populous areas and more interesting social circles, sometimes even landing them in the eastern cities of friends and family.

For the most part, though, recruiting duty was difficult and unrewarding, especially during good economic times, when ample civilian jobs made military service much less appealing. In times of military expansion, recruiting officers faced different but no less challenging problems. As officers from different units moved into an area to compete for the same people, they resorted to innovative stratagems. For example, they could interpret rules regarding minimum physical requirements in imaginative ways to accept recruits whose health barely allowed them to fog a mirror. Though forbidden to enlist men "whilst in a state of intoxication," many recruiters did resort to collecting potential soldiers "from the streets and prisons of the cities."[3]

One prominent historian has mused that given the new government's hostility toward a peacetime army, it was the potential threat posed by Native Americans that resulted in a permanent American army.[4] It was certainly true that the primary duty of officers at isolated frontier posts was to treat with local Indians and prevent conflicts between them and settlers. Many officers came from the East, where more established communities had not seen an Indian for years, so they tended to regard Indians as exotic rather than threatening—sometimes to be rudely awakened. Yet at the outset, most officers were more curious than antagonistic about native populations, which was good, for the government expected them to serve as preliminary diplomats and preserve the peace. To that end, officers were also instructed to remove settlers from Indian lands, an assignment that made them unpopular with the growing numbers of squatters flocking to the frontier. Traders, some unscrupulously intending to sell enlisted men and Indians whiskey, also came under the purview of the commanding officers of frontier forts.

Most officers had time to explore the countryside, read, write letters to family, and socialize with fellow officers. Their mealtime assemblies, called the officers' mess, were convivial gatherings full of stories and lengthy reminiscences. If posted near a town or settlement, they could attend dances, go to dinner parties, receive regular mail, and court local girls. In isolated garrisons, though, officers struggled to create wholesome and varied amusements. Some failed and took to strong drink to break the monotony of their days, with regrettable results.

Itinerant assignments usually promised a level of discomfort, but permanent stations, whether frontier forts or urban garrisons, usually offered officers better quarters, food, clothes, and pay. While they were exempted from the kind of discipline meted out to enlisted men, officers were neither idle nor indulgent. They functioned in a chain of command that had them, in stipulated degrees of authority and responsibility, not only making decisions for everybody in their charge but also regularly explaining those decisions to superiors. In fact, the chores of routine reporting made them as busy as the soldiers under them as officers generated oceans of paper that were dispatched according to closely defined procedures to places where the reports were carefully filed away, usually unread and likely forgotten.

Especially in peacetime, officers shared with their soldiers the reality that army life was extraordinarily tedious. They trained men, filed reports, watched drills, filed more reports, meted out punishments for breaches of discipline, filed additional reports, supervised work parties, filed reports about that, and sat on courts-martial, which required extensive reports. The occasional parley with Indians introduced variety to duties, but such episodes, of course, also entailed filing reports. And even as dense smoke hung over a battlefield and the moans of his wounded men carried across recently contested ground, an officer began to frame the actions of the day in his mind. He would have to recount them in a report.

Even if better than the lot of a lowly private, an officer's life was not very appealing when compared to the opportunities for **Pay** advancement and the better pay available in civilian employment. If they had the chance, enlisted men tended to leave the army during good economic times, and many officers followed suit by resigning their commissions. Given the pay scales for the period, it is not difficult to see why. In 1792 a lieutenant made $26 a month (less than $500 in current value), a captain $40 (a little more than $700 in current value), and a major of infantry $50 (less than $1,000 in current value). This meant that in terms of today's purchasing power, the lieutenant made less than $6,000 a year, the captain about $8,000 a year, and the major less than $12,000 a year. The pay for senior officers was better, of course, but hardly bountiful. At $104 a month, a brigadier general earned the equivalent of $24,000 a year in current value, and a major general's $166 a month could only go as far as about $36,000 of today's money.

In comparison with a comparable civilian job, a junior officer drew about half the pay of an entry-level clerk in a large business or government job. And though the young officer did receive his food and housing and could earn extra-duty pay, if he had plans to marry and have a family, his compensation was simply inadequate.

Officers contrived ways to supplement their paltry salaries. If they were lucky enough to have an extended stay in one place, they could moonlight by taking part-time jobs in the community. Those posted on the frontier might take advantage of the opportunity to snatch up cheap land before settlers moved into the area. After settlers came and the land increased in value, some officers made a nice profit that they then invested in other enterprises. It was the wise officer who did, for there was no fixed retirement system, and officers who had not shown such foresight were compelled to stay in the service until they died, essentially with their "boots on."

Sometimes the ingenuity behind supplementing one's income crossed the line into shadowy areas that were at best dubious and at worst constituted outright misconduct. The senior officer in the army during part of this period serves as an example of both. Major General James Wilkinson was perhaps the most resourceful officer in the history of the service at finding ways to increase his income. In addition to engaging in the usual business activities, he also worked as a secret agent for the Spanish government, accepting regular payments to supply details about American activities on Spain's border in the Southwest, deeds that made him, according to one historian, "the most consummate artist in treason that the nation ever possessed."[5]

Insults and Honor   The relatively small cadre of officers in the American army was a tight-knit group whose members generally knew each other quite well. This intimate circle created many enduring friendships, but it could also make men into bitter enemies. Boredom was the most constant companion of soldiers posted on the frontier, and tedium often increased tensions that in other settings would have been unimportant. Scarcities also contributed to friction: romantic rivalries were exaggerated because of the few women in an area; petty jealousies about who received plum assignments or obtained one of the few available promotions became brooding resentments. Snarling arguments could lead to protracted feuds, and sometimes they were ultimately resolved with violence.

At the center of such touchiness was a sharpened sense of honor that could not tolerate insult. Officers, like other nineteenth-century gentlemen, were taught by the times that to suffer insult without seeking retraction or demanding satisfaction was to invite additional insults and spinelessly accept a ruined reputation.[6] They were further encouraged by their status as commanders to be sensitive about their reputations, seeing themselves as the spiritual heirs of medieval knights for whom the respect of peers and admiration of subordinates was an imperative component of leadership. Quick to perceive slights and interpret them as grave affronts, they were nevertheless presumptively gentlemen and were expected to refrain from brawls, fisticuffs being the remedy for enlisted ranks. If the insult was not personal or was the work of an inferior officer, a common practice was to charge the offender before a military court. Such hearings occurred with remarkable regularity, and both sitting on military courts and being the subject of them occupied a large part of an average officer's time. Because many posts did not have enough officers to constitute a proper military court, an officer might have to travel long distances to sit as a judge or journey to the site of a court to answer charges against him.

Personal offenses against their honor saw officers resorting to the more dignified protocols of violence prescribed by the Code Duello. Duels took place in middle- and upper-class circles of the civilian world (especially in the South and Southwest), but they were far more common in the military.[7] The process worked like this: When an officer felt he was the victim of an insult, he asked its author in writing for a clarification, expressing the hope that the matter was merely a misunderstanding. The tone at this point could be formally cordial or decidedly cool, depending on the seriousness of the offense and the level of acquaintance between the correspondents. If an agreeable explanation was wanting, however, the business became instantly perfunctory and ceremonial with the issuance of a formal challenge, usually rendered in euphemisms that invited the offender to a "conversation," that is, a duel. Friends of the two men acted as their seconds, either to arrange the appointment or to devise an accommodation that would please both principals. Frequently the latter effort was successful, and dueling in both civilian and military circles was often nothing more than a carefully coordinated dance of strange etiquette that settled disputes with sham threats and carefully crafted apologies. Even disputes that reached the dreaded encounter frequently ended in a bloodless exchange of gunfire, a display of bravado that allowed the duelists to leave with both honor and bodies intact. In fact, most officers could in good conscience condone the practice because it was usually harmless. Yet occasionally a dispute was sufficiently serious, and the principals sufficiently angry, to turn the affair deadly. Although dueling declined after 1806 when the War Department formally adopted the Articles of War that made the practice illegal, it did not completely disappear before the Civil War and sometimes involved celebrated figures in tragic disputes. In 1820, for example, Captain James Barron killed naval hero Stephen Decatur in a duel.

Congress usually granted pensions both to enlisted personnel and to officers who served in conflicts, especially those **Pensions** who were disabled, or, in case of their death, to their widows and orphans. The process of granting these annuities was sometimes cumbersome and tardy, though. The congressional Committee on Claims began receiving petitions for the Revolutionary War in 1794 and was supplanted by the Committee on Pensions and Revolutionary War Claims in 1813, a structure that was again revised in 1825. As late as 1875, pension rolls from the Revolutionary War still had 379 widows on them. Yet no fixed national retirement system existed for the military during the period, and those who had not been on the rolls in a war could expect no income beyond their terms of active service.

THE UNITED STATES MILITARY ACADEMY

Origins   The United States Military Academy was established at West Point, New York, in 1802. Even before it received that official designation, President Thomas Jefferson charged its commanding army engineer, Lieutenant Colonel Louis de Tousard, to instruct officer candidates. The cadets' daily routine was accordingly established before the small facility that George Washington had created to teach engineers and artillerists became the military academy. Initially, that routine was haphazardly organized around mathematics classes in the morning and physical and military training in the afternoons. With no age or educational requirements in place, the cadet corps presented a strange cross section of American manhood. Some cadets were 10 or 11 years old, while others were grown men with families. Some had only had the equivalent of an elementary education, while others had already graduated from a civilian college. The primary qualification for admission seems to have been family political connections.

Jefferson wanted to bring order at West Point and to create a curriculum that would benefit the nation. Envisioning an academy that would embrace as well as teach the scientific erudition of the Enlightenment, he appointed celebrated scientist Jonathan Williams superintendent of cadets in 1801. Early in the following year, Congress made everything official by designating West Point as the United States Military Academy and creating the Corps of Engineers, in part to maintain it.

Early Curricula and Practices   The academy physically began its existence when classes commenced in April 1802. Yet the shortage of money and the lack of qualified instructors meant little change in the daily routine of the place and its people. Slowly, though, the curriculum broadened. In addition to mathematics, cadets began to study physics, fortifications, and artillery. Passing examinations that queried their knowledge of these subjects and familiarity with certain basic textbooks qualified cadets for graduation, and if an officer billet was vacant, a cadet received his commission. It was an improvement over the old, narrow system, but as an education, it was not even closely comparable to that for a degree in a civilian college. Gradually, the addition of subjects like French (the language of many military texts) gave cadets a better-rounded education, but the emphasis nevertheless remained on the rote memorization of generally superficial texts.

The wide range of cadet capabilities drove that emphasis, a circumstance that was eventually recognized as a problem. Those who had been to college usually completed their studies at the academy in about a year; others were there for as many as seven years. This mixture of student proficiency made teaching a challenge and encouraged reliance on a daily schedule that primarily focused on slogging through specified texts. It finally became apparent that through no fault of their own, the cadets themselves were thwarting efforts to create a meaningful educational curriculum as well as an effective training regimen. In 1810 new regulations stipulated that an entering cadet had to be between 15 and 20 years old and possess minimal skills in reading, writing, and arithmetic.

Daily life for the average cadet was not made routine until the security threat posed by the War of 1812 forced Congress to reform the academy. Cadets during the war spent their   **Cadet Life** days studying engineering, mathematics, French, drawing, and physics. The penury of Congress meant, however, that the academy was at best supplied with outdated equipment and obsolete textbooks. Furthermore, the demands of the war for an increasing number of officers translated into pressure on instructors to hasten their cadets to graduation. The conflict ended before the reforms could see West Point officers making noticeable contributions to the war effort, but many in Washington mulled over additional reforms. Further changes created a curriculum and training program that placed West Point cadets under the most regimented daily schedule in the United States.

Virtually every waking moment of a cadet's life was planned for him. His day began at 6:00 A.M. roll call, followed by room cleaning and inspection, breakfast, three hours of mathematics, two hours of French, and dinner, the main meal of the day throughout the nation in those days, which took place a bit later than the modern lunch. He then studied two hours of drawing and engineering before his daily drill, a scheduled study time, an evening parade, and supper. A failure to perform according to rigorous standards, not being where he was supposed to be at any given time, or violating any rule drew penalties that ranged from verbal reprimands to walking tours to confinement to quarters. Really serious offenses meant dismissal.

Meals under the new regulations were equally regimented. Cadets marched in and out of meals, sat ramrod straight, and kept silent at the table. The food was bland but nutritious. Breakfast consisted of coffee, bread and butter, and a meat. At dinner cadets ate meat, bread, potatoes, and two vegetables. Supper, the lightest meal of the day, was tea and bread and butter. Once a week cadets received dessert at dinner and supper.

Stricter regimentation did not necessarily mean absolute order, however. For example, prospective cadets received appointments throughout the year and traveled to West Point immediately to begin their studies. Class schedules and orderly lectures were almost impossible, as new cadets arrived who had no background in the subject. On the other hand, cadets left the academy just as irregularly, sometimes through dismissal for disciplinary reasons, but more often because they were judged competent enough to become officers. Under those circumstances, even the stricter program did little to impart a sense of day-to-day continuity in the cadet ranks.

That situation began to change in 1816 when the War Department mandated that all cadets must remain for four years and could enter the academy only in September. In addition, a significant curriculum reform sorted out the course of study according to a cadet's matriculation. Cadets took classes that grew more involved and sophisticated in each of their years until graduation, a system that fostered a sense of class unity important in creating esprit de corps. In their day-to-day experience, cadets took classes with the same cadets through four years of school.

During the next three years, new superintendent Sylvanus Thayer introduced further changes. Daily life became even more regimented to include military training in a summer encampment, a change that made West Point the cadet's exclusive home during his entire four years of attendance. In fact, he was allowed summer leave only once. Superintendent Thayer's goal was to establish a system whereby "the standing of an individual is dependent wholly upon his own merits."[8] Cadets cooperated with this new system not only to escape punishment but also to enhance their daily performance and conduct ratings that ranked them within their classes. Upon graduation, a cadet's ranking determined his assignment, ranging from the elite engineers for the top graduates to the common infantry for the least stellar performances. By 1820, the United States Military Academy had become a prestigious educational institution that was well on its way to providing the United States Army with a majority of its commissioned officers.

ENLISTED MEN

A variety of motives impelled men to enlist in the United States Army during the early Republic. The enlistee usually received some sort of bounty ranging from $2 to $16, a value set by how badly the country needed his services. Bounties could be persuasive inducements, especially for those who were otherwise unemployable. New soldiers also received a uniform and a daily ration of food. The average ration during the early Republic was about a pound of beef or pork, give or take a few ounces, bread or flour, one gill of liquor (four ounces), salt, vinegar, and part of a candle. Soldiers were supposed to be paid anywhere from $3 to $7 a month, but pay was seldom regular. Soldiers received extra pay for additional work beyond combat or garrison duty. Many frontier forts were built far from the usual supply of laborers, and soldiers collected extra pay for constructing their own forts, a practice that probably kept some men in the army by matching the pay received by laborers in a city. The extra financial opportunities and the free clothes and shelter made soldiering an appealing way to make a living for some. As war with Britain loomed, other incentives came into play. In January 1812, for instance, soldiers were exempted from prosecution for debt, an immunity that lured countless debtors into the ranks. Additionally, the British army paid its soldiers considerably less than the American army and treated them far more harshly. Many British soldiers, already knowing the profession, deserted to the United States and joined the American army.

The army promised men a roof over their heads, regular food, and warm clothes, and for some unskilled and illiterate laborers, those were sufficient inducements to sign up. Others joined for adventure, leaping at the chance to see the frontier and perhaps make their fortunes there. Army life, however, could disappoint with open-air encampments, wretched rations, and ragged uniforms. The frontier was often monotonous rather than exhilarating, and fortunes proved as hard to make there as anywhere else. Desertion was always an option for the disillusioned, especially if they had not squandered their bounty money. It and their new clothes might carry them far enough to someplace else in the country where they could avoid capture and make a new start.

New recruits received about four hours of drill instruction each day while they waited to depart for their assignment. After **Duties** the recruiting officer reached his quota, he usually marched his company to its permanent station, which was typically on the frontier. If he were lucky, he would have a couple of noncommissioned officers with him to maintain discipline, because it was during this journey that most men tried to desert. Many who remained in the ranks required constant vigilance to keep them from preying on civilians with crimes that ranged from petty theft to worse.

After soldiers reached their destination, most of their time might be consumed by building the fort they would garrison. The expanding frontier made fort construction one of the army's primary activities, and a special incentive like an extra whiskey ration could help speed the work. Soldiers first cleared the site both to improve observation from the bastion and to provide the materials for its construction. If a structure already existed, soldiers would either refurbish it or add outbuildings such as stables. There was always the need for general maintenance. The strictness of discipline and the importance placed on drill could vary from fort to fort, depending on the taste of the commanding officer. Some insisted on regular drill and practice at the manual of arms at least every other day; others were so easygoing that their garrison's martial skills atrophied while the men spent their days gardening and hunting.

During the early 1800s, the government found important activities to keep its outland army busier in the service of the country. The developing frontier made road building an important function for soldiers, in part to facilitate pioneer travel, but mainly to tie together the growing number of scattered forts. Road building became a particular preoccupation after the War of 1812, when that conflict brought into government hands millions of acres acquired from Indians. In addition, the war's logistical complications had revealed serious difficulties in moving troops and supplies, a consequence of a lack of roads and the abysmal state of extant ones. In the wake of the war, soldiers spent much of their time remedying this problem with picks and shovels.

Also in those years, the frontier soldier was frequently involved in exploratory expeditions. In major expeditions such as the celebrated one conducted by army officers Meriwether Lewis and William Clark into the Pacific Northwest and Zebulon Pike into the Southwest, frontier soldiers trekked into uncharted lands to search out the sources of rivers, locate the best places to build bridges, and determine the best places for forts. In the process, the uncharted lands of the American wilderness became mapped regions with their physical features revealed and their vast distances measured by army engineers, surveyors, and cartographers.

Hardships The typical fort or post was a small concern with only a couple dozen men. When not performing caretaking chores, soldiers cultivated gardens, hunted game, and fished nearby streams to supplement their dreary diet. Civilian contractors hired to supply rations were notoriously haphazard in their vaguely scheduled visits to frontier outposts, and soldiers periodically had to travel long distances to retrieve provender and other supplies. The arrival of a civilian supplier was hardly a cause for celebration, in any case. The rations they brought were usually meager, sometimes spoiled, and always only just edible. In fact, having posted most of its soldiers on the frontier, the government in some ways acted as if they did not exist. Pay was routinely late, supplies sometimes went missing, and uniforms unraveled into rags. Officers tried to remedy these problems, but often all they could do was send detachments to scattered settlements in the hope they might purchase enough supplies to stave off starvation. Irregular pay was a different but no less difficult problem. With depressing frequency, desperate officers, gauging plummeting morale and rising desertions, had to send parties of officers and men hundreds of miles to fetch payrolls that were months in arrears.

Contemplating these problems, soldiers found it easy to feel that the government had abandoned them. Collapsing morale saw some desert, but others remained in place to crawl into whiskey bottles. The trap they set for themselves with this liquid refuge was an insidious one. Whiskey could temporarily ease boredom, blunt anger, and dull frustrations over poor food and tardy pay, but its magic was as consistently fleeting as its grip was increasingly firm. Susceptible officers and enlisted men alike became notorious drunkards. Itinerant traders, their wagons filled with whiskey, followed payrolls to frontier forts to make paydays into spree days that ended with many of the men stumbling drunk. Some officers joined a few civilian authorities to call attention to the problem of soldiers' drinking, but the culture of the times was not inclined to see anything alarming. American men drank a profuse amount of alcohol anyway, and most observers did not regard the presence or absence of a uniform to be pertinent. There were officers, however, who were appalled by the breach of military discipline that drunkenness posed and worried about the overall health and effectiveness of their commands. They might ban from their posts traders with alcohol and build their forts as far as possible from nearby towns with their tempting saloons, but soldiers always found a way around these well-intentioned gestures. With relative ease, they supplemented their whiskey ration.

Officers were more often forced to restore discipline after the fact by leveling severe punishments for drunkenness. Consequences for soldiers guilty of violating regulations or laws were harsh by anyone's standards. During the early Republic, corporal punishment was common for numerous infractions including theft, assault, and insubordination. Under regulations, the maximum number of lashes a soldier could receive was 100, but other physical ordeals could be substituted for or added to a sentence of flogging. On the eve of the War of 1812, the army ceased flogging malefactors, but the practice of branding continued, usually to a visible part of the body like the face or hand, to make readily and permanently apparent its owner had committed a military breach. Trivial offenses could mean reduced rations of food or whiskey, the latter deprivation being regarded by most soldiers as the worse punishment. A violator might have to perform duties while dragging around a log or cannonball chained to his leg. The most serious offenses could mean a death sentence, either by hanging or firing squad, depending on the crime.

Army life was unhealthy. It carried the risk of combat, but there were other perils as well. Poor food, indifferent health care, **Health** insufficient shelter, incipient or outright alcoholism, and the likelihood of being posted to unhealthy locations made soldiering highly dangerous aside from the chance that one might be shot in battle. Those who had the misfortune to be stationed in the South during summer probably suffered most. The heat made physical labor doubly difficult, spoiled food quickly, and carried the constant threat of tropical disease. Yellow fever was prevalent, and physicians were in short supply because most competent doctors would not serve under such conditions. The army made do with poorly trained surgeons.

It was all a prescription for trouble, and in 1809 it a produced a first-class health disaster at Terre aux Boeufs, Louisiana. The commander was General James Wilkinson, later infamous for his wide-ranging corruption, who in this instance displayed a scandalous disregard for the 2,000 men in his charge by refusing to move them to healthier ground. The scandal went beyond dereliction. Wilkinson wanted to remain near New Orleans to cultivate dishonest relationships with civilian contractors in the city. As Wilkinson padded his pocketbook, his men remained on low ground whose main features were bad water, swarming mosquitoes, poor sanitation, and rotten food. The encampment became a nightmare. Delirious with fever, the dying filled the camp with screams while the living endured the stench of feces and unburied, rotting corpses. At last, even Wilkinson could not ignore the calamity unfolding at Terre aux Boeufs. He belatedly acted to move survivors to higher ground. By then, almost half of his command was dead.

Actually, Wilkinson's debacle was only an amplification of a condition that was a chronic blight, though in less spectacular ways, throughout the period. The health and welfare of soldiers at posts throughout the country was of minor importance to the government. After the War of 1812, however, new attitudes appeared in the War Department. The increasing reliance on the regular army to build roads, maintain frontier forts, and treat with Indians required healthy recruits kept fit by positive changes in procedure. The contracting system was improved, and the men's rations were placed on a sounder nutritional basis with the introduction of fruits and vegetables. Even with these changes, soldiers were hardly pictures of health, but they were better off than their fellows of only a few years earlier.

WOMEN

Women helped to alleviate the drudgery and monotony of life at frontier posts. The army provided for up to four laundresses per company of soldiers, not only to clean the men's clothes, bed linens, and quarters, but also to furnish a feminine presence. Many were either already married to, or would marry, enlisted men. Such authorized women workers, who received rations and pay from the army, were considered a civilizing influence, but "loose females" were another matter.[9] It was one of the realities of soldiering that wherever men in uniform gathered, prostitutes would follow. Most officers discouraged the presence of prostitutes because they caused quarrels and transmitted diseases, but at forts located near settlements, they were almost impossible to exclude. It did not help that many officers kept mistresses, possibly emulating European practice, and lost some measure of moral authority to preach sexual abstinence in the process.

On the other hand, the presence of fewer women meant frictions of another sort, such as officers frolicking with subordinates' wives. Some officers discouraged their men from marrying, but because they had no authority to forbid such unions, they were more often than not foolish to oppose them.

Families Soldiers and officers tried to maintain a measure of normal family life while serving on the frontier. The outbreak of war endangered women and children who lived in garrisons, yet when presented with peril, women could prove helpful. Caught in the crossfire as Indians attacked Arthur St. Clair's expedition against the Ohio River tribes, the women lent assistance and even engaged in combat.

In the early nineteenth century, officers more regularly had their wives with them, at least for part of the year. Their companionship not only helped to chase away the blues on the humdrum frontier; the wives themselves also provided medical care of sorts to men frequently without physicians. Theirs was a lonely life, though, because officers' wives likely had few female companions of their social class at the frontier forts. Properly educating their children in such remote sites was a doubtful undertaking at best and at least one of the reasons many wives spent most of the year living with relatives, usually their parents. Those who remained with their husbands did their best to teach their children. In some cases, an educated enlisted man taught them.

Many officers with growing families found they could not support a wife and children on their limited salaries. If not lucky or clever enough to find other sources of income, they were compelled to contemplate leaving the service for a civilian job. Officers also left the army to spare their families the strain of being regularly uprooted as well as the isolation and danger of frontier life. Finally, a military husband and father who died in circumstances other than combat potentially placed his family in an economic crisis. Because there were no official provisions for their upkeep, they were left to fend for themselves.

MILITIA

According to the Militia Act of 1792, states were to maintain a militia force of fit men between the ages of 18 and 45 for national defense in emergencies. Beyond that requirement, how states were to train, equip, and supply these men was entirely up to them. Taking advantage of such lax oversight, states usually neglected the militia, especially during hard economic times, leading one militiaman to comment at the beginning of the War of 1812 that "most of our officers as well as the men are as yet destitute of the qualifications requisite in military life."[10] Communities held militia musters to train and practice firearms drills, but these events gradually transformed into social occasions in which picnicking, drinking, and dancing supplanted most training. Firearms were anything but standardized and not always in good repair. Ammunition and powder were in short supply. Consequently, the militia muster typically consisted of marching and firing practice in the morning, with social activities filling the afternoon.

On the rare occasion when a local militia company was called for duty, its lack of training was instantly apparent. On the march, militiamen straggled behind regular soldiers. Their wretched camp hygiene made them sick. Their poor discipline and inadequate training meant that they often ran from battles. Although the War of 1812 saw militia behaving admirably in some actions, the usual capriciousness of citizen forces compelled the government to rely far less on them in the years after that conflict.

COMBAT

The most extended period of combat for American soldiers during the early Republic was the War of 1812 (1812–1815). Of several Indian conflicts, the most important was the First Seminole War of 1818, which ultimately brought about the acquisition of Florida. While life in frontier forts included the constant threat of conflict with Native Americans and the occasional border skirmish with a European neighbor, American soldiers actually saw little or no combat during the period.

War is always a possibility for soldiers, of course, whether on the frontier or in less remote garrisons, and it is a testimony to the early Republic's complacency that its soldiers were seldom effectively trained to meet the exigencies of combat. Until the War of 1812 forced a reevaluation of the military structure, deficiently trained officers inevitably produced ineffective combat soldiers.

The United States Army and militia practiced offensive and defensive warfare in every conflict during the period. Daily marching over long, often roadless, terrain to attack the enemy generally preceded offensive battles, particularly in the War of 1812. In short, campaigns involved relatively little fighting, most battles generally lasting a few hours at most, and considerable marching. Offensive combat consisted of open-field charges or assaults on fortifications. In both cases, an artillery barrage directed at enemy troops or their fortifications preceded the infantry's advance, usually answered by an artillery bombardment from the enemy. Depending on the skill of gunners, bombardments could be noisy but ineffective or terribly destructive. If the latter, infantry hunkered down to weather the storm of shells interspersed with piercing shrieks from the wounded and the visual horrors, as one witness described, of a ball flying through the air taking "off one man's head."[11] Infantry advanced in straight, parallel lines. If fighting on an open field, the opposing army mirrored these movements. The two forces marched to within firing range of their smoothbore muskets, usually 100 yards or less, and discharged a volley. The casualties from gunshots were typically light because the muskets were notoriously inaccurate at anything but virtually point-blank range. Instead, the volleys threw up dense clouds of smoke from the black gunpowder, an acrid screen that intensified as the sides reloaded and fired additional rounds. One American soldier who fought at the battle of New Orleans on January 8, 1815, said that "the morning had dawned to be sure, but the smoke was so thick that every thing seemed to be covered up in it."[12] At some point, the issue would be pressed by a melee in which the infantry staged a bayonet charge for hand-to-hand combat. Those contests usually decided the fate of battle.

Attacking fortifications required an infantry charge under the cover of continued artillery support lest the fort's guns have free rein to cut down advancing soldiers. The front ranks carried scaling ladders to overrun the fortification's outer works as a prelude to assailing the main fort.

American forces during the War of 1812 more commonly defended a fortified position. During attacks, duties in the fort varied. Some soldiers manned the fort's artillery while others were positioned at gun ports and on the ramparts. Officers either supervised artillery fire or paced behind the men on the walls to give encouragement and to direct their musket volleys. Attacks on fortifications often became formal sieges in which the enemy surrounded the fort and threatened an attack for days extending into weeks. A siege reduced the daily routine of soldiers to the essentials of survival: they took cover during artillery bombardments, kept watch for surprise attacks, and stretched diminishing supplies of rations. Living under siege was considered the most unpleasant of military duties.

Despite the perils, noise, and chaos of battle, many preferred some sort of action to the monotony of garrison life. A well-trained army could function like a machine in battle, fostering a great deal of satisfaction and pride among those who were part of such an organization. Unfortunately for American soldiers during the War of 1812, their armies often operated like broken machines. Large numbers of volunteers and militia with virtually no military experience or training were hurled into offensive and defensive battles against better-trained opponents who were often allied with merciless Indian warriors, leading one discouraged American to lament, "we are doomed to experience nothing but disaster and disgrace where ever our arms are turned."[13] Understandably, if not laudably, Americans simply ran. While there were some notable exceptions, such as the battle of Lundy's Lane in July 1814, when American soldiers charging a British battery engaged in one of the most "gallant acts ever known,"[14] and the battle of New Orleans in January 1815, these few instances did little to persuade against serious reforms in the United States Army. After the war, the government made a determined decision to rely almost entirely on a regular army. The daily life of the average soldier would thereafter involve far more training, conducted by increasingly competent officers.

THE NAVY

The peacetime lives of sailors, whether in the merchant fleet or in the United States Navy, were typically a good deal busier than those of average soldiers. Sailors received on average at least twice as much pay as enlisted soldiers, about $10 to $12 per month during the period. A sailor's pay was higher in part because he was consigned to lengthy tours at sea. Yet sailors on merchant vessels received even higher wages (as much as $15 to $20 a month), making it difficult for the navy to recruit able-bodied, knowledgeable seamen. In wartime, an extra incentive was that navy seamen had the opportunity to win prize money, a portion of a captured ship's value, but it was common knowledge that strict discipline framed shipboard life with punishments that were not only harsh but also violent. The army discontinued flogging in 1812, but sailors were subject to it until 1850. Rank water, spoiled food, and cramped living conditions were the sailor's lot, confirming Samuel Johnson's observation that serving aboard ship was like being in prison, with "the chance of being drowned."[15]

Personnel   Similar to army practice, the captain and his officers had to man their ships by personally recruiting their crews. The British Royal Navy filled out its crews by using impressment—often little more than the forcible abduction of inebriated tavern patrons—but law prohibited American naval officers from forcing men to serve. Accordingly, conditions were usually better in American ships than in British ones, if for no other reason than to induce volunteers to sign on. In peacetime, however, the most liberal enticements could not compete with the far more palatable situation and more generous pay of merchant service, and only the chance for prize money in wartime could offset the advantages of the merchant marine.

Life aboard ship was an unpleasant combination of unthinking obedience and demanding labor. The one discouraged the irritable, and the other disqualified the very young, the very old, and the infirm. Most men who joined the navy were in their late teens or twenties, and they typically signed on as a last resort after failing to find employment at anything else. The unskilled were likely recruits, then, but those whom discrimination and prejudice had made outsiders also found a home in the navy. For example, a large number of African Americans became sailors. Some captains hesitated to recruit black seamen, but manpower shortages usually prevailed over bigotry, and some figures calculate that African Americans made up between 15 and 25 percent of the American navy.

Duties   Ships were incredibly complex and self-contained communities in which each man had a particular place and duty. As in any organization, some duties gave sailors added status and authority. The navy's equivalent of noncommissioned officers had particular responsibilities and held the men under them accountable for their implementation. The boatswain (pronounced "bosun") supervised a boatswain's mate to keep the ship's heavy canvas sails and intricate rigging in working order. The master-at-arms commanded a complement of seamen to maintain order aboard ship and report infractions of the regulations to officers. The ship's carpenter and his assistants could be the busiest people aboard, especially after combat, when extensive damage required repairs. Weather could also inflict dire damage on wooden sailing vessels, and the carpenter and his mates were seldom idle. The purser kept all the ship's money, squared its ledgers with expenses paid during a voyage, and disbursed the men's monthly wages.

Ships functioned best when they were under strictly regulated routines, and crews best abided the tedium of endless days under sail and in confined quarters when they were busy. Every crewman consequently had a set of jobs that required his attention every day, usually in the same order, if not during the same hours. Because ships at sea required some portion of the crew always to be on duty, the men were organized into several work gangs called watches. The duties of watches could range from two to five hours, depending on the time of day. Watches rotated so that nobody always had to work at night. Part of the watch spent its entire time trimming sails according to instructions from officers on the quarterdeck (the part of the vessel nearest the helm) to adapt to changing wind and weather. This could be dangerous work, whether one was heaving lines on deck or scampering aloft in the rigging, and sailors who were able to set and haul in sails during a "blow" (high winds) were more than valuable to a ship; they were essential to its survival. Less perilous work also occupied watches: normal wear and tear required housekeeping chores such as scrubbing the deck with pumice stones, washing away detritus, and painting and polishing woodwork to a high sheen, hence its nautical name of "brightwork." Day watches also honed gunnery skills to meet the American navy's goal of firing "three broadsides to the enemy's two."[16]

The crew was also divided into groups called "messes" for three daily meals. There was neither enough time nor room for **Food** the entire crew to eat at the same time. Depending on the size of the ship and the weather, men usually ate on deck with one or more of the members of the mess dispatched to the galley to retrieve the food. Breakfast, the lightest meal of the day, typically consisted of bread or hardtack and hot tea. Dinner, the largest meal, was eaten at midday and included beef or pork, bread, peas or potatoes, and occasionally cheese. Supper, served in the late afternoon, consisted of leftovers from dinner. After each meal, the men were issued a part of their daily rum ration.

Officers and noncommissioned officers were also divided into messes that were scheduled to avoid conflicts with the watch they commanded. Their meals consisted of freshly cooked food served to them at tables in the wardroom or other quarters belowdecks. Yet neither officers nor crew would have described the food as anything other than fuel. The best that could be said was that only the foulest weather prevented galley fires from making food hot. Otherwise, meat was in varying stages of decay, cheeses always bore evidence of gnawing rats, and weevils squirmed in moldy bread. Long voyages with few stops for provisions meant that both officers and men ate increasingly unpalatable food that was fairly well spoiled by the time it was prepared. A corresponding increase in intestinal complaints toward the end of a voyage was a standard condition for officers and crew.

Officers   The popular perception of life at sea as a dashing adventure attracted middle- and upper-class men to a naval officer's career, and the fact that officers received the lion's share of prize money in wartime was an encouragement as well. A wartime navy, in fact, saw some commissions given to adult men with more regard for their political influence than their naval experience. Most officers, however, received their appointments as teenagers to the lowly rank of midshipman. Influence worked here as well inasmuch as these appointments were usually meted out to the sons or relations of influential men, but at least they were in the form of officer apprenticeships that allowed youngsters literally to learn the ropes before exercising significant command. A midshipman hardly found himself in an exalted position, but he outranked common seamen and could expect from his captain a comprehensive education on seamanship, navigation, and leadership. Most of a midshipman's day was occupied by running errands and performing chores for the captain and other officers. After a midshipman completed his training, he was recommended for a lieutenant's commission, but there was usually a waiting list, especially in peacetime, when few vessels were at sea. Some midshipmen had to wait several years before a lieutenant's commission came available.

A new lieutenant took on part of the crew as his immediate subordinates and commenced to supervise certain functions of the ship. The number of lieutenants aboard ship varied according to its size. The largest American vessels, the so-called superfrigates, usually had a complement of six. The senior lieutenant acted as the captain's second-in-command. At sea, the captain ruled over all aboard as an absolute dictator, his authority backed by centuries of naval tradition and an elaborate set of codes and punishments that preemptively presumed his judgments sound and his disciplinary actions just.

Discipline   The captain wielded unqualified authority out of necessity. Common seamen and officers alike endured the difficulties imposed by living in extremely close quarters, and discipline was essential to maintaining order. Consequently, regulations were strictly enforced, though the typical sailor was prone to violate rules. The tedium of long cruises led to fights, drunkenness, and insubordination. Most offenses were punished with flogging, the number of lashes depending on the seriousness of the transgression. When the captain or a formal court-martial imposed a sentence of flogging, all hands were required to witness the punishment to deter them from straying as well. Yet stray they did, and such punishment scenes regularly occurred aboard American naval vessels.

The United States Navy has never had a mutiny aboard one of its ships, pointing to the fact that these toughened salts were a willing lot, taken as a whole. Harsh punishments, bad food, boring routines, and the potential for horrible death in battle could not deter them from a life at sea. The prospect of adventure doubtless appealed to many, and hard times threw unskilled workers into the martial life, as it did on land as well as at sea, but they took pride in their ships and never embarrassed their country. The American navy during the early Republic carried the flag to far-flung ports in peacetime. In times of trouble, it comported itself with keen efficiency and admirable skill. It began to build a widespread reputation for having the best officers and the most able seamen in the world.

Discipline was crucial to ensure proficient conduct during a naval battle, an event so violent and chaotic that it could paralyze **Battle** an inexperienced crew. Everyone had to be trained to perform his duty during battle not only without hesitation but also with reflexive speed.

At first sight of an enemy vessel, drumbeats sounded the command to clear the decks for action and post to battle stations. Limited space belowdecks typically meant that gun decks were used for sleeping and eating, and an impending engagement required the clearing of hammocks and tables so that gun crews could load and run out their pieces. The upper deck and gun deck quickly became scenes of apparent confusion that were actually highly organized drills practiced hundreds of times. Sailors meanwhile darted through the rigging to set sails best to maneuver the ship into range of the enemy. As the ship closed on the enemy, captain, helmsman, and sailing master worked together to keep the ship's profile from being fully exposed to enemy fire as gun crews began testing their ranges. Ships could maneuver for hours, firing only sporadically, trying to secure the "weather gauge," the upwind position that provided significant advantages over an opponent. The object was to bring all the ship's guns to bear (a broadside) while minimizing the risk posed by enemy fire. Everything depended on the wind and the crew's skill in handling sails, an especially unpredictable chore when enemy shot damaged masts and rigging, making it difficult to maneuver the ship. While the captain shouted instructions to maneuver the ship, he and his officers also barked orders regarding the ordnance: starting with "cast loose your guns" to ensure that the guns were no longer lashed to the bulwarks, followed with orders to load, "run" (put the muzzle out of the gun port), "aim," "prime" (put powder in the touchhole), and finally "fire!"[17]

If the ships closed, they increased their rates of fire, and engagements often became slugfests of endurance. Shouting officers paced among seamen loading and firing heavy cannons whose concussions shivered every timber in the ship and whose recoil snapped taut straining ropes that barely kept the weapons in place. Salvos from the enemy hurtled with ear-splitting shrieks and found their target with horrifying results, ripping wide holes in planking and throwing up large splinters of wood that could be deadlier than shot and shell. Gun deck crews continued firing in intense heat and choking smoke as explosions and debris maimed those they did not kill. Sand spread on decks prevented them from becoming slick with blood, but dismembered bodies impeded work and were either shoved to the side or sent to the surgeon's table. The frenzy panicked many, especially those new to battle, but if they tried to flee, the ship offered few avenues of retreat. Officers and their noncommissioned mates had the duty of forcing the frightened back to their posts. An officer confronting unreasoning terror might even resort to killing an escaping sailor with his sword or pistol as an example to everyone else that it was safer to fight the enemy.

Men aloft handled the sails, or what was left of them, and those on deck prepared to repel boarders if the enemy grappled his ship to theirs. Every warship had a complement of marines whose primary job was to take positions in the rigging to shoot enemy officers and to fend off and fight boarders. Marines took charge of prisoners if a ship surrendered without being boarded.

Depending on advantages in size, guns, and wind, naval battles could be over in minutes or lengthen into hours, especially ones with relatively equal opponents. Prolonged fights inflicted staggering damage to both ship and crew, and officers suffered especially high mortality rates.

The ship's surgeon and his mates tended to the wounded. They did their best to remove casualties while the engagement raged around them, and those with a chance for survival were rushed to the sickbay, where the surgeon amputated mangled limbs and stitched up wounds. Many who survived this initial trauma died either of shock or from infections that were a common consequence of unsanitary medical practices.

Health   The surgeon's most frantic periods were during and immediately following battles, but he was constantly busy at other times as well. Close quarters, spoiled food, foul water, and fetid air belowdecks meant that there were always plenty of sick sailors. Some surgeons were trained physicians, while others learned their craft through apprenticeship like many civilian doctors. They employed at sea the same medicines and techniques as their civilian counterparts on land: bleeding and purgatives were the most common remedies, treatments that never cured and sometimes killed. If the ship had one, a chaplain conducted the funerals that were sadly regular events; the captain did so otherwise. With the entire ship's company assembled, appropriate readings from the scriptures preceded the tipping of the corpse, wrapped in a canvas shroud, into its watery grave.

Prizes   As for soldiers, battle was hardly a daily occurrence for sailors, even in wartime. Much of a warship's time was spent cruising over vast stretches of open, empty seas. If lucky, it would encounter an enemy merchant vessel, an easily captured quarry to sell for prize money. If near an American port, part of the crew was detached to sail the prize to that haven for sale. A midshipman typically took command of a prize crew because the captain needed all his officers if he happened on an enemy warship. A merchant vessel captured far from an American port was usually burned and its crew put off at the nearest stop.

CONCLUSION

Military life could be arduous and unforgiving during the early Republic just as in all times. Daily routines were usually monotonous, discipline was severe, food was often scant and spoiled, and quarters were cramped and dirty. Danger was not a typical element of daily life, but circumstances could make it so at a moment's notice and without warning. What drew men to soldiering or to the sea, then as now, were the timeless appeals that have always attracted those seeking adventure or fellowship or escape. Brothers in arms came from all occupations and circumstances and included all types of people: men who were courageous or merely audacious, men on the lam and those for whom a bad marriage was a greater peril than bullets on a battlefield. In short, the martial life with all its uncertainties was for some an adventure, an escape, an opportunity, or a sentence. Occasionally they all had to find out what they were made of, either when battling the debilitating tedium of routines or the terrifying figures of violent enemies. Then as now, they served and protected their country, and then as now, they too often were disdained or, worse, forgotten.

NOTES

1. Edward M. Coffman, *The Old Army: A Portrait of the American Army in Peacetime, 1784–1898* (New York: Oxford University Press, 1986), 7.

2. Ibid., 18.

3. Ibid., 14, 15.

4. Francis Paul Prucha, *The Sword of the Republic: The United States Army on the Frontier, 1783–1846* (Lincoln: University of Nebraska Press, 1969), 1–5.

5. Frederick Jackson Turner, quoted in Malcolm Muir Jr., "James Wilkinson," in *Encyclopedia of the War of 1812*, ed. David S. Heidler and Jeanne T. Heidler (Santa Barbara: ABC-Clio, 1997), 555.

6. A solid explanation of dueling and its connection to reputation is in Bertram Wyatt-Brown, *Southern Honor: Ethics and Behavior in the Old South* (Oxford: Oxford University Press, 1982).

7. The most famous duel in American history occurred in 1804 at Weehawken, New Jersey, between former secretary of the treasury Alexander Hamilton and sitting vice president Aaron Burr, an encounter that left Hamilton mortally wounded and Burr under indictment. Burr was never prosecuted for killing Hamilton, but the deed further tarnished his already blemished reputation.

8. Stephen E. Ambrose, *Duty, Honor, Country: A History of West Point* (Baltimore: Johns Hopkins University Press, 1966), 75.

9. Coffman, *The Old Army*, 25.

10. James M. Merrill, ed., *Uncommon Valor: The Exciting Story of the Army* (Chicago: Rand McNally, 1964), 79.

11. Ibid., 95.

12. Joseph T. Cox, ed., *The Written Wars: American War Prose through the Civil War* (North Haven, Conn.: Archon Books, 1996), 128.

13. Richard C. Knopf, ed., *Document Transcriptions of the War of 1812 in the Northwest*, vol. 3 (Columbus: Ohio Historical Society, 1957), 166.

14. Cox, *Written Wars*, 114.

15. James Boswell, *Boswell's Life of Johnson, together with Boswell's Journal of a Tour of the Hebrides and Johnson's Diary of a Journey into North Wales*, ed. Lawrence Fitzroy Powell, vol. 1 (Oxford: Clarendon Press, 1934), 266.

16. Edward L. Beach, *The United States Navy: A 200-Year History* (Boston: Houghton Mifflin, 1986), 75.

17. Frances Diane Robotti and James Vescovi, *The USS* Essex *and the Birth of the American Navy* (Holbrook, Mass.: Adams Media Corporation, 1999), 83–86.

EPILOGUE

The only unconditional laws of human existence are those of change and imperfection. Numerous ancient fables and modern tales revolve around the simple wisdom of the indisputable constant in all human affairs: "This too shall pass." Equally numerous stories point to the reality that all things are alloyed. The years of the early Republic were no exception. By the early 1800s, almost 200 years of European settlement had steadily made its mark on the land of America, first on the eastern seaboard, then on its interior. The remarkable progress of settlement, however, was often at the expense of lands left barren and exhausted by overplanting, and its advance frequently deprived Indian populations of birthrights and dignity.

As colonies became states and the Confederation became the constitutional republic, agriculture remained the chief occupation throughout the nation, but as the first two decades of the nineteenth century ended, a remarkable revolution in farming was already taking place. Farmers used more and better implements to increase yields. Experiments in novel farming techniques revealed a continuing American fascination with innovation and improvement. Meanwhile, other Americans strode westward, clearing fields and notching logs for windowless cabins, attracted to that hard life by the expectation that hard work would make them prosperous and keep them free. After the War of 1812, Americans exhibited a renewed dedication to their experiment in liberty and even more confidence in the apparently boundless possibilities for their country. Crops filled the fields, factories prospered as their numbers increased, canals and turnpikes lured investment and hurried commerce, and nothing seemed beyond the reach of a new nation whose unofficial motto might have been "We can do anything."

Yet the people of the early Republic could not do some things at all, at least for the time being. They could not ease the plight of native peoples for whom expanding white settlements posed an increasing threat. Unable to fashion a satisfactory solution to this cultural as well as physical collision of Indians and whites, Americans would resort to the shameful program of taking Indian lands and removing their inhabitants to regions beyond the Mississippi River. In a similar way, the immorality of slavery in their free republic left them more stymied about resolving this inconsistency with each passing year. Slavery by 1820 was peculiar to the South, but the question of whether it could expand into territories already loomed in the angry debates over Missouri's admission to the Union. To the enslaved, the troubling contradiction of slavery and freedom was more than a disruptive social, economic, and political question. For them, it regulated every aspect of their existence. For those blacks who had shaken the bonds of slavery, or even for those who had never known it, its taint still cast a huge pall over their lives. Farmers guiding their plows across dawn-lit fields in Ohio, planters watching the gangs trudge to the cotton rows, and the slaves themselves with callused hands and burlap bags slung over their shoulders could not have known the terrible cost this moral dilemma would exact. In 1820 freedom was more than a generation away for these people, a freedom that would be bought with more than 600,000 American lives. All things, good and evil, are alloyed.

Nor did these Americans realize that the Industrial Revolution was dawning, its effects and consequences destined to change forever the lives of everyone. With its impressive technological advances, the coming industrialism would make goods previously reserved for the wealthy staples of everyday households. It would also create a new type of laborer, the factory worker. These men and women did not farm or learn arcane skills or ply special trades. They instead adjusted their lives to clocks, clanging bells, shrill steam whistles, and the unremitting din of well-oiled, tireless machinery. Their workplaces were at first in rural settings because running streams provided the first sources of power, but cities often grew around these early factories, eventually transforming the surrounding countryside into bustling junctions of trade, culture, and people. There would be new theaters, museums, and art galleries; but there would also be squalid slums with hollow-eyed children, broken men, and women old before their time.

Yet the revolution in what later generations called consumerism—people of the early Republic would have called it material progress—crushed eighteenth-century social and economic theories about the rigidity of class systems. What happened in these pivotal years in America should also discourage the modern tendency to dismiss the buying and selling of things as coarse consumerism and exploitative commercialism. European intellectuals asserted that only necessity made poor people work, but the American experience revealed that theory to be nothing more than condescending hogwash, to use an Americanism grating to European ears. In America, aspirations to a better life encouraged and emboldened all classes, a circumstance that was a true break from old European ideas of society and the proper place for people in it. By acquiring the material comforts of more elevated social classes, one could reach a state of gentility. The result might be seen as a paradox for the earnest republicans who rejected kings and disdained aristocrats, but it was not really. By making gentility the normal course of progress for ordinary people, Americans turned the trappings of aristocracy into a hallmark of democracy. In America, where anybody could achieve the status of "gentleman" or "lady" through hard work, anything was possible, even the emancipation of slaves, eventually. European observers might have assumed that the reward for hard work—the accumulation of material comfort—was merely another example of America's lack of refinement, but that snobbish attitude missed the point. In America, the accumulation of material comfort was an evolutionary step to the creation of a society far different from that imagined in the doomsday predictions of a Malthus and more egalitarian than any envisioned by the violent prescriptions of a Marx.

The changes that marked America during these years were not entirely about the getting of things. Americans were a literate people, a result of religious convictions, economic necessities, and political obligations. Foremost they believed that only educated citizens could preserve free government. Inherited as part of the Puritan legacy of learning, America's thirst for knowledge either matched or surpassed any other place in the world. Furthermore, the concerns prompted by religious revivalism meant a growing compassionate impulse that found expression in charitable institutions, embryonic abolitionism, and reform movements fighting alcoholism and rampant gambling. Rather than the product of persistent, grim Puritanism, these efforts were a demonstration of buoyant faith in the betterment of mankind, a logical melding of Enlightenment rationalism with romantic optimism. In any case, Americans were not always toiling to better themselves or improve others. They took time to court, to marry, to make love, to raise children, to laugh, to stroll country lanes or city parks.

The ordinary American in 1820 might well have described his or her life by distilling it to such essentials. Americans' philosophical embrace of the principles that had driven the Revolution a generation earlier did not mean that they were necessarily a philosophical people. They inclined toward action rather than introspection, and the liberties they enjoyed were tangible evidence of sacrifices, not abstract rhetorical flourishes for a

political speech. The dangers of the world they held at bay, the boiling dis-
contents of home they ignored or tried to alleviate, the timeless routines of
life, love, and death they experienced in joy and sorrow—such was the
stuff of that life so many years ago, the changeless exception to the
absolute law of change, reminding us that in its essentials, the play is
always the same, and only the actors, with each generation, are different.

BIBLIOGRAPHY

AFRICAN AMERICANS

Ashworth, John. *Slavery, Capitalism, and Politics in the Antebellum Republic*. New York: Cambridge University Press, 1995.

Berlin, Ira. *Many Thousands Gone: The First Two Centuries of Slavery in North America*. Cambridge: Belknap Press of Harvard University Press, 1998.

———. *Slaves without Masters: The Free Negro in the Antebellum South*. New York: Pantheon Books, 1974.

Berlin, Ira, and Philip D. Morgan. *Cultivation and Culture: Labor and the Shaping of Slave Life in the Americas*. Charlottesville: University Press of Virginia, 1993.

Blassingame, John. *The Slave Community*. New York: Oxford University Press, 1979.

Bradley, Patricia. *Slavery, Propaganda, and the American Revolution*. Jackson: University Press of Mississippi, 1998.

Clifford, Mary Louise. *From Slavery to Freedom: Black Loyalists after the American Revolution*. Jefferson, N.C.: McFarland, 1999.

Dillon, Merton Lynn. *Slavery Attacked: Southern Slaves and Their Allies, 1619–1865*. Baton Rouge: Louisiana State University Press, 1990.

Fehrenbacher, Don Edward. *The Slaveholding Republic: An Account of the United States Government's Relations to Slavery*. New York: Oxford University Press, 2001.

Fladeland, Betty. *Men and Brothers: Anglo-American Antislavery Cooperation*. Urbana: University of Illinois Press, 1972.

Foner, Philip Sheldon, and Robert J. Branham. *Lift Every Voice: African American Oratory, 1787–1900*. Tuscaloosa: University of Alabama Press, 1998.

Genovese, Eugene D. *Roll, Jordan, Roll: The World the Slaves Made*. New York: Vintage Books, 1972.

Greenberg, Kenneth S. *Masters and Statesmen: The Political Culture of American Slavery.* Baltimore: Johns Hopkins University Press, 1986.

Horton, James Oliver. *Free People of Color inside the African American Community.* Washington, D.C.: Smithsonian Institution Press, 1993.

King, Wilma. *Stolen Childhood: Slave Youth in Nineteenth-Century America.* Bloomington: Indiana University Press, 1995.

Levine, Lawrence. *Black Culture and Black Consciousness: Afro-American Folk Thought from Slavery to Freedom.* New York: Oxford University Press, 1977.

Litwack, Leon. *North of Slavery: The Negro in the Free States, 1790–1860.* Chicago: University of Chicago Press, 1961.

Morgan, Kenneth. *Slavery and Servitude in North America, 1607–1800.* Edinburgh: Edinburgh University Press, 2000.

Murphy, Thomas. *Jesuit Slaveholding in Maryland, 1717–1838.* New York: Routledge, 2001.

Newman, Richard, and Patrick Rael. *Pamphlets of Protest: An Anthology of Early African-American Protest Literature, 1790–1860.* New York: Routledge, 2001.

Richards, Leonard L. *The Slave Power: The Free North and Southern Domination, 1780–1860.* Baton Rouge: Louisiana State University Press, 2000.

Thomas, Velma Maia. *Lest We Forget: The Passage from Africa to Slavery and Emancipation.* New York: Crown, 1997.

Wiencek, Henry. *An Imperfect God: George Washington, His Slaves, and the Creation of America.* New York: Farrar, Straus and Giroux, 2003.

Wilson, Carol. *Freedom at Risk: The Kidnapping of Free Blacks in America, 1780–1865.* Lexington: University Press of Kentucky, 1994.

AGRICULTURE

Atack, Jeremy, and Fred Bateman. *To Their Own Soil: Agriculture in the Antebellum North.* Ames: Iowa State University Press, 1987.

Bidwell, Percy W., and John I. Falconer. *History of Agriculture in the Northern United States, 1620–1860.* Washington, D.C.: Carnegie Institution, 1925; New York: Peter Smith, 1941.

Cochrane, Willard Wesley. *The Development of American Agriculture: A Historical Analysis.* Minneapolis: University of Minnesota Press, 1979.

Ferleger, Lou. *Agriculture and National Development: Views on the Nineteenth Century.* Ames: Iowa State University Press, 1990.

Fussell, G. E. *Farming Technique from Prehistoric to Modern Times.* Oxford: Pergamon Press, 1966.

Gates, Paul Wallace. *The Farmers Age: Agriculture, 1815–1860.* Armonk, N.Y.: M. E. Sharpe, 1989.

Grey, Lewis C. *History of Agriculture in the Southern United States to 1860.* Washington, D.C.: Carnegie Institution, 1933; New York: Peter Smith, 1958.

Howard, Robert West. *Two Billion Acre Farm: An Informal History of American Agriculture.* Garden City, N.Y.: Doubleday, 1945.

Hurt, R. Douglas. *American Agriculture: A Brief History.* Ames: Iowa State University Press, 1994.

Kelsey, Darwin, ed. *Farming in the New Nation: Interpreting American Agriculture.* Washington, D.C.: Agricultural History Society, 1972.

Kulikoff, Allan. *The Agrarian Origins of American Capitalism.* Charlottesville: University Press of Virginia, 1992.

Opie, John. *The Law of the Land: Two Hundred Years of American Farmland Policy.* Lincoln: University of Nebraska Press, 1994.

Otto, John Solomon. *The Southern Frontiers, 1607–1860: The Agricultural Evolution of the Colonial and Antebellum South.* New York: Greenwood Press, 1989.

Paulsen, Gary. *Farm: A History and Celebration of the American Farmer.* Englewood Cliffs, N.J.: Prentice-Hall, 1977.

Power, Richard Lyle. *Planting Corn Belt Culture: The Impress of the Upland Southerner and the Yankee in the Old Northwest.* Indianapolis: Indiana Historical Society, 1953.

Rubnow, John, and Carol Ward Knox. *The Growing of America: Two Hundred Years of U.S. Agriculture.* Fort Atkinson, Wis.: Johnson Hill Press, 1975.

Russell, Howard S. *A Long, Deep Furrow: Three Centuries of Farming in New England.* Hanover, N.H.: University Press of New England, 1976.

Schafer, Joseph. *The Social History of American Agriculture.* New York: Macmillan, 1936.

Schapsmeier, Edward L., and Frederick H. Schapsmeier. *Encyclopedia of American Agricultural History.* Westport, Conn.: Greenwood Press, 1975.

Schlebecker, John T. *Bibliography of Books and Pamphlets on the History of Agriculture in the United States, 1607–1967.* Santa Barbara: ABC-Clio, 1969.

———. *Whereby We Thrive: A History of American Farming, 1607–1972.* Ames: Iowa State University Press, 1975.

ARCHITECTURE

Cummings, Abbott Lowell. *Architecture in Early New England.* Sturbridge, Mass.: Old Sturbridge Village, 1984.

Gillon, Edmund Vincent. *Early Illustrations and Views of American Architecture.* New York: Dover, 1971.

Glassie, Henry. *Folk Housing in Middle Virginia: A Structural Analysis of Historic Artifacts.* Knoxville: University of Tennessee Press, 1975.

Hafertepe, Kenneth, and James F. O'Gorman. *American Architects and Their Books to 1848.* Amherst: University of Massachusetts Press, 2001.

Handlin, David P. *The American Home: Architecture and Society, 1815–1915.* Boston: Little, Brown, 1979.

Hitchcock, Henry Russell, and Edgar Kaufmann. *The Rise of American Architecture.* New York: Praeger, 1970.

Kennedy, Roger G. *Architecture, Men, Women, and Money in America, 1600–1860.* New York: Random House, 1985.

Maynard, W. Barksdale. *Architecture in the United States, 1800–1850.* New Haven: Yale University Press, 2002.

McMurry, Sally Ann. *Families and Farmhouses in Nineteenth-Century America: Vernacular Design and Social Change.* New York: Oxford University Press, 1988.

Morrison, Hugh. *Early American Architecture: From the First Colonial Settlements to the National Period.* New York: Dover Publications, 1987.

Naylor, David, and Joan Dillon. *American Theaters: Performance Halls of the Nineteenth Century.* New York: Wiley and Sons, 1997.

Noble, Allen G. *Wood, Brick, and Stone: The North American Settlement Landscape.* Vol. 1, *Houses.* Amherst: University of Massachusetts Press, 1984.

Sutton, Robert Kent. *Americans Interpret the Parthenon: The Progression of Greek Revival Architecture from the East Coast to Oregon, 1800–1860.* Niwot: University Press of Colorado, 1992.

Woods, Mary N. *From Craft to Profession: The Practice of Architecture in Nineteenth-Century America.* Berkeley: University of California Press, 1999.

CHILDREN

Ashby, LeRoy. *Endangered Children: Dependency, Neglect, and Abuse in American History.* New York: Twayne, 1997.

Avery, Gillian. *Behold the Child: American Children and Their Books, 1621–1922.* Baltimore: Johns Hopkins University Press, 1994.

Bremner, Robert Hamlett, ed. *Children and Youth in America: A Documentary History.* 3 vols. Cambridge: Harvard University Press, 1970–1974.

Cable, Mary. *The Little Darlings: A History of Child Rearing in America.* New York: Scribner, 1975.

Calvert, Karin. *Children in the House: The Material Culture of Early Childhood, 1600–1900.* Boston: Northeastern University Press, 1992.

Graff, Harvey J. *Conflicting Paths: Growing Up in America.* Cambridge: Harvard University Press, 1995.

Haviland, Virginia, and Margaret N. Coughlan. *Yankee Doodle's Literary Sampler of Prose, Poetry and Pictures; Being an Anthology of Diverse Works Published for the Edification and/or Entertainment of Young Readers in America before 1900.* New York: Crowell, 1974.

Hiner, N. Ray, and Joseph M. Hawes. *Growing Up in America: Children in Historical Perspective.* Urbana: University of Illinois Press, 1985.

Kiefer, Monica Mary. *American Children through Their Books, 1700–1835.* Philadelphia: University of Pennsylvania, 1948.

Larkin, Jack. *Children Everywhere: Dimensions of Childhood in Rural New England.* Sturbridge, Mass.: Old Sturbridge Village, 1987.

Pollock, Linda A. *Forgotten Children: Parent-Child Relations from 1500 to 1900.* New York: Cambridge University Press, 1983.

Reinier, Jacqueline S. *From Virtue to Character: American Childhood, 1775–1850.* New York: Twayne, 1996.

Thompson, Kathleen, and Hilary Austin. *America's Children: Picturing Childhood from Early America to the Present.* New York: W. W. Norton, 2003.

Welch, d'Alté A. *A Bibliography of American Children's Books Printed Prior to 1821.* Worcester, Mass.: American Antiquarian Society, 1972.

Youcha, Geraldine. *Minding the Children: Child Care in America from Colonial Times to the Present.* New York: Scribner, 1995.

Zeilizer, Viviana A. Rotman. *Pricing the Priceless Child: The Changing Social Value of Children.* New York: Basic Books, 1985.

CITIES

Barth, Gunther Paul. *City People: The Rise of Modern City Culture in Nineteenth-Century America.* New York: Oxford University Press, 1980.

Bender, Thomas. *Toward an Urban Vision: Ideas and Institutions in Nineteenth-Century America.* Lexington: University Press of Kentucky, 1975.

Blumin, Stuart M. *The Emergence of the Middle Class: Social Experience in the American City, 1760–1900.* New York: Cambridge University Press, 1989.

———. *The Urban Threshold: Growth and Change in a Nineteenth-Century American Community.* Chicago: University of Chicago Press, 1976.

Griffith, Ernest Stacey, and Charles R. Adrian. *History of American City Government: The Formation of Traditions, 1775–1870.* Washington, D.C.: National Municipal League and University Press of America, 1983.

Kramer, Simon Paul, and Frederick L. Holborn. *The City in American Life: A Historical Anthology.* New York: Putnam, 1970.

Lingeman, Richard R. *Small Town America: A Narrative History, 1620–the Present.* New York: Putnam, 1980.

McKelvey, Blake. *The City in American History.* London: Allen and Unwin, 1969.

Moehring, Eugene P. *Urban America and the Foreign Traveler, 1815–1855.* New York: Arno Press, 1974.

Mohl, Raymond A. *The Making of Urban America.* Wilmington, Del.: Scholarly Resources, 1997.

Monkkonen, Eric H. *America Becomes Urban: The Development of U.S. Cities and Towns, 1780–1980.* Berkeley: University of California Press, 1988.

Monti, Daniel J. *The American City: A Social and Cultural History.* Malden, Mass.: Blackwell Publishers, 1999.

Pred, Allan. *Urban Growth and the Circulation of Information: The United States System of Cities, 1790–1840.* Cambridge: Harvard University Press, 1973.

Richardson, James F. *Urban Police in the United States.* Port Washington, N.Y.: Kennikat Press, 1974.

Rishel, Joseph Francis. *American Cities and Towns: Historical Perspectives.* Pittsburgh: Duquesne University Press, 1992.

Schultz, Stanley K. *Constructing Urban Culture: American Cities and City Planning, 1800–1920.* Philadelphia: Temple University Press, 1989.

Shumsky, Neil L. *Encyclopedia of Urban America: The Cities and Suburbs.* Santa Barbara, Calif.: ABC-Clio, 1998.

Smith, Page. *As a City upon a Hill: The Town in American History.* New York: Knopf, 1966.

DEATH

Coffin, Margaret. *Death in Early America: The History and Folklore of Customs and Superstitions of Early Medicine, Funerals, Burials, and Mourning.* Nashville: Nelson, 1976.

Farrell, James J. *Inventing the American Way of Death, 1830–1920.* Philadelphia: Temple University Press, 1980.

Hume, Janice. *Obituaries in American Culture.* Jackson: University Press of Mississippi, 2000.

Isenberg, Nancy, and Andrew Burstein. *Mortal Remains: Death in Early America.* Philadelphia: University of Pennsylvania Press, 2003.

Jackson, Charles O., ed. *Passing: The Vision of Death in America.* Westport, Conn.: Greenwood Press, 1977.

Stannard, David E., ed. *Death in America*. Philadelphia: University of Pennsylvania Press, 1975.

Steiner, Michael J. *A Study of the Intellectual and Material Culture of Death in Nineteenth-Century America*. Lewiston, N.Y.: Edwin Mellen Press, 2003.

EDUCATION

Friedman, Jean E., Glenna R. Schroeder-Lein, and Rachel Mordecai Lazarus. *Ways of Wisdom: Moral Education in the Early National Period*. Athens: University of Georgia Press, 2001.

Geiger, Roger L. *The American College in the Nineteenth Century*. Nashville: Vanderbilt University Press, 2000.

Kaestle, Carl F. *Pillars of the Republic: Common Schools and American Society, 1780–1860*. New York: Hill and Wang, 1983.

Montgomery, Scott L. *Minds for the Making: The Role of Science in American Education, 1750–1990*. New York: Guilford Press, 1994.

Parkerson, Donald Hugh, and Jo Ann Parkerson. *The Emergence of the Common School in the U.S. Countryside*. Lewiston, N.Y.: Edwin Mellen Press, 1998.

Rothblatt, Sheldon, and Bjorn Wittrock. *The European and American University since 1800: Historical and Sociological Essays*. New York: Cambridge University Press, 1993.

Salvatori, Mariolina Rizzi. *Pedagogy: Disturbing History, 1819–1929*. Pittsburgh, Pa.: University of Pittsburgh Press, 1996.

Soltow, Lee, and Edward Stevens. *The Rise of Literacy and the Common School in the United States: A Socioeconomic Analysis to 1870*. Chicago: University of Chicago Press, 1981.

Stone, Lawrence. *The University in Society*. Princeton: Princeton University Press, 1974.

Winterer, Caroline. *The Culture of Classicism: Ancient Greece and Rome in American Intellectual Life, 1780–1910*. Baltimore: Johns Hopkins University Press, 2002.

FAMILY

Albin, Mel, and Dominick Cavallo. *Family Life in America, 1620–2000*. St. James, N.Y.: Revisionary Press, 1981.

Benson–von der Ohe, Elizabeth, and Valmari M. Mason. *An Annotated Bibliography of U.S. Scholarship on the History of the Family*. New York: AMS Press, 1986.

Cashin, Joan E. *A Family Venture: Men and Women on the Southern Frontier*. New York: Oxford University Press, 1991.

Coontz, Stephanie. *The Social Origins of Private Life: A History of American Families, 1600–1900*. New York: Verso, 1988.

Cott, Nancy F. *Public Vows: A History of Marriage and the Nation*. Cambridge: Harvard University Press, 2000.

Davis, Peggy Cooper. *Neglected Stories: The Constitution and Family Values*. New York: Hill and Wang, 1997.

D'Emilio, John, and Estelle B. Freedman. *The History of the Family and the History of Sexuality in America*. Washington, D.C.: American Historical Association, 1997.

Demos, John. *Past, Present, and Personal: The Family and the Life Course in American History.* New York: Oxford University Press, 1986.

Farrell, Betty. *Family: The Making of an Idea, an Institution, and a Controversy in American Culture.* Boulder, Colo.: Westview Press, 1999.

Fox, Vivian C., and Martin H. Quitt. *Loving, Parenting, and Dying: The Family Cycle in England and America, Past and Present.* New York: Psychohistory Press, 1980.

Frank, Stephen M. *Life with Father: Parenthood and Masculinity in the Nineteenth-Century American North.* Baltimore: Johns Hopkins University Press, 1998.

Garrett, Elisabeth Donaghy. *At Home: The American Family, 1750–1870.* New York: H. N. Abrams, 1990.

Godbeer, Richard. *Sexual Revolution in Early America.* Baltimore: Johns Hopkins University Press, 2002.

Gordon, Michael. *The American Family in Social-Historical Perspective.* New York: St. Martin's Press, 1973.

Hamilton, Phillip. *The Making and Unmaking of a Revolutionary Family: The Tuckers of Virginia, 1752–1830.* Charlottesville: University Press of Virginia, 2003.

Hareven, Tamara K. *Family and Kin in Urban Communities, 1700–1930.* New York: New Viewpoints, 1977.

Hareven, Tamara K., and Maris Vinovskis, eds. *Family and Population in Nineteenth-Century America.* Princeton: Princeton University Press, 1978.

Hawes, Joseph M., and Elizabeth I. Nybakken. *Family and Society in American History.* Urbana: University of Illinois Press, 2001.

Jabour, Anya. *Marriage in the Early Republic: Elizabeth and William Wirt and the Companionate Ideal.* Baltimore: Johns Hopkins University Press, 1998.

Luchetti, Cathy. *"I Do!": Courtship, Love, and Marriage on the American Frontier; A Glimpse at America's Romantic Past through Photographs, Diaries, and Journals, 1715–1915.* New York: Crown, 1996.

Lystra, Karen. *Searching the Heart: Women, Men, and Romantic Love in Nineteenth-Century America.* New York: Oxford University Press, 1989.

McCall, Laura, and Donald Yacovone. *A Shared Experience: Men, Women, and the History of Gender.* New York: New York University Press, 1998.

McKune, Amy. *To Love and to Cherish: The Great American Wedding.* New York: Museums at Stony Brook, 1991.

Mintz, Steven, and Susan Kellogg. *Domestic Revolutions: A Social History of American Family Life.* New York: Free Press, 1988.

Moran, Gerald F., and Maris Vinovskis. *Religion, Family, and the Life Course: Explorations in the Social History of Early America.* Ann Arbor: University of Michigan Press, 1992.

Muncy, Raymond Lee. *Sex and Marriage in Utopian Communities: Nineteenth Century America.* Bloomington: Indiana University Press, 1973.

O'Day, Rosemary. *The Family and Family Relationships, 1500–1900: England, France, and the United States of America.* New York: St. Martin's Press, 1994.

Rothman, Ellen K. *Hands and Hearts: A History of Courtship in America.* New York: Basic Books, 1984.

Ryan, Mary P. *Cradle of the Middle Class: The Family in Oneida County, New York, 1790–1835.* New York: Cambridge University Press, 1981.

Scott, Donald M., and Bernard Wishy, eds. *America's Families: A Documentary History.* New York: Harper and Row, 1982.

Tufte, Virginia, and Barbara G. Myerhoff. *Changing Images of the Family.* New Haven: Yale University Press, 1979.

Wells, Robert V. *Revolutions in Americans' Lives: A Demographic Perspective on the History of Americans, Their Families, and Their Society.* Westport, Conn.: Greenwood, 1982.

———. *Uncle Sam's Family: Issues and Perspectives in American Demographic History.* Albany: State University of New York Press, 1986.

Wolf, Stephanie G. *Urban Village: Population, Community, and Family Structure in Germantown, Pennsylvania, 1683–1800.* Princeton: Princeton University Press, 1976.

FOOD

Cummings, Richard Osborne. *The American and His Food.* Chicago: University of Chicago Press, 1940.

Levenstein, Harvey A. *Revolution at the Table: The Transformation of the American Diet.* New York: Oxford University Press, 1988.

McIntosh, Elaine N. *American Food Habits in Historical Perspective.* Westport, Conn.: Praeger, 1995.

Nissenbaum, Stephen. *Sex, Diet, and Debility in Jacksonian America: Sylvester Graham and Health Reform.* Westport, Conn.: Greenwood Press, 1980.

Root, Waverley Lewis, and Richard De Rochemont. *Eating in America: A History.* New York: Morrow, 1976.

Schremp, Geraldine. *Celebration of American Food: Four Centuries in the Melting Pot.* Golden, Colo.: Fulcrum, 1996.

GENERAL

Boorstin, Daniel M. *The Americans: The National Experience.* New York: Random House, 1964.

Brown, Richard D. *Modernization: The Transformation of American Life.* New York: Hill and Wang, 1976.

Bruce, Dickson D. *Violence and Culture in the Antebellum South.* Austin: University of Texas Press, 1979.

Demos, John. *Circles and Lines: The Shape of Life in Early America.* Cambridge: Harvard University Press, 2004.

Fischer, David Hackett. *Growing Old in America.* New York: Oxford University Press, 1977.

Glenn, Myra C. *Campaigns against Corporal Punishment: Prison, Sailors, Women, and Children in Antebellum America.* Albany: State University of New York Press, 1984.

Haultunen, Karen. *Confidence Men and Painted Women: A Study of Middle-Class Culture in America, 1830–1870.* New Haven: Yale University Press, 1982.

Henretta, James A. *The Evolution of American Society, 1700–1815: An Interdisciplinary Analysis.* Lexington, Mass.: D.C. Heath, 1973.

Horn, James P., and Jan Lewis. *The Revolution of 1800: Democracy, Race, and the New Republic.* Charlottesville: University Press of Virginia, 2002.

Hunt, Gaillard. *Life in America One Hundred Years Ago.* New York: Harper and Brothers, 1914.

Kennon, Donald R. *A Republic for the Ages: The United States Capitol and the Political Culture of the Early Republic.* Charlottesville: University Press of Virginia, 1999.

Mayfield, John. *The New Nation, 1800–1845.* Rev. ed. New York: Hill and Wang, 1986.

McClelland, Peter D., and Richard J. Zeckenhauser. *Demographic Dimensions of the New Republic: American Interregional Migration, Vital Statistics, and Manumissions, 1800–1860.* New York: Cambridge University Press, 1982.

McCutcheon, Marc. *Everyday Life in the 1800s: A Guide for Writers, Students, and Historians.* Cincinnati: Writer's Digest Books, 1993.

Mesick, Jane Louise. *The English Traveller in America, 1785–1835.* New York: Columbia University Press, 1922.

Miller, John C. *The Federalist Era, 1789–1801.* New York: Harper and Row, 1960.

Nye, Russell Blaine. *The Cultural Life of the New Nation, 1776–1830.* New York: Harper Torchbooks, 1960.

Purvis, Thomas L. *Revolutionary America: 1763–1800.* New York: Facts on File, 1995.

Saum, Lewis O. *The Popular Mood of Pre–Civil War America.* Westport, Conn.: Greenwood Press, 1980.

Simpkins, Francis Butler, and Charles Pierce Roland. *A History of the South.* 4th ed. New York: Knopf, 1972.

Smelser, Marshall. *The Democratic Republic, 1801–1815.* New York: Harper and Row, 1968.

Smith, Jeffery Alan. *Franklin and Bache: Envisioning the Enlightened Republic.* New York: Oxford University Press, 1990.

Tyler, Alice Felt. *Freedom's Ferment: Phases of American Social History from the Colonial Period to the Outbreak of the Civil War.* New York: Harper and Row, 1962.

Vickers, Anita. *The New Nation.* Westport, Conn.: Greenwood Press, 2002.

Wiebe, Robert H. *The Opening of American Society: From the Adoption of the Constitution to the Eve of Disunion.* New York: Vintage Books, 1985.

Wright, Louis B. *Everyday Life in the New Nation, 1787–1860.* New York: Putnam, 1972.

Young, James Sterling. *The Washington Community, 1800–1828.* New York: Harcourt, Brace, 1966.

HEALTH

Blake, John B. *Public Health in the Town of Boston, 1630–1822.* Cambridge: Harvard University Press, 1959.

Burbick, Joan. *Healing the Republic: The Language of Health and the Culture of Nationalism in Nineteenth-Century America.* New York: Cambridge University Press, 1994.

Cayleff, Susan E. *Wash and Be Healed: The Water-Cure Movement and Women's Health.* Philadelphia: Temple University Press, 1987.

Duffy, John. *From Humors to Medical Science: A History of Medicine.* Urbana: University of Illinois Press, 1993.

Estes, J. Worth, Philip Cash, and Eric H. Christianson, eds. *Medicine in Colonial Massachusetts, 1620–1820.* Boston: Colonial Society of Massachusetts, 1980.

Fett, Sharla M. *Working Cures: Healing, Health, and Power on Southern Slave Plantations.* Chapel Hill: University of North Carolina Press, 2002.

Gillett, Mary C. *The Army Medical Department, 1775–1818*. Washington, D.C.: Center for Military History, 1990.

Grob, Gerald N. *The Deadly Truth: A History of Disease in America*. Cambridge: Harvard University Press, 2002.

———. *The Mad among Us: A History of the Care of America's Mentally Ill*. New York: Free Press, 1994.

Mohr, James C. *Abortion in America: The Origins and Evolution of National Policy, 1800–1900*. New York: Oxford University Press, 1978.

Moss, Kay. *Southern Folk Medicine, 1750–1820*. Columbia: University of South Carolina Press, 1999.

Nissenbaum, Stephen. *Sex, Diet, and Debility in Jacksonian America: Sylvester Graham and Health Reform*. Westport, Conn.: Greenwood, 1980.

Norwood, William Frederick. *Medical Education in the United States before the Civil War*. New York: Arno Press, 1971.

Numbers, Ronald L., and Todd Lee Savitt. *Science and Medicine in the Old South*. Baton Rouge: Louisiana State University Press, 1989.

Powell, J. H. *Bring Out Your Dead: The Great Plague of Yellow Fever in Philadelphia in 1793*. New York: Time, 1965.

Risse, Gunter, Ronald L. Numbers, and Judith Walzer Leavitt, eds. *Medicine without Doctors: Home Health Care in American History*. New York: Science History Publications, 1978.

Riznik, Barnes. *Medicine in New England, 1790–1840*. Sturbridge, Mass.: Old Sturbridge Village, 1965.

Rothman, David J. *The Discovery of the Asylum: Social Order and Disorder in the Early Republic*. Boston: Little, Brown, 1971.

Sax, Margaret F. *Complaints and Cures: The Search for Health in Nineteenth Century America*. Hartford: Trinity College, 1990.

Shryock, Richard H. *Medicine and Society in America, 1660–1860*. New York: New York University Press, 1960.

Starr, Paul. *The Social Transformation of American Medicine*. New York: Basic Books, 1982.

Valencius, Conevery Bolton. *The Health of the Country: How American Settlers Understood Themselves and Their Land*. New York: Basic Books, 2002.

Vinovskis, Maris. *Fertility in Massachusetts from the Revolution to the Civil War*. New York: Academic Press, 1981.

Whitaker, Robert. *Mad in America: Bad Science, Bad Medicine, and Enduring Mistreatment of the Mentally Ill*. Cambridge: Perseus, 2002.

Whorton, James C. *Nature Cures: The History of Alternative Medicine in America*. Oxford: Oxford University Press, 2002.

IMMIGRANTS

Baseler, Marilyn C. *"Asylum for Mankind": America, 1607–1800*. Ithaca, N.Y.: Cornell University Press, 1998.

Bayor, Ronald H. *Race and Ethnicity in America: A Concise History*. New York: Columbia University Press, 2003.

Daniels, Roger. *Coming to America: A History of Immigration and Ethnicity in American Life*. New York: HarperCollins, 1990.

Diner, Hasia R. *A New Promised Land: A History of Jews in America.* New York: Oxford University Press, 2003.

Dinnerstein, Leonard, and David M. Reimers. *Ethnic Americans: A History of Immigration and Assimilation.* New York: Dodd, Mead, 1975.

Dinnerstein, Leonard, Roger L. Nichols, and David M. Reimers. *Natives and Strangers: A Multicultural History of the Americas.* New York: Oxford University Press, 1996.

Dublin, Thomas. *Immigrant Voices: New Lives in America, 1773–1986.* Urbana: University of Illinois Press, 1993.

Erickson, Charlotte. *Invisible Immigrants: The Adaptation of English and Scottish Immigrants in Nineteenth-Century America.* Coral Gables, Fla.: University of Miami Press, 1972.

———. *Leaving England: Essays on British Emigration in the Nineteenth Century.* Ithaca, N.Y.: Cornell University Press, 1994.

Filby, P. William. *Passenger and Immigration Lists Bibliography, 1538–1900: Being a Guide to Published Lists of Arrivals in the United States and Canada.* Detroit, Mich.: Gale Research, 1988.

Handlin, Oscar. *The Uprooted: The Epic Story of the Great Migrations That Made the American People.* Boston: Little, Brown, 1951.

Kenny, Kevin. *The American Irish: A History.* New York: Longman, 2000.

Lehmann, Hartmut, and Hermann Wellenreuther. *In Search of Peace and Prosperity: New German Settlements in Eighteenth-Century Europe and America.* University Park: Pennsylvania State University Press, 2000.

McCaffrey, Lawrence John. *The Irish Catholic Diaspora in America.* Washington, D.C.: Catholic University of America Press, 1997.

Trommler, Frank, and Elliott Shore. *The German-American Encounter: Conflict and Cooperation between Two Cultures, 1800–2000.* New York: Berghahn Books, 2001.

LANGUAGE

Barnhart, David K., and Allan A. Metcalf. *America in So Many Words: Words That Have Shaped America.* Boston: Houghton Mifflin, 1997.

Bryson, Bill. *Made in America: An Informal History of the English Language in the United States.* New York: W. Morrow, 1994.

Cmiel, Kenneth. *Democratic Eloquence: The Fight over Popular Speech in Nineteenth-Century America.* New York: W. Morrow, 1990.

Dillard, J. L. *A History of American English.* New York: Longman, 1992.

———. *Toward a Social History of American English.* New York: Mouton, 1985.

Flexner, Stuart Berg. *Listening to America: An Illustrated History of Words and Phrases from Our Lively and Splendid Past.* New York: Simon and Schuster, 1982.

Flexner, Stuart Berg, and Anne H. Soukhanov. *Speaking Freely: A Guided Tour of American English from Plymouth Rock to Silicon Valley.* New York: Oxford University Press, 1997.

Friend, Joseph H. *The Development of American Lexicography, 1798–1864.* Paris: Mouton, 1967.

Gustafson, Thomas. *Representative Words: Politics, Literature, and the American Language, 1776–1865.* New York: Cambridge University Press, 1992.

Kramer, Michael P. *Imagining Language in America: From the Revolution to the Civil War.* Princeton: Princeton University Press, 1992.

Lepore, Jill. *A Is for American: Letters and Other Characters in the Newly United States.* New York: Alfred A. Knopf, 2002.

Mathews, M. M., ed. *The Beginnings of American English: Essays and Comments.* Chicago: University of Chicago Press, 1931.

Mencken, H. L. *The American Language.* New York: Knopf, 1936.

Micklethwait, David. *Noah Webster and the American Dictionary.* Jefferson, N.C.: McFarland, 2000.

Monaghan, E. Jennifer. *A Common Heritage: Noah Webster's Blue-Back Speller.* Hamden, Conn.: Archon Books, 1983.

Read, Allen Walker, and Richard W. Bailey. *Milestones in the History of English in America.* Durham, N.C.: Duke University Press, 2002.

Robertson, Andrew W. *The Language of Democracy: Political Rhetoric in the United States and Britain, 1790–1900.* Ithaca, N.Y.: Cornell University Press, 1995.

Sperry, Kip. *Reading Early American Handwriting.* Baltimore: Genealogical Publishing, 1998.

LEISURE

Ade, George. *The Old-Time Saloon: Not Wet—Not Dry, Just History.* New York: R. Long and R. R. Smith, 1931.

Apperson, G. L. *The Social History of Smoking.* New York: G. P. Putnam's Sons, 1916.

Aron, Cindy Sondik. *Working at Play: A History of Vacations in the United States.* New York: Oxford University Press, 1999.

Batterberry, Michael, and Ariane Batterberry. *On the Town in New York from 1776 to the Present.* New York: Charles Scribner's Sons, 1973.

Braden, Donna R. *Leisure and Entertainment in America.* Dearborn, Mich.: Henry Ford Museum and Greenfield Village, 1988.

Brown, John Hull. *Early American Beverages.* New York: Bonanza Books, 1966.

Burnham, John C. *Bad Habits: Drinking, Smoking, Taking Drugs, Gambling, Sexual Misbehavior, and Swearing in American History.* New York: New York University Press, 1993.

Chafetz, Henry. *Play the Devil: A History of Gambling in the United States, 1492–1955.* New York: Clarkson N. Potter, 1960.

Chambers, Thomas A. *Drinking the Waters: Creating an American Leisure Class at Nineteenth-Century Mineral Springs.* Washington, D.C.: Smithsonian Institution Press, 2002.

Chase, Gilbert. *America's Music from the Pilgrims to the Present.* 2nd rev. ed. New York: McGraw-Hill, 1966.

Coffin, Tristram P. *The British Traditional Ballad in North America.* Rev. ed. Philadelphia: University of Pennsylvania Press, 1963.

Crawford, Richard. *America's Musical Life: A History.* New York: Norton, 2001.

Cross, Gary. *A Social History of Leisure since 1600.* State College, Pa.: Venture Publishing, 1990.

Crunden, Robert M. *A Brief History of American Culture.* New York: Paragon House, 1994.

Cullen, Jim. *The Art of Democracy: A Concise History of Popular Culture in the United States.* New York: Monthly Review Press, 1996.

Dulles, Foster Rhea. *A History of Recreation: America Learns to Play.* New York: Appleton-Century-Crofts, 1965.

Eisen, George, and David Kenneth Wiggins. *Ethnicity and Sport in North American History and Culture.* Westport, Conn.: Greenwood Press, 1994.

Epstein, Dena J. *Sinful Tunes and Spirituals: Black Folk Music to the Civil War.* Urbana: University of Illinois Press, 1977.

Fairholt, F. W. *Tobacco: Its History and Associations, Including an Account of the Plant and Its Manufacture, with Its Modes of Use in All Ages and Countries.* Detroit: Singing Tree Press, 1968.

Fisher, Donald M. *Lacrosse: A History of the Game.* Baltimore: Johns Hopkins University Press, 2002.

Gately, Iain. *Tobacco: The Story of How Tobacco Seduced the World.* New York: Grove Press, 2001.

Goodman, Jordan. *Tobacco in History: The Cultures of Dependence.* New York: Routledge, 1993.

Gorn, Elliott J., and Warren Goldstein. *A Brief History of American Sports.* New York: Hill and Wang, 1993.

Hampel, Robert L. *Temperance and Prohibition in Massachusetts, 1813–1852.* Ann Arbor: UMI Research Press, 1982.

Heintze, James R. *American Musical Life in Context and Practice to 1865.* New York: Garland, 1994.

Hewitt, Barnard. *Theatre U.S.A., 1868–1957.* New York: McGraw-Hill, 1959.

Hotaling, Edward. *The Great Black Jockeys: The Lives and Times of the Men Who Dominated America's First National Sport.* Rocklin, Calif.: Forum, 1999.

Kroeger, Karl. *American Fuging-Tunes, 1770–1820: A Descriptive Catalog.* Westport, Conn.: Greenwood Press, 1994.

Lathrop, Elise. *Early American Inns and Taverns.* New York: Tudor Publishing, 1946.

Lender, Mark E., and James Kirby Martin. *Drinking in America: A History.* New York: Free Press, 1976.

Lock, Stephen, and L. A. Reynolds. *Ashes to Ashes: The History of Smoking and Health.* Atlanta: Rodopi, 1998.

Lowens, Irving. *Music and Musicians in Early America.* New York: W. W. Norton, 1964.

McConachie, Bruce. "American Theatre in Context, from the Beginnings to 1870." In *The Cambridge History of American Theatre,* ed. Don B. Wilmeth and Christopher Bigsby, vol. 1. Cambridge: Cambridge University Press, 1998.

Nasaw, David. *Going Out: The Rise and Fall of Public Amusements.* New York: Basic Books, 1993.

Pencak, William, and Matthew Dennis. *Riot and Revelry in Early America.* University Park: Pennsylvania State University Press, 2002.

Rader, Benjamin G. *American Sports: From the Age of Folk Games to the Age of Spectators.* Englewood Cliffs, N.J.: Prentice-Hall, 1983.

Rice, Kym S. *Early American Taverns: For the Entertainment of Friends and Strangers.* Chicago: Regnery Gateway, 1983.

Riess, Steven A. *City Games: The Evolution of American Urban Society and the Rise of Sports.* Urbana: University of Illinois Press, 1989.

Robert, Joseph C. *The Story of Tobacco in America.* New York: Knopf, 1952.

Rorabaugh, William J. *The Alcoholic Republic: An American Tradition.* New York: Oxford University Press, 1979.

Sherow, Victoria, and Laura LoTurco. *Huskings, Quiltings, and Barn Raisings: Work-Play Parties in Early America.* New York: Walker, 1992.

Sonneck, Oscar George Theodore. *Early Concert-Life in America (1731–1800).* Leipzig: Breitkopf and Hartel, 1907.

Spivey, Donald. *Sport in America: New Historical Perspectives.* Westport, Conn.: Greenwood Press, 1985.

Steiner, Jesse Frederick. *Americans at Play.* New York: Arno Press, 1970.

Stiles, Henry Reed. *Bundling: Its Origin, Progress, and Decline in America.* Albany, N.Y., 1871.

Struna, Nancy L. *People of Prowess: Sport, Leisure, and Labor in Early Anglo-America.* Urbana: University of Illinois Press, 1996.

Tawa, Nicholas E. *High-Minded and Low-Down: Music in the Lives of Americans, 1800–1861.* Boston: Northeastern University Press, 2000.

———. *Sweet Songs for Gentle Americans: The Parlor Song in America, 1790–1860.* Bowling Green, Ohio: Bowling Green University Popular Press, 1980.

Tyrell, Ian R. *Sobering Up: From Temperance to Prohibition in Antebellum America, 1800–1860.* Westport Conn.: Greenwood Press, 1979.

Wiggins, David Kenneth. *Sport in America: From Wicked Amusements to National Obsession.* Champaign, Ill.: Human Kinetics, 1995.

MATERIAL CULTURE

Ames, Kenneth L., and Thomas J. Schlereth. *Material Culture: A Research Guide.* Lawrence: University Press of Kansas, 1985.

Deetz, James J. F. *In Small Things Forgotten: The Archaeology of Early American Life.* Garden City, N.J.: Anchor Press, 1977.

Haines, Carol L. *"Forms to Sett On": A Social History of Concord Seating Furniture.* Concord, Mass.: Concord Antiquarian Museum, 1984.

Kidwell, Claudia, and Margaret B. Christman. *Suiting Everyone: The Democratization of Clothing in America.* Washington, D.C.: Smithsonian Institution Press, 1974.

Langdon, William Chauncy. *Everyday Things in American Life, 1776–1876.* New York: Scribner, 1941.

Martin, Ann Smart, and J. Ritchie Garrison. *American Material Culture: The Shape of the Field.* Knoxville: University of Tennessee Press, 1997.

Mayhew, Edgar de Noailles, and Minor Meyers Jr. *A Documentary History of American Interiors: From the Colonial Era to 1915.* New York: Scribners, 1980.

McClellan, Elisabeth. *History of American Costume, 1607–1870.* New York: Tudor Publishing, 1937.

Quimby, Ian M. G. *Material Culture and the Study of American Life.* New York: W. W. Norton, 1978.

Schiffer, Margaret B. *Chester County, Pennsylvania Probate Inventories, 1684–1850.* Exton, Pa.: Schiffer, 1974.

Schlereth, Thomas J. *Cultural History and Material Culture: Everyday Life, Landscapes, Museums.* Ann Arbor: UMI Research Press, 1990.

———. *Material Culture Studies in America.* Nashville: American Association for State and Local History, 1982.

St. George, Robert Blair. *Material Life in America, 1600–1860.* Boston: Northeastern University Press, 1988.

Memoirs, Diaries, Letters, Sermons, Speeches

Adams, John Quincy. *Diary of John Quincy Adams.* 2 vols. Ed. David Grayson Allen. Cambridge: Belknap Press of Harvard University Press, 1981.

Allen, Richard. *The Life Experience and Gospel Labors of the Rt. Rev. Richard Allen: To Which Is Annexed the Rise and Progress of the African Methodist Episcopal Church in the United States of America: Containing a Narrative of the Yellow Fever in the Year of Our Lord 1793: With an Address to the People of Color in the United States.* New York: Abingdon Press, 1960.

Arksey, Laura, Nancy Pries, and Marcia Reed, eds. *American Diaries: An Annotated Bibliography of Published American Diaries and Journals.* Detroit: Gale Research, 1983.

Audubon, John James. *Writings and Drawings.* Ed. Christoph Irmscher. New York: Penguin Putnam, 1999.

Berger, Josef. *Diary of America: The Intimate Story of Our Nation, Told by 100 Diarists—Public Figures and Plain Citizens, Natives and Visitors—Over the Five Centuries from Columbus, the Pilgrims, and George Washington to Thomas Edison, Will Rogers, and Our Own Time.* New York: Simon and Schuster, 1957.

Cartwright, Peter, and W. P. Strickland. *Autobiography of Peter Cartwright: The Backwoods Preacher.* New York: Carlton and Porter, 1956.

Clyman, James. *Journal of a Mountain Man.* Ed. Linda M. Hasselstrom. Missoula, Mont.: Mountain Press, 1984.

Cox, Joseph T., ed. *The Written Wars: American War Prose through the Civil War.* North Haven, Conn.: Archon Books, 1996.

De Voto, Bernard A., ed. *The Journals of Lewis and Clark.* Boston: Houghton Mifflin, 1953.

DeWolfe, Barbara. *Discoveries of America: Personal Accounts of British Emigrants to North America during the Revolutionary Era.* New York: Cambridge University Press, 1997.

Fremantle, Elizabeth Wynne, ed. *The Wynne Diaries, 1789–1820.* London: Oxford University Press, 1952.

Frey, Sylvia R., and Marian J. Morton. *New World, New Roles: A Documentary History of Women in Pre-industrial America.* New York: Greenwood Press, 1986.

Glass, Anthony. *Journal of an Indian Trader: Anthony Glass and the Texas Trading Frontier, 1790–1810.* Ed. Dan L. Flores. College Station: Texas A&M University Press, 1985.

Glass, Patrick. *The Journals of Patrick Glass: Member of the Lewis and Clark Expedition.* Ed. Carol Lynn MacGregor. Missoula, Mont.: Mountain Press, 1997.

Grant, C. L., ed. *Letters, Journals, and Writings of Benjamin Hawkins.* 2 vols. Savannah, Ga.: Beehive Press, 1980.

Hart, Albert Bushnell, ed. *American History Told by Contemporaries.* 5 vols. New York: Macmillan, 1897–1929.

Hulbert, Archer Butler, ed. *Southwest on the Turquoise Trail: The First Diaries on the Road to Santa Fe.* Colorado Springs: Steward Commission of Colorado College, 1933.

Humez, Jean McMahon. *Mother's First-Born Daughters: Early Shaker Writings on Women and Religion.* Bloomington: Indiana University Press, 1993.

Hunt, Gaillard. *The First Forty Years of Washington Society in the Family Letters of Margaret Bayard Smith.* New York: Frederick Ungar, 1965.

Jackson, Donald Dean, ed. *Letters of the Lewis and Clark Expedition, with Related Documents, 1783–1854.* Urbana: University of Illinois Press, 1962.

Kagle, Steven E. *American Diary Literature, 1620–1799.* Boston: Twayne, 1979.

Keetley, Dawn, and John Pettegrew. *Public Women, Public Words: A Documentary History of American Feminism.* Madison: Madison House, 1997.

Kierner, Cynthia A. *Revolutionary America, 1750–1815: Sources and Interpretation.* Upper Saddle River, N.J.: Prentice-Hall, 2003.

———. *Southern Women in Revolution, 1776–1800: Personal and Political Narratives.* Columbia: University of South Carolina Press, 1998.

King, Duane H. *The Cherokee Indian Nation: A Troubled History.* Knoxville: University of Tennessee Press, 1979.

Lewis, Jon E., ed. *The Mammoth Book of Eye-Witness History.* New York: Carroll and Graf, 1998.

———. *The Mammoth Book of War Diaries and Letters: Life on the Battlefield in the Words of the Ordinary Soldier, 1775–1991.* New York: Carroll and Graf, 1999.

McNemar, Richard. *The Kentucky Revival, or, A Short History of the Late Extraordinary Out-Pouring of the Spirit of God, in the Western States of America, Agreeably to Scripture Promises, and Prophecies concerning the Latter Day: With a Brief Account of the Entrance and Progress of What the World Call Shakerism, among the Subjects of the Late Revival in Ohio and Kentucky. Presented to the True Zion-Traveller, as a Memorial of the Wilderness Journey.* Albany, N.Y.: E. E. Hosford, 1808.

Meltzer, Milton, ed. *The Jewish Americans: A History in Their Own Words, 1650–1950.* New York: Crowell, 1982.

Merrill, James M., ed. *Uncommon Valor: The Exciting Story of the Army.* Chicago: Rand McNally, 1964.

M'Gillivray, Duncan. *The Journal of Duncan M'Gillivray.* Fairfield, Wash.: Ye Galleon Press, 1989.

Miller, Kerby A. *Irish Immigrants in the Land of Canaan: Letters and Memoirs from Colonial and Revolutionary America, 1675–1815.* New York: Oxford University Press, 2003.

Mondy, Robert William. *Pioneers and Preachers: Stories of the Old Frontier.* Chicago: Nelson-Hall, 1980.

Morgan, Speer, and Greg Michalson. *For Our Beloved Country: American War Diaries from the Revolution to the Persian Gulf.* New York: Atlantic Monthly Press, 1994.

Newman, Richard, and Patrick Rael. *Pamphlets of Protest: An Anthology of Early African-American Protest Literature, 1790–1860.* New York: Routledge, 2001.

Phillips, Joyce B., and Paul Gary Phillips. *The Brainerd Journal: A Mission to the Cherokees, 1817–1823.* Lincoln: University of Nebraska Press, 1998.

Rae, Noel, ed. *Witnessing America: The Library of Congress Book of Firsthand Accounts of Life in America, 1600–1900.* New York: Stonesong Press, 1996.

Rasmussen, Wayne David, comp. *Agriculture in the United States: A Documentary History.* New York: Random House, 1975.

Richardson, James D. *A Compilation of the Messages and Papers of the Presidents, 1789–1897.* 10 vols. Washington, D.C.: Government Printing Office, 1896–1899.

Ridge, Martin, and Ray Allen Billington, eds. *America's Frontier Story: A Documentary History of Westward Expansion.* New York: Holt, Rinehart, and Winston, 1969.

Ripley, C. Peter. *Witness for Freedom: African American Voices on Race, Slavery, and Emancipation*. Chapel Hill: University of North Carolina Press, 1993.
Sweet, William Warren, ed. *The Baptists, 1783–1830: A Collection of Source Material*. New York: H. Holt, 1931.
———. *The Presbyterians, 1783–1840: A Collection of Source Materials*. New York: Harper and Brothers, 1936.
Tucher, Andie, ed. *Agriculture in America, 1622–1860: Printed Works in the Collections of the American Philosophical Society, the Historical Society of Pennsylvania, the Library Company of Philadelphia*. New York: Garland, 1984.
Woodson, Carter G., ed. *The Mind of the Negro As Reflected in Letters Written during the Crisis, 1800–1850*. New York: Russell and Russell, 1969.

Men

Clawson, Mary Ann. *Constructing Brotherhood: Class, Gender, and Fraternalism*. Princeton: Princeton University Press, 1989.
Kimmel, Michael S. *Manhood in America: A Cultural History*. New York: Free Press, 1997.
Pugh, David G. *Sons of Liberty: The Masculine Mind in Nineteenth-Century America*. Westport, Conn.: Greenwood Press, 1983.
Rotundo, E. Anthony. *American Manhood: Transformations in Masculinity from the Revolution to the Modern Era*. New York: Basic Books, 1993.

The Military

Ambrose, Stephen E. *Undaunted Courage: Meriwether Lewis, Thomas Jefferson, and the Opening of the American West*. New York: Simon and Schuster, 1996.
Coakley, Robert W. *The Role of Federal Military Forces in Domestic Disorders, 1789–1878*. Washington, D.C.: Center of Military History, 1988.
Coffman, Edward M. *The Old Army: A Portrait of the American Army in Peacetime, 1784–1898*. New York: Oxford University Press, 1986.
Crackel, Theodore J. *Mr. Jefferson's Army: Political and Social Reform of the Military Establishment, 1801–1809*. New York: New York University Press, 1987.
Cress, Lawrence Delbert. *Citizens in Arms: The Army and Militia in American Society to the War of 1812*. Chapel Hill: University of North Carolina Press, 1982.
Dudley, William S., and Michael J. Crawford. *The Early Republic and the Sea: Essays on the Naval and Maritime History of the Early United States*. Washington, D.C.: Brassey's, 2001.
Fowler, William M. *Jack Tars and Commodores: The American Navy, 1783–1815*. Boston: Houghton Mifflin, 1984.
Gillett, Mary C. *The Army Medical Department, 1775–1818*. Washington, D.C.: Center of Military History, 1990.
Heidler, David S., and Jeanne T. Heidler, eds. *Encyclopedia of the War of 1812*. Santa Barbara, Calif.: ABC-Clio, 1997.
———. *Old Hickory's War: Andrew Jackson and the Quest for Empire*. Mechanicsburg, Pa.: Stackpole Books, 1996; Baton Rouge: Louisiana State University Press, 2003.
———. *The War of 1812*. Westport, Conn.: Greenwood Publishing, 2002.

Kochan, James, and David Rickman. *The United States Army, 1783–1811*. Oxford: Osprey Military, 2001.

Long, David Foster. *Gold Braid and Foreign Relations: Diplomatic Activities of U.S. Naval Officers, 1798–1883*. Annapolis: Naval Institute Press, 1988.

McKee, Christopher. *A Gentlemanly and Honorable Profession: The Creation of the U.S. Naval Officer Corps, 1794–1815*. Annapolis: Naval Institute Press, 1991.

Merrill, James M. *Quarter-Deck and Fo'c's'le: The Exciting Story of the Navy*. Chicago: Rand McNally, 1963.

Palmer, Dave Richard. *1794: America, Its Army, and the Birth of the Nation*. Novato, Calif.: Presidio, 1994.

Prucha, Francis Paul. *Broadax and Bayonet: The Role of the United States Army in the Development of the Northwest, 1815–1860*. Madison: State Historical Society of Wisconsin, 1953.

———. *A Guide to the Military Posts of the United States, 1789–1895*. Madison: State Historical Society of Wisconsin, 1964.

———. *The Sword of the Republic: The United States Army on the Frontier, 1783–1846*. New York: Macmillan, 1968.

Resch, John Phillips. *Suffering Soldiers: Revolutionary War Veterans, Moral Sentiment, and Political Culture in the Early Republic*. Amherst: University of Massachusetts Press, 1999.

Robotti, Frances Diane, and James Vescovi. *The USS Essex and the Birth of the American Navy*. Holbrook, Mass.: Adams Media Corporation, 1999.

Silverstone, Paul H. *The Sailing Navy, 1775–1854*. Annapolis: Naval Institute Press, 2001.

Skeen, Carl Edward. *Citizen Soldiers in the War of 1812*. Lexington: University Press of Kentucky, 1999.

Skelton, William B. *An American Profession of Arms: The Army Officer Corps, 1784–1861*. Lawrence: University Press of Kansas, 1992.

Tucker, Spencer. *The Jeffersonian Gunboat Navy*. Columbia: University of South Carolina Press, 1993.

Valle, James E. *Rocks and Shoals: Order and Discipline in the Old Navy, 1800–1861*. Annapolis: Naval Institute Press, 1980.

Native Americans

Benn, Carl. *The Iroquois in the War of 1812*. Toronto: University of Toronto Press, 1998.

Braund, Kathryn E. Holland. *Deerskins and Duffels: The Creek Indian Trade with Anglo-America, 1685–1815*. Lincoln: University of Nebraska Press, 1993.

Chapman, George. *Chief William McIntosh: A Man of Two Worlds*. Atlanta: Cherokee Publishing, 1988.

Crosby, Alfred W., Jr. *The Columbian Exchange: Biological and Cultural Consequences of 1492*. Westport, Conn.: Greenwood Press, 1969.

———. *Ecological Imperialism: The Biological Expansion of Europe, 900–1900*. New York: Cambridge University Press, 1986.

Doster, James Fletcher. *The Creek Indians and Their Florida Lands, 1740–1823*. New York: Garland, 1974.

Ethridge, Robbie Franklyn. *Creek Country: The Creek Indians and Their World*. Chapel Hill: University of North Carolina Press, 2003.

Griffith, Benjamin W. *McIntosh and Weatherford, Creek Indian Leaders.* Tuscaloosa: University of Alabama Press, 1988.

Hoxie, Frederick E., and Ronald Hoffman. *Native Americans and the Early Republic.* Charlottesville: University Press of Virginia, 1999.

Hurt, R. Douglas. *Indian Agriculture in America: Prehistory to the Present.* Lawrence: University Press of Kansas, 1987.

———. *The Indian Frontier, 1763–1846.* Albuquerque: University of New Mexico Press, 2002.

King, Duane H. *The Cherokee Indian Nation: A Troubled History.* Knoxville: University of Tennessee Press, 1979.

Littlefield, Daniel F. *Africans and Creeks: From the Colonial Period to the Civil War.* Westport, Conn.: Greenwood, 1979.

Martin, Joel W. *Sacred Revolt: The Muskogees' Struggle for a New World.* Boston: Beacon Press, 1991.

McLoughlin, William Gerald. *Cherokee Renascence in the New Republic.* Princeton: Princeton University Press, 1986.

———. *Cherokees and Missionaries, 1789–1839.* Norman: University of Oklahoma Press, 1995.

Perdue, Theda. *Cherokee Women: Gender and Culture Change, 1700–1835.* Lincoln: University of Nebraska Press, 1998.

———. *Slavery and the Evolution of Cherokee Society, 1540–1866.* Knoxville: University of Tennessee Press, 1979.

Prucha, Francis Paul. *American Indian Policy in the Formative Years: The Indian Trade and Intercourse Acts, 1780–1834.* Cambridge: Harvard University Press, 1962.

———. *The Great Father: The United States Government and the American Indians.* Lincoln: University of Nebraska Press, 1984.

Ronda, James P. *Lewis and Clark among the Indians.* Lincoln: University of Nebraska Press, 1984.

Saunt, Claudio. *A New Order of Things: Property, Power, and the Transformation of the Creek Indians, 1733–1816.* New York: Cambridge University Press, 1999.

Skaggs, David C., and Larry L. Nelson, eds. *The Sixty Years' War for the Great Lakes, 1754–1814.* East Lansing: Michigan State University Press, 2001.

Southerland, Henry DeLeon, and Jerry Elijah Brown. *The Federal Road through Georgia, the Creek Nation, and Alabama, 1806–1836.* Tuscaloosa: University of Alabama Press, 1989.

Swanton, John Reed. *Early History of the Creek Indians and Their Neighbors.* Gainesville: University Press of Florida, 1998.

Vennum, Thomas. *American Indian Lacrosse: Little Brother of War.* Washington, D.C.: Smithsonian Institution Press, 1994.

Wright, J. Leitch. *Creeks and Seminoles: The Destruction and Regeneration of the Muscogulge People.* Lincoln: University of Nebraska Press, 1986.

Newspapers

Ashley, Perry J. *American Newspaper Journalists, 1690–1872.* Detroit: Gale, 1985.

Brown, Walt. *John Adams and the American Press: Politics and Journalism at the Birth of the Republic.* Jefferson, N.C.: McFarland, 1995.

Dicken Garcia, Hazel. *Journalistic Standards in Nineteenth-Century America.* Madison: University of Wisconsin Press, 1989.

Humphrey, Carol Sue. *The Press of the Young Republic, 1783–1833.* Westport, Conn.: Greenwood, 1996.

Lee, Alfred McClung. *The Daily Newspaper in America: The Evolution of a Social Instrument.* New York: Macmillan, 1937.

Pasley, Jeffrey L. *"The Tyranny of Printers": Newspaper Politics in the Early American Republic.* Charlottesville: University Press of Virginia, 2001.

Phillips, Kim Tousley. *William Duane, Radical Journalist in the Age of Jefferson.* New York: Garland, 1989.

Riley, Sam G. *American Magazine Journalists, 1741–1850.* Detroit: Gale, 1988.

Rutland, Robert Allen. *The Newsmongers: Journalism in the Life of the Nation, 1690–1972.* New York: Dial Press, 1973.

Schudson, Michael. *Discovering the News: A Social History of American Newspapers.* New York: Basic Books, 1978.

Tebbel, John William. *The Compact History of the American Newspaper.* New York: Hawthorn Books, 1963.

Reform

Adams, A.D. *The Neglected Period of Anti-slavery in America (1808–1831).* Williamstown, Mass.: Corner House Publishers, 1973.

Degler, Carl N. *The Other South: Southern Dissenters in the Nineteenth Century.* New York: Harper and Row, 1974.

Dillon, Merton Lynn. *The Abolitionists: The Growth of a Dissenting Minority.* De Kalb: Northern Illinois University Press, 1974.

Epstein, Barbara Leslie. *The Politics of Domesticity: Women, Evangelism, and Temperance in Nineteenth-Century America.* Middletown, Conn.: Wesleyan University Press, 1981.

Fox, Early Lee. *The American Colonization Society, 1817–1840.* New York: AMS Press, 1971.

Frick, John W. *Theatre, Culture, and Temperance Reform in Nineteenth-Century America.* New York: Cambridge University Press, 2003.

Hampel, Robert L. *Temperance and Prohibition in Massachusetts, 1813–1852.* Ann Arbor: UMI Research Press, 1982.

Hirsch, Adam J. *The Rise of the Penitentiary: Prisons and Punishments in Early America.* New Haven: Yale University Press, 1992.

Lewis, Orlando F. *The Development of American Prisons and Prison Customs, 1776–1845.* Montclair, N.J.: Patterson Smith, 1967.

Lowance, Mason I. *A House Divided: The Antebellum Slavery Debates in America, 1776–1865.* Princeton: Princeton University Press, 2003.

Macy, Jesse. *The Anti-slavery Crusade: A Chronicle of the Gathering Storm.* New Haven: Yale University Press, 1919.

Newman, Richard S. *The Transformation of American Abolitionism: Fighting Slavery in the Early Republic.* Chapel Hill: University of North Carolina Press, 2002.

Parsons, Elaine Frantz. *Manhood Lost: Fallen Drunkards and Redeeming Women in the Nineteenth-Century United States.* Baltimore: Johns Hopkins University Press, 2003.

Strong, Douglas M. *Perfectionist Politics: Abolitionism and the Religious Tensions of American Democracy.* Syracuse: Syracuse University Press, 1999.

Zilversmit, Arthur. *The First Emancipation: The Abolition of Slavery in the North.* Chicago: University of Chicago Press, 1967.

Religion

Ahlstron, Sydney E. *A Religious History of the American People.* New Haven: Yale University Press, 1972.

Andrews, Dee. *The Methodists and Revolutionary America, 1760–1800: The Shaping of an Evangelical Culture.* Princeton: Princeton University Press, 2000.

Berens, John F. *Providence and Patriotism in Early America, 1640–1815.* Charlottesville: University Press of Virginia, 1978.

Bilhartz, Terry D. *Urban Religion and the Second Great Awakening: Church and Society in Early National Baltimore.* Cranbury, N.J.: Fairleigh Dickinson University Press, 1986.

Bodo, John R. *The Protestant Clergy and Public Issues, 1812–1848.* Princeton, N.J.: Princeton University Press, 1954.

Boyland, Anne M. *Sunday School: The Formation of an American Institution, 1790–1880.* New Haven: Yale University Press, 1988.

Brekus, Catherine A. *Strangers and Pilgrims: Female Preaching in America, 1740–1845.* Chapel Hill: University of North Carolina Press, 1998.

Bressler, Ann Lee. *The Universalist Movement in America, 1770–1880.* New York: Oxford University Press, 2001.

Brown, Candy Guther. *The Word in the World: Evangelical Writing, Publishing, and Reading in America, 1789–1880.* Chapel Hill: University of North Carolina Press, 2004.

Bruce, Dickson D. *And They All Sang Hallelujah: Plain-Folk Camp Meeting Religion, 1800–1845.* Knoxville: University of Tennessee Press, 1974.

Campbell, James T. *Songs of Zion: The African Methodist Episcopal Church in the United States and South Africa.* New York: Oxford University Press, 1995.

Cross, Whitney R. *The Burned-Over District: The Social and Intellectual History of Enthusiastic Religion in Western New York, 1800–1850.* New York: Harper Torchbooks, 1965.

DeBerg, Betty A. *Ungodly Women: Gender and the First Wave of American Fundamentalism.* Minneapolis: Fortress Press, 1990.

Dorrien, Gary J. *The Making of American Liberal Theology: Imagining Progressive Religion, 1805–1900.* Louisville, Ky.: Westminster John Knox Press, 2001.

Elsbree, Oliver Wendell. *The Rise of the Missionary Spirit in America, 1790–1815.* Williamsport: Williamsport Printing and Binding Co., 1928; Philadelphia: Porcupine Press, 1980.

Foster, Lawrence. *Women, Family, and Utopia: Communal Experiments of the Shakers, the Oneida Community, and the Mormons.* Syracuse, N.Y.: Syracuse University Press, 1991.

Fraser, James W. *Pedagogue for God's Kingdom: Lyman Beecher and the Second Great Awakening.* Lanham, Md.: University Press of America, 1985.

Gaustad, Edwin S. *Faith of Our Fathers: Religion and the New Nation.* San Francisco: Harper and Row, 1987.

George, Carol V. R. *Segregated Sabbaths: Richard Allen and the Emergence of Independent Black Churches, 1760–1840.* New York: Oxford University Press, 1973.

Gribbin, William. *The Churches Militant: The War of 1812 and American Religion.* New Haven: Yale University Press, 1973.

Hamm, Thomas D. *The Transformation of American Quakerism: Orthodox Friends, 1800–1907.* Bloomington: Indiana University Press, 1988.

Hardman, Keith. *Seasons of Refreshing: Evangelism and Revivals in America.* Grand Rapids, Mich.: Baker Books, 1994.

Hutchison, William R. *Religious Pluralism in America: The Contentious History of a Founding Ideal.* New Haven: Yale University Press, 2003.

Hutson, James H. *Religion and the Founding of the American Republic.* Washington, D.C.: Library of Congress, 1998.

Jenkins, Philip. *Mystics and Messiahs: Cults and New Religions in American History.* New York: Oxford University Press, 2000.

Johnson, Paul E. *A Shopkeeper's Millennium: Society and Revivals in Rochester, New York, 1815–1837.* New York: Hill and Wang, 1978.

Keller, Charles Roy. *The Second Great Awakening in Connecticut.* Hamden, Conn.: Archon Books, 1968.

Longenecker, Stephen L. *Piety and Tolerance: Pennsylvania German Religion, 1700–1850.* Metuchen, N.J.: Scarecrow Press, 1994.

Luchetti, Cathy. *Under God's Spell: Frontier Evangelists, 1772–1915.* San Diego: Harcourt Brace Jovanovich, 1989.

McLoughlin, William Gerald, comp. *The American Evangelicals, 1800–1900: An Anthology.* New York: Harper and Row, 1968.

Miller, William Lee. *The First Liberty: Religion and the American Republic.* New York: Knopf, 1986.

Noll, Mark A. *America's God: From Jonathan Edwards to Abraham Lincoln.* New York: Oxford University Press, 2002.

Payne, Daniel Alexander. *History of the African Methodist Episcopal Church.* New York: Arno Press, 1969.

Richey, Russell E. *Early American Methodism.* Bloomington: Indiana University Press, 1991.

Rohrer, James R. *Keepers of the Covenant: Frontier Missions and the Decline of Congregationalism, 1774–1818.* New York: Oxford University Press, 1995.

Roth, Randolph A. *The Democratic Dilemma: Religion, Reform, and the Social Order in the Connecticut River Valley of Vermont, 1791–1850.* New York: Cambridge University Press, 1987.

Singleton, George A. *The Romance of African Methodism: A Study of the African Methodist Episcopal Church.* New York: Exposition Press, 1952.

Thomas, George M. *Revivalism and Cultural Change: Christianity, Nation Building, and the Market in the Nineteenth-Century United States.* Chicago: University of Chicago Press, 1989.

Washington, Joseph R. *Race and Religion in Early Nineteenth Century America, 1800–1850: Constitution, Conscience, and Calvinist Compromise.* Lewiston, N.Y.: E. Mellen, 1988.

Wigger, John H. *Taking Heaven by Storm: Methodism and the Rise of Popular Christianity in America.* New York: Oxford University Press, 1998.

Rural and Frontier America

Ambrose, Stephen E., and Douglas Brinkley. *The Mississippi and the Making of a Nation: From the Louisiana Purchase to Today.* Washington, D.C.: National Geographic, 2002.

Bartlett, Richard A. *The New Country: A Social History of the American Frontier, 1776–1890.* New York: Oxford University Press, 1974.

Billington, Ray Allen. *Westward Expansion: A History of the American Frontier.* New York: Macmillan, 1967.

Carlson, Laurie M. *Seduced by the West: Jefferson's America and the Lure of the Land beyond the Mississippi.* Chicago: Ivan R. Dee, 2003.

Cayton, Andrew R. L., and Fredrika J. Teute. *Contact Points: American Frontiers from the Mohawk Valley to the Mississippi, 1750–1830.* Chapel Hill: University of North Carolina Press, 1998.

Chittenden, Hiram Martin. *The American Fur Trade of the Far West.* 2 vols. Stanford: Academic Reprints, 1954.

Davis, James Edward. *Frontier America, 1800–1840: A Comparative Demographic Analysis of the Settlement Process.* Glendale, Calif.: A. H. Clark, 1977.

Davis, William C. *The American Frontier: Pioneers, Settlers, and Cowboys, 1800–1899.* New York: Smithmark, 1992.

DeVoto, Bernard A. *The Course of Empire.* Boston: Houghton Mifflin, 1952.

Dick, Everett. *The Dixie Frontier: A Social History of the Southern Frontier from the First Transmontane Beginnings to the Civil War.* New York: Alfred A. Knopf, 1948; New York: Capricorn Books, 1964.

Gates, Paul Wallace, Allan G. Bogue, and Margaret Beattie Bogue. *The Jeffersonian Dream: Studies in the History of American Land Policy and Development.* Albuquerque: University of New Mexico Press, 1996.

Goodwin, Cardinal Leonidas. *The Trans-Mississippi West, 1803–1853: A History of Its Acquisition and Settlement.* New York: Russell and Russell, 1967.

Hafen, Le Roy Reuben, and Harvey Lewis Carter. *Mountain Men and Fur Traders of the Far West: Eighteen Biographical Sketches.* Lincoln: University of Nebraska Press, 1982.

Heidler, David S., and Jeanne T. Heidler. *Manifest Destiny.* Westport Conn.: Greenwood Press, 2003.

Hyslop, Stephen G. *Bound for Santa Fe: The Road to New Mexico and the American Conquest, 1806–1848.* Norman: University of Oklahoma Press, 2002.

Jones, Mary Ellen. *The Nineteenth Century American Frontier.* Westport, Conn.: Greenwood Press, 1998.

Maguire, James H., and Peter Wild. *A Rendezvous Reader: Tall, Tangled, and True Tales of the Mountain Men, 1805–1850.* Salt Lake City: University of Utah Press, 1997.

Mancall, Peter C. *American Eras: Westward Expansion, 1800–1860.* Detroit: Gale, 1999.

Merk, Frederick. *History of the Westward Movement.* New York: Knopf, 1978.

Moring, John. *Early American Naturalists: Exploring the American West, 1804–1900.* New York: Cooper Square Press, 2002.

Osborn, William M. *The Wild Frontier: Atrocities during the American-Indian War from Jamestown Colony to Wounded Knee.* New York: Random House, 2000.

Otto, John Solomon. *The Southern Frontiers, 1607–1860: The Agricultural Evolution of the Colonial and Antebellum South.* New York: Greenwood Press, 1989.

Paxson, Frederic L. *History of the American Frontier, 1763–1893.* Boston: Houghton Mifflin, 1924.

Ronda, James P. *Thomas Jefferson and the Changing West: From Conquest to Conservation.* Albuquerque: University of New Mexico Press, 1997.

Sandoz, Mari. *The Beaver Men: Spearheads of Empire.* New York: Hastings House, 1964.

Stegner, Page. *Winning the Wild West: The Epic Saga of the American Frontier, 1800–1899.* New York: Free Press, 2002.

Terrell, John Upton. *The Six Turnings: Major Changes in the American West, 1806–1834.* Glendale, Calif.: A. H. Clark, 1968.

Turner, Frederick Jackson. *The Frontier in American History.* New York: Holt, Rinehart, and Winston, 1962.

Van Every, Dale. *Ark of Empire: The American Frontier, 1784–1803.* New York: Morrow, 1963.

Weber, David J. *New Spain's Far Northern Frontier: Essays on Spain in the American West, 1540–1821.* Albuquerque: University of New Mexico Press, 1979.

Wishart, David J. *The Fur Trade of the American West, 1807–1840: A Geographical Synthesis.* Lincoln: University of Nebraska Press, 1979.

Wright, J. Leitch. *Britain and the American Frontier, 1783–1815.* Athens: University of Georgia Press, 1975.

Travel

Bourne, Russell. *Americans on the Move: A History of Waterways, Railways, and Highways: With Maps and Illustrations from the Library of Congress.* Golden, Colo.: Fulcrum, 1995.

Cole, Harry Ellsworth, and Louise Phelps Kellogg. *Stagecoach and Tavern Tales of the Old Northwest.* Cleveland: Arthur H. Clark, 1930.

Dorsey, Leslie, and Janice Devine. *Fare Thee Well: A Backward Look at Two Centuries of Historic American Hostelries, Fashionable Spas, and Seaside Resorts.* New York: Crown, 1964.

Dunbar, Seymour. *A History of Travel in America.* 4 vols. Indianapolis: Bobbs-Merrill, 1915.

Haas, Irvin. *America's Historic Inns and Taverns.* New York: Arco, 1972.

Holmes, Oliver W., and Peter T. Rohrbach. *Stagecoach East: Stagecoach Days in the East from the Colonial Period to the Civil War.* Washington, D.C.: Smithsonian Institution Press, 1983.

Jordan, Philip D. *The National Road.* Indianapolis: Bobbs-Merrill, 1948.

Olcott, William. *The Greenbrier Heritage.* Philadelphia: Arndt, Preston, Chapin, Lamb and Keen, 1967.

Parks, Roger. *Roads and Travel in New England, 1790–1840.* Sturbridge, Mass.: Old Sturbridge Village, 1967.

Taylor, George Rogers. *The Transportation Revolution, 1815–1860.* Vol. 4 of *The Economic History of the United States.* New York: Rinehart, 1951.

Williamson, Jefferson. *The American Hotel: An Anecdotal History.* New York: Knopf, 1930.

Withey, Lynne. *Grand Tours and Cook's Tours: A History of Leisure Travel, 1750 to 1915.* London: Aurum Press, 1998.

Women

Abramovitz, Mimi. *Regulating the Lives of Women: Social Welfare from Colonial Times to the Present.* Boston, Mass.: South End Press, 1988.

Applewhite, Harriet Branson, and Darline Gay Levy. *Women and Politics in the Age of the Democratic Revolution.* Ann Arbor: University of Michigan Press, 1990.

Barker-Benfield, G. J. *The Horrors of the Half-Known Life: Male Attitudes toward Women and Sexuality in Nineteenth-Century America.* New York: Harper and Row, 1976.

Baym, Nina. *American Women Writers and the Work of History, 1790–1860.* New Brunswick, N.J.: Rutgers University Press, 1995.

Blair, Karen J. *The History of American Women's Voluntary Organizations, 1810–1960: A Guide to Sources.* Boston: G. K. Hall, 1989.

Cherniavsky, Eva. *That Pale Mother Rising: Sentimental Discourses and the Imitation of Motherhood in Nineteenth Century America.* Bloomington: Indiana University Press, 1995.

Clinton, Catherine E. *The Plantation Mistress: Women's World in the Old South.* New York: Pantheon Books, 1982.

Conway, Jill K. *The Female Experience in Eighteenth- and Nineteenth-Century America: A Guide to the History of American Women.* New York: Garland, 1982.

Cott, Nancy F. *The Bonds of Womanhood: "Woman's Sphere" in New England, 1780–1835.* New Haven: Yale University Press, 1977.

Degler, Carl N. *At Odds: Women and the Family in America from the Revolution to the Present.* New York: Oxford University Press, 1980.

Delamont, Sara, and Lorna Duffin. *The Nineteenth-Century Woman: Her Cultural and Physical World.* London: Croom Helm, 1978.

Dudden, Faye E. *Serving Women: Household Service in Nineteenth Century America.* Middletown, Conn.: Wesleyan University Press, 1983.

———. *Women in the American Theatre: Actresses and Audiences, 1790–1870.* New Haven: Yale University Press, 1994.

Elred, Janet Carey, and Peter Mortensen. *Imagining Rhetoric: Composing Women of the Early United States.* Pittsburgh: University of Pittsburgh Press, 2002.

Glenn, Evelyn Nakano. *Unequal Freedom: How Race and Gender Shaped American Citizenship and Labor.* Cambridge: Harvard University Press, 2002.

Groneman, Carol, and Mary Beth Norton. *"To Toil the Livelong Day": America's Women at Work, 1780–1980.* Ithaca, N.Y.: Cornell University Press, 1987.

Halem, Lynne Carol. *Divorce Reform: Changing Legal and Social Perspectives.* New York: Free Press, 1980.

Harris, Sharon M. *American Women Writers to 1800.* New York: Oxford University Press, 1996.

———. *Redefining the Political Novel: American Women Writers, 1797–1901.* Knoxville: University of Tennessee Press, 1995.

Hoffert, Sylvia D. *Private Matters: American Attitudes toward Childbearing and Infant Nurture in the Urban North, 1800–1860.* Urbana: University of Illinois Press, 1989.

Jensen, Joan M. *Loosening the Bonds: Mid-Atlantic Farm Women, 1750–1850.* New Haven: Yale University Press, 1986.

Johnson, Mary. *An Alternative Agenda to Male-Dominated History: Material Culture and Women's History.* Wellesley, Mass.: Wellesley College, Center for Research on Women, 1983.

Kelley, Mary. *Private Woman, Public Stage: Literary Domesticity in Nineteenth-Century America.* New York: Oxford University Press, 1984.

Kerber, Linda K. *No Constitutional Right to Be Ladies: Women and the Obligations of Citizenship.* New York: Hill and Wang, 1998.

———. *Toward an Intellectual History of Women.* Chapel Hill: University of North Carolina Press, 1997.

Leavitt, Judith Walzer. *Brought to Bed: Childbirth in America, 1750–1950*. New York: Oxford University Press, 1986.

Matthews, Glenna. *"Just a Housewife": The Rise and Fall of Domesticity in America*. New York: Oxford University Press, 1987.

McMillen, Sally Gregory. *Motherhood in the Old South: Pregnancy, Childbirth, and Infant Rearing*. Baton Rouge: Louisiana State University Press, 1990.

Misner, Barbara. *Highly Respectable and Accomplished Ladies: Catholic Women Religious in America, 1790–1850*. New York: Garland, 1988.

Norton, Mary Beth. *Liberty's Daughters: The Revolutionary Experience of American Women, 1750–1850*. Boston: Little, Brown, 1980.

Ogden, Annegret S. *The Great American Housewife: From Helpmate to Wage Earner, 1776–1986*. Westport, Conn.: Greenwood Press, 1986.

Premo, Terri L. *Winter Friends: Women Growing Old in the New Republic, 1785–1835*. Urbana: University of Illinois Press, 1990.

Rendall, Jane. *The Origins of Modern Feminism: Women in Britain, France, and the United States, 1780–1860*. New York: Schocken Books, 1984.

Richards, Jeffrey H. *Mercy Otis Warren*. New York: Twayne, 1995.

Samuels, Shirley. *Romances of the Republic: Women, the Family, and Violence in the Literature of the Early American Nation*. New York: Oxford University Press, 1996.

Scherr, Arthur. *I Married Me a Wife: Male Attitudes toward Women in the American Museum, 1787–1792*. Lanham, Md.: Lexington Books, 1999.

Schloesser, Pauline E. *The Fair Sex: White Women and Racial Patriarchy in the Early American Republic*. New York: New York University Press, 2002.

Scholten, Catherine M. *Childbearing in American Society, 1630–1850*. New York: New York University Press, 1985.

Stansell, Christine. *City of Women: Sex and Class in New York, 1789–1860*. New York: Knopf, 1986.

Theriot, Nancy M. *Mothers and Daughters in Nineteenth-Century America: The Biosocial Construction of Femininity*. Lexington: University Press of Kentucky, 1996.

Todd, Jan. *Physical Culture and the Body Beautiful: Purposive Exercise in the Lives of American Women, 1800–1870*. Macon, Ga.: Mercer University Press, 1998.

Verbrugge, Martha H. *Able-Bodied Womanhood: Personal Health and Social Change in Nineteenth-Century Boston*. New York: Oxford University Press, 1988.

Weil, Dorothy. *In Defense of Women: Susanna Rowson (1762–1824)*. University Park: Pennsylvania State University Press, 1976.

Work

Applebaum, Herbert A. *The American Work Ethic and the Changing Work Force: An Historical Perspective*. Westport, Conn.: Greenwood Press, 1998.

Atherton, Lewis S. *The Pioneer Merchant in Mid-America*. New York: Greenwood Press, 1968.

———. *The Southern Country Store, 1800–1860*. Baton Rouge: Louisiana State University Press, 1949.

Bezís-Selfa, John. *Forging America: Ironworkers, Adventurers, and the Industrious Revolution*. Ithaca, N.Y.: Cornell University Press, 2004.

Cowan, Ruth Schwartz. *A Social History of American Technology*. New York: Oxford University Press, 1997.

Donkin, Richard. *Blood, Sweat, and Tears: The Evolution of Work.* New York: Texere, 2001.

Faler, Paul. *Mechanics and Manufacturers in the Early Industrial Revolution: Lynn, Massachusetts, 1780–1860.* Albany, N.Y.: State University of New York Press, 1981.

Gilje, Paul A. *Wages of Independence: Capitalism in the Early American Republic.* Madison: Madison House, 1997.

Hamilton, Milton W. *The Country Printer: New York State, 1785–1830.* Port Washington, N.Y.: I. J. Freidman, 1964.

Hirsch, Susan E. *Roots of the American Working Class: The Industrialization of Crafts in Newark, 1800–1860.* Philadelphia: University of Pennsylvania Press, 1978.

Jeremy, David J. *Artisans, Entrepreneurs, and Machines: Essays on the Early Anglo-American Textile Industries, 1770–1840s.* Aldershot: Ashgate, 1998.

———. *Transatlantic Industrial Revolution: The Diffusion of Textile Technologies between Britain and America, 1790–1830s.* Cambridge: MIT Press, 1981.

Joyce, William L., ed. *Printing and Society in Early America.* Worcester, Mass.: American Antiquarian Society, 1983.

Laurie, Bruce, and Eric Foner. *Artisans into Workers: Labor in Nineteenth-Century America.* New York: Hill and Wang, 1989.

Licht, Walter. *Industrializing America: The Nineteenth Century.* Baltimore: Johns Hopkins University Press, 1995.

Montgomery, David. *Citizen Worker: The Experience of Workers in the United States with Democracy and the Free Market during the Nineteenth Century.* New York: Cambridge University Press, 1993.

Prude, Jonathan. *The Coming of Industrial Order: Town and Factory Life in Rural Massachusetts, 1810–1860.* New York: Cambridge University Press, 1983.

Puig, Francis J., and Michael Conforti. *The American Craftsman and the European Tradition, 1620–1820.* Minneapolis: Minneapolis Institute of Arts, 1989.

Rigal, Laura. *The American Manufactory: Art, Labor, and the World of Things in the Early Republic.* Princeton: Princeton University Press, 1998.

Rock, Howard. *Artisans of the New Republic: The Tradesmen of New York in the Age of Jefferson.* New York: New York University Press, 1981.

Rock, Howard B., and Paul A. Gilje. *American Artisans: Crafting Social Identity, 1750–1850.* Baltimore: Johns Hopkins University Press, 1995.

Rorabaugh, William J. *The Craft Apprentice in America: From Franklin to the Machine Age.* New York: Oxford University Press, 1986.

Sellers, Charles Grier. *The Market Revolution: Jacksonian America, 1815–1846.* New York: Oxford University Press, 1991.

Silver, Rollo P. *The American Printer, 1787–1825.* Charlottesville: University Press of Virginia, 1967.

Steinberg, Theodore. *Nature Incorporated: Industrialization and the Waters of New England.* New York: Cambridge University Press, 1991.

Tucker, Barbara M. *Samuel Slater and the Origins of the American Textile Industry, 1790–1860.* Ithaca, N.Y.: Cornell University Press, 1984.

Wilentz, Sean. *Chants Democratic: New York City and the Rise of the American Working Class, 1788–1850.* New York: Oxford University Press, 1984.

Wishart, David J. *The Fur Trade of the American West, 1807–1840: A Geographical Synthesis.* Lincoln: University of Nebraska Press, 1979.

INDEX

About the Authors

DAVID S. HEIDLER is a renowned award-winning historian. He is on the faculty at Colorado State University, Pueblo. He is co-author with Jeanne T. Heidler of many well-respected books and reference works, including *The Civil War, The Mexican American War, Manifest Destiny,* and *The War of 1812.*

JEANNE T. HEIDLER is Professor of History at the United States Air Force Academy. She is co-author with David S. Heidler of many well-respected books and reference works, including *The Civil War, The Mexican American War, Manifest Destiny,* and *The War of 1812.*